COVERING DISSENT

COVERING DISSENT

THE MEDIA AND
THE ANTI-VIETNAM WAR
MOVEMENT

MELVIN SMALL

RUTGERS UNIVERSITY PRESS
NEW BRUNSWICK, NEW JERSEY

Library of Congress Cataloging-in-Publication Data

Small, Melvin.
    Covering dissent : the media and the anti-Vietnam War movement /
Melvin Small.
        p.   cm.—(Perspectives on the sixties)
    Includes bibliographical references and index.
    ISBN 0-8135-2106-8 (cloth)—ISBN 0-8135-2107-6 (pbk.)
    1. Vietnamese Conflict, 1961–1975—Protest movements—United
States.   2. Vietnamese Conflict, 1961–1975, in mass media—United
States.   I. Title.   II. Series.
DS559.62.U6S64   1994
959.704'3373—dc20   94-195
                                                                               CIP

British Cataloging-in-Publication information available

*For Sarajane Miller-Small
and the millions of other women and men
whose antiwar activities
the media often misrepresented*

CONTENTS

PREFACE

As I was working on *Johnson, Nixon, and the Doves*, a study of the impact of the antiwar movement on decisionmakers, I realized that one important part of the story that had not been told, which I simply could not incorporate in that book, concerned the relationship between the media and the movement. Indeed, that relationship was central to the question of how antiwarriors influenced policy because their effectiveness depended on the way the media brought their activities to the attention of the public and the people in power. After all, if no one had been impressed with their marches, rallies, and speeches, Presidents Johnson and Nixon would have enjoyed a much freer hand in Southeast Asia.

After completing *Johnson, Nixon, and the Doves*, I turned to this related study, on which I have worked off and on since 1988. I have received a good deal of essential assistance from many people and institutions over the past few years. Aside from series editor Barbara L. Tischler, who was one of the very helpful readers for Rutgers University Press, Natalie Atkin, Charles Chatfield, George Herring, Chris Johnson, Ralph Levering, and Lynn Parsons have commented on all or large portions of the manuscript.

The Lyndon Baines Johnson Foundation once again generously supported my work at the Lyndon Baines Johnson Presidential Library in Austin, Texas, where David Humphrey and Regina Greenwell guided me through the materials. Byron Parham was helpful during my visit to the Richard M. Nixon Presidential Materials Project in Alexandria, Virginia. Michael Gibson at Vanderbilt University's Television News Archive assisted in preparing taped materials used for the illustrations. Bill Klein of CBS helped me gain access to his company's news archives in New York City.

Wayne State University's Graduate School and History Department provided grants to help defray expenses for photographs and permissions and the university awarded me sabbaticals in 1988 and 1992 during which time I worked on this project. The photography unit at the university, under the able direction of Deborah Kingery, produced most of the photographs that illustrate the volume. Gerry Dervish, an old antiwarrior who now owns Troy Video, took some of the video shots, Judith Legosky of the Royal Oak Public Library permitted some of her valuable microfilm to leave the building, and the Wayne State History Department's excellent office staff of Ginny Corbin,

Gayle McReedy, Delinda Neal, and Amanda Rayha assisted in a variety of ways.

I am grateful as well to the permissions departments of the *Daily Tribune*, the *New York Times*, the *Washington Post*, *Newsweek*, the United Press International, and Capital Cities/ABC Broadcasting Company, and to Linnea Lannon and Chip Visci for helping me obtain permission from the *Detroit Free Press* to reproduce the cover photograph.

Central to the entire process was, as always, my best friend, Sarajane Miller-Small. A veteran of the antiwar movement, she helped with the original concept, encouraged me as I went along, and spent untold hours poring over the manuscript and galleys polishing the finished product.

November 1993
Royal Oak, Michigan

1

INTRODUCTION

T he anti-Vietnam War movement was the largest and most effective antiwar movement in American history.[1] Despite its successes in influencing opinion leaders, decisionmakers, ordinary citizens—and Hanoi—it never captured the support of a majority of the American people, even when a majority began expressing opposition to continued involvement in Vietnam. If anything, some movement activities, especially mass demonstrations, may have retarded the growth of antiwar sentiment.[2]

Throughout much of the period, most Americans opposed antiwar activities, and many even opposed the doves' right to march or peacefully assemble.[3] Moreover, administration denunciations of dissenters as unpatriotic, violent radicals wounded the movement. Americans' innate wariness of left-wing protesters and their leaders' offensives against such opponents were reenforced by the way the media treated antiwar activities.

Reenforcement may be too weak a term to describe the media's role in affecting public attitudes. Indeed, many Americans would probably agree with former Detroit Piston center Bill Laimbeer who asserts simply, "media creates public opinion."[4] Social scientists who study the complicated relationship between leaders, the fourth estate, and the public find that formulation too simple. Yet, there is no doubt that the media, which brought both antiwar and administration activities to the attention of the public, constituted the single most important influence on the way people viewed mass demonstrations in particular and the antiwar movement in general during the era of the Vietnam War.[5]

Despite the publication of five convincing scholarly studies on the American media's generally prowar position through much of the period, critics still contend that the United States could have won the war had it not been for the press's embrace of antiwar arguments and perspectives.[6] So pervasive is this view that the media themselves were nervous about offering favorable or extensive coverage of antiwar activities during the Gulf War in 1991, particularly the January 26, 1991, rally in Washington that drew at least one hundred thousand doves.[7]

Although previous studies touch upon the relationship between the media and the antiwar movement, they concentrate on the way the media treated military activities in Vietnam.[8] In this study, I concentrate exclusively on the movement as I explain how newspapers, magazines, and the television networks contributed to the development of popular attitudes about antiwar activities. I try to shed light as well on general problems confronted by all dissenting groups attempting to attract supporters through adequate and accurate coverage of their activities.[9]

Oppositional mass movements have a difficult time obtaining fair, much less favorable, coverage from establishment media, even in the freest of democracies. For a variety of economic, political, and institutional reasons, journalists and their employers tend to denigrate those out of the mainstream, despite the fact that they themselves may doubt the wisdom of administration policies. The Right's offensives against the media over the past quarter century have obscured the fact that most newspapers, magazines, and television news services are bulwarks of the status quo whose attitude toward dissent and unusual political ideas is generally negative.

As we shall see time and time again, those who reported major antiwar demonstrations concentrated on violent and radical—albeit colorful—behavior on the fringes of the activity, undercounted the crowds, and ignored political arguments the protesters' leadership presented. In addition, because of a misapplication of the "fairness doctrine," especially on television, journalists bent over backwards to present the views and activities of counterdemonstrators and administration spokespersons in order to balance those of the doves. Such unfavorable coverage of the movement's activities and objectives slowed the growth of anti-Vietnam War sentiment in the United States from 1965 through 1971, since many of those who had begun to approve of the dovish message disapproved of the media-caricatured movement more.

The media caricature suggested as well a monolithic antiwar movement. But this "hydra-headed movement" was composed of thousands of formal and informal, permanent and temporary, and local and national organizations and coalitions that changed over time.[10] Antiwarriors generally found themselves supporting one of two general tendencies, a liberal tendency that concentrated on ending the Vietnam War and a radical tendency that hoped to transform the entire political system. The former was in the ascendancy within the movement from 1965 through 1967, although not always perceived as such by the media; the latter gained more and more adherents from 1968 through 1971 because of widespread frustration with the unresponsiveness of the government to earlier campaigns. Periodically, the two tendencies joined forces in the same locale to stage ever-more-spectacular mass demonstrations.[11]

This amorphous and complex movement constituted more than just mediagenic mass demonstrations. For example, some Americans decided to join its ranks because of grassroots, door-to-door campaigning by individuals who tirelessly canvassed neighborhoods and workplaces, while others were influenced by pamphlets, advertisements, and local lectures. Such activities were virtually invisible to the press, which treated demonstrations as synonymous with the movement and thus ignored or misunderstood their relationship to other political strategies and tactics. Images of rallies and marches that drew media attention comprised Americans' only exposure to an antiwar movement that was far less monolithic than it appeared on television screens and newspaper front pages. And that exposure did not often lead to a positive impression of the antiwarriors.

Did things have to turn out that way? Is it in the nature of such movements to adopt strategies that produce generally counterproductive media coverage? These issues, which appear frequently in the pages to follow, are as important now to the proper functioning of a democracy as they were during the Vietnam War.

Methodological Issues

The analysis of the media's handling of antiwar activities raises numerous methodological problems. Among the most difficult are the determination of the media to be examined, the sampling method, and the identification of important antiwar activities.

If the impact of the media on decision-making through their perceived impact on the public is the primary concern, then the problem of sources is a surprisingly simple one. Both Lyndon Johnson and Richard Nixon were obsessed with the coverage of dissenting activities in newspapers and magazines and on radio and television. Although interested in all media, they were convinced that seven counted most in the business of opinion-making. Both paid special attention to the *New York Times* and *Washington Post* among newspapers, *Time* and *Newsweek* among magazines, and the three national networks' evening newscasts on television. Despite a variety of attempts to punish, isolate, and subvert the independence of these very influential institutions, and despite repeated campaigns to favor and promote other newspapers and magazines, Johnson and Nixon reluctantly returned to these seven media as the most important in the United States.[12] Students of American journalism tend to agree with both presidents' judgments.

In terms of newspapers, almost everyone who was anyone in Washington and beyond read (and still reads) the *Times* and the *Post*.[13] Moreover, other major newspapers, as well as magazines and television networks, accept their definition of what is "news." In a somewhat different fashion (beginning with their celebrated covers), *Time* and *Newsweek* similarly help set the national opinion agenda. Both magazines enjoy large circulations among influential Americans.[14] Finally, the television networks' nightly newscasts are watched regularly by millions of Americans.[15]

To be sure, both the Johnson and the Nixon administrations evinced concern about prominent columnists in other newspapers and magazines, as well as such publications as the *Wall Street Journal*, *Los Angeles Times*, *Chicago Tribune*, and *U.S. News and World Report*. In addition, both monitored wire-service reports and their daily news budgets to which thousands of publications subscribed. Yet, in the end, they devoted special attention to the aforementioned seven media.[16]

By concentrating on what the presidents concentrated on, I will ignore the more traditional approach to media analysis that samples journals with an eye toward balancing liberal and conservative, highbrow and lowbrow, and regional interests. I could, for example, also examine the *Nation* and the *National Review* among magazines, and the *New York Daily News*, *Chicago Tribune*, and *New Orleans Times-Picayune* among newspapers, and so on, in order to give a more well-rounded view of the media's portrayal of the anti-Vietnam War movement.[17] I am concerned here, however, with the relationship between the antiwar movement, the press, and public opinion and not simply with a valid cross-section of media views of the movement. Opinion in America was affected most by the influential media, which either affected the perceptions of opinion leaders directly or affected other media, which in turn affected their readers, some of whom were local opinion leaders.[18]

This study differs from many other media studies as well because I am less concerned about editorial opinion than the straight news coverage of an event, which may or not have been colored by the editorial stance of a newspaper, magazine, or a television station.[19] People are influenced more by news stories than editorials or columns identified as opinion. This has come to be the case more and more as cities are left with only one major newspaper that people buy for local news, not necessarily because they agree with or even read its editors' opinions. If editorial positions were that important, few Democrats would have been elected president in this century.

For print media, headlines, lead paragraphs, and pictures that appear on the front pages are the most important influencers of opinion. A photograph of a very large crowd or a headline that mentions violence has much more impact than an editorial or the lengthy description of an event on the jump page that few people read carefully.[20] If this is the case, then an empirical content analysis that evaluates an entire story may reveal a journalist's overall slant but may not be very useful in gauging the impact of that slant on the reader. For example, when a newspaper headline declares that two hundred thousand people attended a rally, that bit of information is far more important than material buried deep in the story that offers other estimates as high as five hundred thousand. Or, as a candidate in the 1993 Detroit mayoral race complained to the *Detroit Free Press*, "On September 16, you carried a front-page story entitled 'Candidates fire opening shots.' All of the space on Page One was devoted to Dennis Archer's criticism of me. This placement favors my opponent. Many people do not turn the page but do read what appears on Page One."[21]

In the pages that follow, I concentrate on news accounts in these seven major media and pay attention to the wire services as well. Each section begins with a description of an antiwar activity based primarily on memoirs and secondary accounts.[22] This description covers the origins and organization of the event, the venue, crowd size, and major activities, and concludes with an appraisal of its significance. Obviously, given the often chaotic and ad hoc nature of many dissenting activities, and the strong partisan feelings they aroused in observers and participants alike, it is difficult, if not impossible, to capture accurately all that happened at such events. Nevertheless, enough years have passed and enough monographs and memoirs have been written to reconstruct major antiwar actions more precisely than was the case at the time.

Following the description of the event, I examine how the *New York Times*, *Washington Post*, *Time*, and *Newsweek* dealt with it in terms of story placement and length, descriptions of the size and nature of the crowd and its activities, and the general evaluation of significance. In addition, I have examined two suburban dailies in Michigan, the *Daily Tribune* (Royal Oak) and the *Macomb Daily* (Warren) for the manner in which they handled wire-service reports of the events.[23] I selected the two Michigan papers as a matter of convenience and assumed that, taken together, they represent the way many other comparable papers throughout the country treated wire-service feeds. The wire services themselves do not maintain historical archives that permit comparisons between their original stories and the material chosen by local editors for publication.[24]

After I completed the penultimate draft of this book, a reader suggested that I look as well at contemporary movement or left-wing media analyses of antiwar activities. I had earlier dismissed them as sources because they had little impact on the general public and its leaders; moreover, I presumed that they would be far less objective than more "professional" media. Nevertheless, out of curiosity, well after I had completed my research, I examined the *Village Voice* and the *National Guardian*, two weeklies with wide readership among movement supporters. I soon discovered, to my astonishment, that their treatment of antiwar demonstrations was often more detailed, accurate, and objective, if more breezy, than that of the seven mainstream sources I previously analyzed.[25]

Writers for the *Voice* and the *Guardian* usually were closer to the event than reporters for the mainstream media. They knew more about the movement, its leadership, and its many internecine political conflicts, and covered demonstrations as participant-observers. Further, because they were antiwar partisans talking to the already convinced, they saw their task as judging the effectiveness of each event from the inside. There was little reason for them to inflate crowd size or promote the high quality of the speeches or music. In addition, as journalists for weeklies, they had the luxury of time to produce stories that also examined the way newspapers and television had earlier covered the events, a major variable in judging political effectiveness.

Thus, at the eleventh hour, I decided to incorporate material from the *Voice* and the *Guardian* into the narrative. Their surprisingly dispassionate accounts, reflecting what journalists from within the movement thought had been accomplished, serve as a counterpoint to and a critique of the elite media.

From print media I turn to the networks and their three nightly telecasts. Unfortunately, the Vanderbilt University Television News Archive's comprehensive videotape collection extends back only to 1968. In addition, the archivists occasionally missed a weekend newscast when Nashville stations chose to run a sporting event instead. And sometimes, two or even all three of the networks cancelled their Saturday or Sunday newscasts because of football or baseball games. Almost all of the mass demonstrations of the era took place on Saturdays. One should also note that the Tennessee-based institution only taped newscasts from the Eastern time zone. West Coast viewers often received somewhat different feeds three hours later.

Of the three networks, only CBS maintains a readily accessible archive for pre-1968 broadcasts. However, for the period prior to Vanderbilt's startup date, CBS did not keep tapes of its shows in entirety, but organized its archive around specific news clips. It is not always possible to determine how much of the raw footage was aired.[26] On the other hand, the schedule for each day's newscasts and summaries of stories are available in the valuable *CBS News Daily News Broadcasts* series.

I do not consider the fact that NBC and ABC do not offer resources comparable to CBS's less-than-satisfactory operation a major problem. Despite the administrations' beliefs that one network was more hostile than others during certain times, their coverages were remarkably similar. It is true that in 1965 and 1966, ABC ran only a fifteen-minute evening newscast against its competitors' half-hour shows. But this difference is not as important as it seems; all through the period, ABC came in a distant third in viewer polls.[27]

Television is more difficult to evaluate than print because of the need to determine the impact of both the words (and the narrator's affect) and the film and photographic footage. Sometimes, visuals belie the narration such as, for example, when crowds are described as mostly young but pictures reveal scores of older people. Ironically, the narration on this visual medium may be more important than the pictures since many "viewers" only listen to the evening news. One can imagine families preparing, eating, or cleaning up from dinner while the network news is on, glancing at it only when an especially interesting story is presented. Another scenario sees busy working people, relaxing with their evening newspapers, or reading their mail, with the newscast only a background factor. On the other hand, of course, viewers trust seemingly objective pictures more than correspondents' narratives when they do pay attention to what is on their screens.

As with print media, I report on the placement of a story in the newscast; the first few stories are considered analogous to the front pages of newspapers. Both the newspapers and networks tended to evaluate the importance of stories in the same fashion. Rarely did a movement story make the front pages of the *Times* and not the *Post*. Even more rarely did one network lead with a story that the other two placed near the end of their telecasts. The networks frequently positioned their stories in identical time slots and devoted roughly the same number of minutes to them. This is not surprising since their news budgets were determined in part by the way the *Times*, *Post*, and wire services had been treating stories during the day. Indeed, this conformity between the networks and the newspapers reenforces the Nixon administration's belief that a conspiracy was afoot to control American minds, with a handful of executives in New York and Washington with the same world view agreeing on what news was fit to print or air.[28]

It is my assumption that the further a story is removed from the front pages or from featured positions on newscasts, the more the audience tends to discount or ignore it. Headlines or leads that introduce the stories appear to be especially important. Segments of the viewing and reading audience lose interest the longer the story continues. That is the time-honored assumption behind the pyramid approach to news reporting, in which the most important information appears at the beginning of the story.

The relative significance of and viewer attitude toward news items may also be affected by the items surrounding it. For example, the networks tend to group similar stories between commercial breaks. Thus, a two-minute feature on a genteel antiwar demonstration might be followed by one on campus violence unrelated to the war issue. The connection is young people and demonstrations. Similarly, an editor might air a poignant story about American soldiers dying in ambush in Vietnam after an account of other young Americans demonstrating against the war. In both cases, the demonstration stories might have been perceived negatively when viewers implicitly compared them to adjacent stories.

Following my own media analyses, I turn briefly to those of the presidential administrations. The media are important because they influence the public but also because they influence the people in power. My media analyses do not always agree with those conducted by the White House. Where they differ constitutes an important part of this study. Unfortunately, White House analyses are fragmentary, particularly for the Johnson administration, which was not as sophisticated—or as driven—as the Nixon administration in this area. Nevertheless, even those fragmentary analyses offer indications of the often curious way the presidents reacted to the media.

Sampling Procedures

The determination of the media to be examined and the analytical method to be employed solves only part of the methodological equation. I also must select a representative sample of movement activities, an easier task but one that also poses problems.

First, I have to establish chronological parameters. The scattered opposition to American involvement in the Vietnam War began to become a "movement" in the late winter of 1965, after Lyndon Johnson ordered the sustained bombing of North Vietnam. Prior to that point, antiwarriors had organized no successful mass demonstrations, even after the Gulf of Tonkin incident the previous August, and no permanent group had formed devoted exclusively to the cause of American deescalation or withdrawal.

The media virtually ignored a small demonstration sponsored by the Women Strike for Peace and the Women's International League for Peace and Freedom in Washington on February 10, 1965.[29] It took an outpouring of more than twenty thousand doves in the Students for a Democratic Society (SDS) Washington demonstration on April 17, 1965, for antiwar activities to receive serious media attention. Thus, I begin with that demonstration. I could also discuss the absence of attention to scattered manifestations of antiwar sentiment prior to that date, but there is little else to say other than that the press did not consider them newsworthy.

The identification of a termination date poses a different sort of problem. The last large antiwar demonstration took place in May, 1971. As the Nixon administration brought its troops home, American casualties declined, the draft came to an end, the intelligence services successfully penetrated and harassed radical and liberal organizations, and détente marked relations with Russia and China, antiwar coalitions broke apart and relatively few people could be cajoled into coming out for yet another protesting activity.

On the other hand, organizers maintain that the years from 1971 through 1973 witnessed intense antiwar activity, which took the form of many small decentralized campaigns instead of twice-yearly mass demonstrations in New York and San Francisco.[30] The media, however, did not cover most of these. The war was winding down and demonstrations were no longer considered interesting or "news."[31] Indeed, as antiwar leader Dave Dellinger notes, the media themselves contributed to the decline of the movement through self-fulfilling prophecy when they announced that the movement had faded away.[32]

No doubt, Richard Nixon felt restrained by the potential of a rejuvenated antiwar movement as he planned his military strategies in 1972.[33] Yet his mining of Hanoi and Haiphong harbors in the spring of that year produced little organized opposition compared, for example, to his invasion of Cambodia just two years earlier.

It is not my purpose here to debate movement claims that historians underestimated the amount of organizing and the number of effective campaigns that took place in the United States from the second half of 1971 through Nixon's reelection. The media did not cover these activities, however meaningful or exciting they may have been. This is an important issue, but as with the pre-1965 opposition, what can one write about it, particularly since the media themselves are the main contemporary sources for the evaluation of the political significance of an event? Thus, I begin my analysis of the way the media viewed antiwar activities in April, 1965 and end six years later in May, 1971.

In *Johnson, Nixon, and the Doves,* I gauged the importance of antiwar activities by their size and the amount of attention they received from the media and the administrations.[34] In general, I was most interested in nationally-organized demonstrations that took place in Washington and New York. Because of space limitations and also to avoid repetitive analyses, I will examine selected antiwar activities every other year during my chosen period. Thus, I will start in 1965 and move on to 1967 for the Johnson years and concentrate on 1969 and 1971 in the Nixon years. I will, however, summarize developments in movement activities and media coverage for 1966, 1968, and 1970. For 1970, I will devote more than passing attention to the important Washington protest over the invasion of Cambodia and the killings at Kent State.

The events chosen for detailed analysis are, in 1965: the SDS Washington demonstration on April 17, the Washington teach-in on May 15, and the International Days of Protest on October 15–16; in 1967: the March on the Pentagon on October 21–22; in 1969: the Moratorium on October 15 and the Mobilization on November 15; and in 1971: the demonstrations in Washington from April 19 through May 5.[35]

For most years during this period, antiwar organizations held at least two large gatherings, one in the spring and one in the fall. New York, in particular, was a regular locale for mass spring demonstrations every year from 1966 through 1970. Quickly becoming keen students of the media, movement leaders planned activities that would attract the most attention. Moreover, they naturally worried that their constituents—as well as the media—would become bored with too many activities in the same venue over a brief period of time.

Antiwar leaders were concerned about making the greatest possible impact on American attitudes. How to accomplish that goal was a matter of controversy among those who planned demonstrations and other actions.

The Impact of the Media on Their Audiences

One of the most difficult problems confronting a historian interested in the media's relationship to a political movement involves the assessment of the impact of the media on their various audiences.[36] This is not just the historian's problem—it remains a primary research interest of all scholars who study public opinion and the media. Despite the attention of several generations of experts on the subject, we still don't know very much about the impact of a newspaper story or newscast on an audience. Even after working in an administration that prided itself on its sophisticated understanding of the media, Richard Nixon's director of communications, Herbert G. Klein, suggested that the government—and the media—cannot measure the impact of media on the citizenry.[37]

Nevertheless, we can make some educated guesses, based upon hundreds of studies, about how the media may have influenced Americans during the period of intense debate about the war in Vietnam. In the first place, materials in the Johnson and Nixon presidential archives, as well as in the many memoirs of people associated with these administrations, offer clues as to how leaders interpreted media coverage. This may not tell us about media impact on public opinion but it certainly suggests what decision-makers (who were affected by that opinion) thought about the reportage of Vietnam War politics. Those concerned only with the impact of opinion on policy need look no further than the White House, because whatever the "real" impact was and whatever "real" opinion was, effective opinion was whatever the president thought it was. If Lyndon Johnson erroneously presumed that Walter Lippmann was a major opinion-maker in 1965, then his columns were influential in affecting White House strategies.[38] Indeed, journalists who know they are read by the president often aim their columns directly at him.[39]

Here, however, I am not just interested in how opinion was analyzed by the White House but how the media affected that opinion as it was reflected in the public opinion polls that were gathered assiduously by Johnson and Nixon. That is, the media affected political officials indirectly, through their impact on opinion registered in polls, as well as directly, through official media monitors' impressionistic evaluations of a story or a newscast.

Most observers agree that although the media are not generally successful in telling their audiences what to think, they are undoubtedly successful in telling them what to think about. Few doubt the importance of the agenda-setting role of newspapers, magazines, and the electronic media.[40] Although that role is affected by what readers and viewers bring with them to a news story,[41] in general, when it appears in several media in a prominent position, people will begin thinking about that story. Since most media tend to agree about the relative importance of news, readers and viewers are exposed to a national agenda that is reenforced, wherever they look, day after day. Thus, if a demonstration makes the front page of the *New York Times* and receives more than thirty seconds on a newscast, millions in the audience undoubtedly conclude that the demonstration is an important event.

When, on February 10, 1965, at the beginning of the bombing campaign against North Vietnam, the activities of several hundred picketers outside of the White House went virtually uncovered by the press, the antiwar movement was on few Americans' news agendas. At that juncture, the media had decided it was not an important story. Later, when demonstrations received lead placement in all media, Americans had to conclude that the antiwar movement was a major issue about which they began to develop attitudes.[42]

This does not mean that most members of the audience instantly became informed about the movement and its programs. Indeed, studies of viewers of newscasts suggest a surprisingly low recall rate for the specifics reported.[43] Nevertheless, once having been placed on the agenda of those concerned about what is going on in the world, news stories of antiwar activities had to leave a general impression of the movement.

The media also create opinion by reporting opinion.[44] When television anchors state that the country is in a conservative mood, they cause some members of their audience, who do not know what mood they are in, to think that they are in a conservative mood. More specifically, when a CBS/*New York Times* poll suggested that antiwar sentiment was growing, some who were nervous about holding an allegedly unpatriotic or unpopular view decided to come out of the closet with their opposition to the war.

In addition, the media have a profound impact on political movements and their strategies. Learning from earlier demonstrations, for example, organizers of the massive April 24, 1993, Gay Rights march in Washington put their most conventional-looking people in the front rows and relegated groups like "Dykes on Bikes" to the distant rear. This does not always guarantee that the media will ignore such fringe elements. One television critic refers to the way "producers often succumb to a temptation to drop in a striking clip or two from a Gay Pride float" in any story dealing with homosexuals.[45]

How a demonstration is reported, who is quoted, and what events make the front pages all influence the direction a movement takes. Thus, during the period in question the media chose leaders from often leaderless or anarchic coalitions and promoted them and their ideas. No doubt, given the media's penchant for drama, the rhetoric of these appointed leaders was more militant than that of others because journalists were not attracted to moderate, un-dramatic—and therefore apparently boring—language.[46]

Complicating any analysis of media impact from 1965 through 1971 is the fact that public attitudes toward the media began to change after 1968 in response to the attacks launched by politicians against them.[47] The media had more of an impact on their audiences during the Johnson years than during the Nixon years when readers and viewers had become more skeptical about the reliability and objectivity of newspapers, and especially, the nightly newscasts. It was precisely during this later period, in the years after the Tet Offensive, that more and more news-gathering institutions began to adopt antiwar editorial positions.[48] This did not necessarily mean that they had become supportive of the antiwar movement.

As we shall see in the next chapter, journalists and editors generally disapproved of political movements not associated with one or the other of the major parties. Beginning with their distaste for the countercultural and sometimes unkempt "beatniks" of the late 1950s, whom they confused with both the early "Vietniks" and the emerging "hippies," most members of the fourth estate were concerned about the potential destabilizing effects of the antiwar movement. That concern, which still confronts any mass oppositional movement out of the political mainstream, made it difficult for the doves to get their messages across in the media during the period of the Vietnam War.

2

THE MEDIA AND OPPOSITIONAL MOVEMENTS

D espite popular impressions created by a few authors and many government officials, the media generally do not look favorably upon movements that oppose official policy.[1] Although reporters and journalists may be disproportionately liberal, or at least moderate, and Democratic, their bosses, the gatekeepers in television and the newspapers, tend to be conservative, especially when it comes to instability or disorder in society.[2] Although few go as far as Edward S. Herman and Noam Chomsky in their depiction of the American media as a propaganda arm of the government, there is something to be said for the five factors they identify that lead the media to defend the status quo: their size and wealth, the role of advertising, their reliance upon government and other elite officials for information, the government's ability to pressure them, and an anticommunist, procapitalist bias.[3] In general, Herbert Gans agrees with Herman and Chomsky when he identifies ethnocentrism, responsible capitalism, small-town pastoralism, moderation, and social order as the values dominating journalistic institutions.[4] For his part, Lewis Lapham dismisses the media as simply fawning courtiers to the oligarchs, the Rosencrantz and Guildenstern of contemporary power-holders.[5]

The media tend to support those who operate within the system and denigrate oppositional activities of ordinary citizens.[6] In most newspapers and television newscasts, middle-class values or those of middle-aged professionals prevail.[7] According to two students of oppositional movements, "The media set limits on what is acceptable protest activity and behavior, and those limits usually reflect community standards."[8]

All of this suggests that antiwar demonstrations run by mostly antiestablishment young people would not receive favorable treatment in the American media of the sixties. Mass demonstrations could become unruly and lead to major societal disruptions. Most system-defending antiwar critics in the media preferred to see the war attacked at the ballot box or in Congress, not in the streets.[9] Of course, the more decorous the mass antiwar activity and the more its leadership involved prominent adult reference figures, the more likely the media would treat it favorably.

Here we encounter one of the great paradoxes of this study. Those who run the media personally prefer civilized, adult, dissenting activities where rowdies do not use profanity and carry Viet Cong or Cuban flags. But such decorous affairs are not very exciting or newsworthy. Although a large meeting of prominent individuals opposing the war politely might receive favorable attention, after a while, unless such meetings or marches become even larger or new glamorous leaders join them, they will start to appear in shorter stories toward the back of the newspaper or at the end of the newscast. Even large, somewhat violent or undisciplined, activities receive short shrift in terms of space and placement when they become routine.[10]

Middle-class values and support for the status quo clearly affect what is news and the way that it is reported. But these are not the only factors. After all, newspaper editors reject 75 percent of all potential news that crosses their desks each day while television rejects a much higher percentage because of time limitations.[11] The media lean toward covering stories that are relevant and fit into some frame or current theme, stories of human drama, especially those involving tragedy, disaster, violence, and death, and stories that are accessible.[12]

The frame or current theme is a most important factor in deciding what is news. Journalists simplify their work by creating an implicit finite group of media frames into which stories fit. Anything outside those frames makes little sense to them. Previous events are crucial in defining and altering frames.[13] In a famous play on words, Johan Galtung and Mari Ruge once noted that there is no such thing as news, only "olds." Of course, olds is ultimately boring so that news ends up being olds with unusual or deviant aspects highlighted.[14] If a story that fits into the proper frame contains no deviant, unusual, or dramatic aspects, it might not be covered.

Although such philosophical and political criteria are crucial in determining what gets reported by whom in what format, the accessibility factor is often paramount, especially for television. It is very costly to maintain permanent camera crews in all major cities in this huge country. To a lesser degree, the same situation holds true for newspapers and newsmagazines that have permanent offices in a few cities and only a handful of "stringers" in other venues.[15] Those who want to get into the newspapers or on prime time know this and plan actions that will be easy and cheap to cover.[16]

A related issue has to do with providing advance texts of speeches to the media, particularly television, to satisfy their need to have as much of their daily output planned in advance as possible.[17] This practice often results in journalists identifying the sentence or two most exciting or newsworthy in advance and then filming only that sequence rather than some other part of the speech, which, for example, might have received the greatest crowd reaction.

When covering political demonstrations without advance copies of speeches, reporters sometimes refuse to remain at the scene to listen to hours of rambling commentaries, due to the need to move their camera crews elsewhere.

Overall then, the coverage of a mass dissenting activity is bound to be affected by the media's generally conservative or moderate approach to change in society, the drama of the activity, and the costs of covering that activity.[18] Simple organizational and business criteria relating to production cost-effectiveness, especially for television, are often the most important. And all of these factors generally caused problems for the anti-Vietnam War movement.

Journalistic "Bias"

Despite compelling evidence that most media supported official policy during much of the Vietnam era and despite convincing theoretical explanations for that support, critics still assail the media for alleged antiwar bias.[19] Like Richard Nixon, they point to the fact that the private political views of a majority of journalists on prestige papers and the networks during the sixties ranged from liberal to moderate. More important, most personally opposed the escalation of the American commitment to Vietnam after 1965.[20] Logically, those journalists should have given a favorable accounting of the activities of the movement, irrespective of the conservative tendencies of their institutions. This was not the case for many of them.

In the first place, some journalists may have personally opposed the war, but they worked for editors and publishers who tried to be evenhanded at the least, and were supportive of the administration at most. For example, although *New York Times* editorial-page editor John Oakes was known for his opposition to the war, publisher Arthur Ochs Sulzberger was more circumspect. Another proadministration *Times* editor, A. M. Rosenthal, sometimes altered or refused to run stories that were at variance with his views of the war. At *Time*, editor Henry Grunwald occasionally changed correspondents' reports because he felt that "on certain major issues the reader has a right not to be confused as to where *Time* magazine as a whole stands."[21]

Even had conservative editors or publishers not been a problem, antiwar journalists who worked for establishment media were not especially fond of the protestors whom they labeled "Vietniks" and treated derisively.[22] In their early reporting, especially, they were not impressed with SDS and other left-wing organizations that attacked the bourgeois media and liberal values.[23] No doubt reporters had to be cautious about embracing the radicals because they relied upon official sources for much of their material. However, like much of middle-class America, they too were disturbed by the activities of the cultural and political revolutionaries in the antiwar van. Those young people were "violators of adult traditions" hallowed to liberal journalists.[24]

On the other hand, from the start, several low-circulation liberal publications like the *Nation* and the *New Republic* offered favorable views of antiwar activists. Given the widespread influence of those weeklies in the left-liberal community in 1965 and 1966, a period when the mainstream media scorned the movement, their stories helped to recruit more respectable protestors whose activities soon attracted favorable attention from newspapers like the *Times* and the *Post*.[25]

Differences between Print and Broadcast Media

Comparative analyses of newspaper, magazine, and television content must reflect the differences and similarities among these media. At first glance, the differences between print and electronic journalism would appear to outweigh the similarities. Newspapers and magazines reach far smaller audiences than the nightly newscasts, have much more space to develop a story, rely less on pictures than prose, are perceived differently by their audiences, and, of course, offer far more editorial or op-ed opinion.

Nevertheless, students of journalism emphasize the general consensus on the daily news agenda for all media. Most newspaper editors and television producers rely heavily on the *New York Times* and *Washington Post*, the wire services, a few morning columnists, and more generally, the covers of *Time* and *Newsweek* for indicators of important news.[26] The *Times* is preeminent, compared by one expert to Harvard in the educational field.[27] Each night the newscasts contain late-breaking items that did not make the morning papers, but producers prepare the majority of their material well in advance of air time. That material is largely dictated by headlines from the prestige papers and the news budgets of the wire services. This makes good sense considering the complications of putting together an expensive newscast on nationwide television at the last moment.[28]

Although it is difficult to overestimate the importance of the *Times* and the *Post* to the other media as well as to government officials and national elites, television newscasts were, in the period under discussion, and still are more influential with the vast majority of the population than newspapers and magazines.[29] Similarly, no print journalist or columnist can ever be as powerful as television anchors Walter Cronkite or David Brinkley, even if they were only transmitters, not interpreters of the news.[30] According to one industry executive of the period, the power of television news "astonishes even those of us who work for it."[31] Of course, as Richard Nixon, a careful student of the media, pointed out, television may be more important than print journalism, but the latter influences dramatically what appears on telecasts.[32]

Most Americans then and now relied more heavily on television than print media for their news. On the other hand, those who wanted serious news coverage relied more on the prestige papers than on television, with its brief stories often delivered in sensational packages that lacked context. Since the readership of prestige papers includes the most influential members of the public and since many of them express disdain for broadcast media, the importance of television in affecting public opinion may be exaggerated. Complicating matters is the fact that most officials think that television is more important than print in affecting the public debate.[33]

During the period of the Vietnam War, no print medium was seen by as many Americans as the nightly newscasts. In 1967, seventeen million Americans watched NBC news nightly, fourteen million watched CBS, and six million watched ABC. The figures for 1970 were about nineteen million for CBS, eighteen million for NBC, and eight million for ABC.[34] Scholars agree that television newscasts do shape the public's opinions, especially when they serve as platforms for presidents or respected experts.[35] Finally, of interest here is the fact that, during the years from 1968 through 1973, television devoted 25 percent of its air time to Vietnam-related stories, compared to only 7 percent of their total space for such stories in the newsmagazines.[36]

Most observers, including this one, have concluded that, despite fierce competition between the newscasts, they all run the same stories with similar news frames in the same time slots night after night.[37] There are, of course, some variations, often due to the anchors' travels. During the Bosnian crisis in 1993, for example, ABC sent Peter Jennings to the region and consequently ran much more on that issue than either CBS or NBC.[38]

The general conformity of views about what is news is a product of several factors, including the networks' reliance on the same sources to validate what is important as well as the relative interchangeability of their on-air and production staffs. This lack of difference in much of the content of the competing newscasts is an important matter since there is no news for many Americans if it is not on television, or, as one commentator notes: "News is whatever the media tells us is news . . . and to a degree, what is not presented is prevented from becoming news."[39]

Given the similarity of their programming and the fact that the three networks reached so many politically active middle-class Americans who trusted them for the news of the day, it was more important—and far easier—for a presidential administration to intimidate the networks than newspapers and magazines. Since networks are federally licensed and newspapers are not, the government has more weapons in its arsenal when it confronts television news executives. Such was the case with Richard Nixon's offensive against the media, which was far more successful with television than with print media.[40]

Although editors of print media also try to sell their product with banner headlines and exciting front-page photos, the dramatic visual is fundamental for telecast editors.[41] This means that a story with visual interest may be more important to television news editors than a story that results merely in a talking head in front of the White House or the Department of Justice. Talking heads do appear on nightly newscasts, but editors try to balance them with action footage. Because the stories are far briefer than comparable newspaper stories and because of the need for striking visuals, television news stories often revolve around one simplistic idea or theme.[42] Nevertheless, one should not ignore the narrative that comes along with the visual for it suggests how that visual is to be interpreted.[43] On occasion, however, narratives do not correspond to visuals, thus confounding the determination of viewers' reactions to the coverage of complicated events such as mass demonstrations, the most popular tactic of the anti-Vietnam War movement.

The Purpose of Mass Demonstrations

Mass demonstrations, rallies, and marches are essential tactics of dissenting political movements in a democratic society. According to one chronicler of the antiwar movement: "Demonstrations are to activist groups what football games are to colleges: major sources of publicity and money."[44] Further, for a decentralized "movement," they provide an opportunity for all activists to come together periodically under one banner. Peace historian Charles Chatfield contends that the movement held mass demonstrations "to attract people whose energy it could not really direct: it provided the decentralized heterogeneous movement a focal point for growth."[45] They also reinvigorated those toiling anonymously in local communities, who returned to their canvassing and leafletting secure in the knowledge that they were not alone.

Demonstrations are used to popularize organizations and their ideas, raise money, extend membership potential, offer psychic rewards to participants, and send a message to the government.[46] Few of these goals can be accomplished without adequate and even favorable coverage by the media, especially television.[47]

Participating in a demonstration can be exhilarating for the foot soldiers of a movement who labor much of the time in small groups or by themselves— they can at last feel as if they are part of a much larger and often quite impressive coalition of people. It is even more exhilarating when they can see themselves on television or in the newspapers the next day.[48] Yippie leader and media specialist Jerry Rubin asked:

> Have you ever seen a boring demonstration on TV? Just being on TV makes it exciting. Even picket lines look breathtaking. Television creates myths bigger than reality.

> Demonstrations last hours, and most of that time nothing happens. After the demonstration we rush home for the six o'clock news. The drama review. TV packs all the action into two minutes—a commercial for the revolution.[49]

Although, unlike Rubin, some participants might find a demonstration itself exciting, it loses much of its political impact if none but the converted ever hear about it.

Especially when one is launching a movement, media attention, even if it is not entirely favorable or fair, can be comforting.[50] Someone is paying attention—we are having some impact, is the feeling. Some political strategists, however, are nervous about the amount of energy and resources that their organizations must invest in demonstrations in order to make them successful. Given the likelihood of either media inattention or criticism, these Woodstock-type carnivals may not be worth the effort, especially in an economic sense.[51] Frequently, all of the unusually large amounts of money raised prior to and during such events are needed to cover expenses incurred by the event itself. Moreover, for logistic reasons, most of the major demonstrations have to be held on weekends. Since weekends are perceived by many in and out of the media as a time for fun, the typical Saturday march might not be taken very seriously. Johnson's press secretary, George Reedy, reported that his surveys revealed that most people did not pay much attention to "hard" news in their newspapers on weekends.[52]

Politicos who may be unsure of the effectiveness of mass demonstrations compared to community organizing and grassroots activities, for example, also point to the difficulty in controlling demonstrations. Unsuccessful demonstrations can hurt a movement that has spent months in painstaking political organization and public-relations campaigns. For example, they could produce disappointingly small crowds after a large buildup, they could receive negative media coverage, concentrating on weird-looking people, violence, and conflict between groups that make up the typical unwieldy coalition, and the most radical members of the group might be elected by the media as the "leaders" whom they choose to quote and photograph because "they are what sells."[53] Above all, when the "movement" became synonymous with demonstrations for many Americans because of the press's inattention to less glamorous dovish activities, negative images of them, as seen through media filters, often made the task of grassroots organizers more difficult.

This critique suggests that demonstrations may not necessarily lead to the mobilization of general public opinion for one's cause. Indeed, during the Vietnam War period, some antiwar leaders did not expect large segments of the public to be positively affected by seeing demonstrations on television or reading about them in their newspapers. They knew that most Americans are suspicious of oppositional mass demonstrations, which seem undemocratic since the majority has apparently already spoken through the electoral process. Also, many Americans viewed the demonstrations of the sixties as disruptive or dangerous.[54]

Rather than influence millions of apolitical Americans, leaders of demonstrations hope to impress the government, either directly or through the media, with the strength of their commitment and the potential power of a significant number of significant people. Nevertheless, Lyndon Johnson and Richard Nixon could still rally a majority of the population around them after they were confronted by huge antiwar demonstrations, especially when they questioned the demonstrators' patriotism and middle-class values. Nevertheless, they worried about these highly visible symbols of dissent, particularly when demonstrations were large and attracted support from national leaders, celebrities, and their student children.[55]

Moreover, demonstrations helped to inspire those in opposition to government policy who would have never considered marching on Washington. The pictures of huge crowds made them realize that they were not alone; if those students and mothers could do something like that, they could fight the war in their own way as well. On the other hand, it is highly unlikely that administration supporters would begin questioning their positions when they saw or read about a large and impressive antiwar protest.

During the late 1960s, demonstrations aimed at attracting the attention of the administration as well as potential allies in the general public came to be judged by their size and their relative civility. Here, movement leaders were at the mercy of the media, which established "official" crowd counts and characterized an event on a continuum from violent to peaceful. These two factors tended to dominate media frames at the expense of more substantive issues.[56]

Crowd Counts

Political organizers agree that the size of the crowd they draw to their events is of prime importance, especially to the media.[57] But what constitutes a large crowd and how does one go about counting it?

One thousand people protesting the Vietnam War in front of the White House in the fall of 1964 might have appeared to the media as a large crowd because no previous gathering had attracted more than fifty picketers.[58] On the other hand, a turnout of one hundred thousand in 1970 no longer impressed the media since previous crowds for such events had been larger.

A recent example sheds light on how crowd size affects the way a demonstration is reported in the media. In trying to explain why he placed a story about a relatively small protest at Michigan State University in 1989 on page three rather than page one, the publisher of the *Detroit Free Press* called attention to its size as a prime factor. He did, however, allow that had his photographer shot a "tight picture," the crowd would have seemed larger and thus might have justified a page-one story. What made his decision even more difficult, he noted, was the amount of drama and emotion in the protest, elements that also might catapult a small demonstration from the interior pages to the front page.[59]

The relative quality and quantity of other news occurring on the day an important antiwar activity takes place compounds the problem. What would have happened to the coverage of a domestic political protest that attracted several thousand demonstrators on October 16, 1964, the day when media in the United States were overwhelmed by three other important stories: the Chinese exploding their first atomic bomb, the replacement of Soviet Premier Nikita S. Khrushchev, and the dismissal of pennant-winning New York Yankees manager Yogi Berra. Similarly, the massive Gay Rights march on April 24, 1993 had to share front-page space in the Sunday papers with the Russian election, in which the future of President Boris Yeltsin's reforms were at stake.

During the period under analysis, some antiwar activities might have received more generous coverage had they not had to compete for space with other big stories. For example, Lyndon Johnson purposefully stole headlines from the Senate Foreign Relations Committee's hearings in early February of 1966 by staging a conference on the war in Honolulu. That fall, the story of Secretary of Defense Robert S. McNamara's harrowing encounter with radical students at Harvard was pushed from the lead position by the national elections. Similarly, although the 1968 Democratic convention in Chicago was big news, it would have received even more play had not the Soviets and their allies chosen the convention period to invade Czechoslovakia.

Accurate crowd enumeration represents an even more difficult issue.[60] It is one thing to count a crowd in a theater or even a stadium and quite another to count participants in a march down a city street or standing in a large open area such as Central or Golden Gate Park.[61] During the Vietnam era, government officials, march leaders, and journalists alike experimented with a variety of crowd-counting methods, including aerial shots and enumerators employing mechanical counters at entrances to an event. No method was truly successful; seat-of-the-pants' estimates were the rule.

There are so many ways even the most fair-minded crowd counter can go astray. During the era of the civil rights marches, for example, reporters tended to count all black people in the vicinity, even those who were bystanders on the sidewalks.[62] But what else could they do? This is a tricky business, especially for a reporter in the middle of an undisciplined group of people—milling about, arriving, leaving, returning—whose numbers have been inflated by scores of media people and plainclothes police officers monitoring the event.[63]

Often, crowd-size estimates depend upon the motivations of those making the estimates. During the period of the antiwar demonstrations, police and government officials underestimated crowd size, movement leaders overestimated.[64] Sympathetic to the left, Students for a Democratic Society (SDS) chronicler Kirkpatrick Sale arrived at his crowd estimates by simply doubling police figures. On the other hand, the *New York Times*'s Tom Wicker halved the estimates of the officials in charge of events.[65] This is not just an American phenomenon. During a major labor-management conflict in Sweden in the fall of 1983, Danish newspapers differed in crowd estimates by a factor of 100 percent depending upon their political orientation.[66] Moreover, the left is not the only group that complains about the press's underestimation of the number of people who show up at its mass political gatherings. Conservative radio commentator Rush Limbaugh began his May 24, 1993 broadcast by expressing concern about how his Fort Collins, Colorado rally the previous Saturday (Dan's Bake Sale) was undercounted by the media.[67]

Demonstration organizers, who know better, often exaggerate crowd size to improve group morale. This causes problems when journalists listen to those obvious exaggerations and then doubt the overall reliability of the organizers.[68]

However the media finally arrive at their estimates, what are readers and viewers to make of reports of large crowds at political demonstrations? Suppose an event is covered because it is massive in relation to previous activities. Readers might be told that two hundred thousand people turned out in Washington, a throng that constituted the largest peace-demonstrating crowd in the history of the United States. Should they be impressed? That two hundred thousand represents only a tiny percentage of the total population of adult Americans, and if the demonstrators are college students, then they are an even less representative body. If the demonstration in question took place on a Saturday in the fall, a likely time, the crowds gathering in football stadiums in Ann Arbor and Stanford would rival those at the demonstration.

Yet, to bring 200,000 Americans to one place on one day from distant cities without financial subsidy is an impressive logistic feat, considering the fact that such a crowd might never have gathered for that reason before. How should the media evaluate the significance of this event? Should television stations cover it live? Is the mere reporting of the "largest" of its kind sufficient? How impressed should the reader have been with the previous largest, perhaps 50,000 in 1967 or even 35,000 in 1965? Or what should he or she make of a later demonstration that drew "only" 175,000?

A final issue has to do with counterdemonstrators. Obviously, evenhanded reporters should note their presence.[69] But how much space or time should 1000 counterdemonstrators receive compared to 100,000 demonstrators?

These are not easy questions. Fair-minded observers then and now may sympathize with journalists trying to estimate and evaluate the size of a crowd at a demonstration. No doubt size was an important—and appropriate—criterion to judge the success of an event for demonstrators, the people in power, the media, and their audience. It became so important that movement organizers constantly worried that they would be perceived as failing or would not be covered by the media if their crowds did not continue to get larger and larger. The need to bring out ever larger crowds to interest the media often determined the activities and messages promoted at demonstrations. The larger and more heterogeneous the crowd, the less control exercised by leaders, and the more likely radicals, crazies, and other fringe participants would attract unwanted attention.

Violent Behavior

The size and, to some degree, composition of the crowd at an antiwar demonstration was the most important factor determining its relative success in the eyes of the media, the administration, and the public. Yet no matter how large the crowd or how diverse its constituents, that apparent success was always weakened substantially by the perceived presence of uncivil or violent behavior.

By the mid-sixties, the absence or presence of violence and arrests was a major element for most journalists and their audiences in stories on political demonstrations. Over the previous decade, civil rights demonstrations had captured headlines due to arrests, and sometimes violence, often produced by the police or counterdemonstrators. The "hook" that made a civil rights protest newsworthy soon became the number of arrests or injuries that occurred during the demonstration. Civil rights leaders understood this unpleasant fact, and were torn between the need to gain publicity for their activities and the danger that provocative marches posed for demonstrators, often women and children.[70]

From the perspective of journalists and editors, a large demonstration that was entirely peaceful might be interesting the first time, but after many such uneventful events, the story began to lose its dramatic quality. This was especially true for television with its need for exciting visuals, but the print media also looked for confrontations or potential confrontations between demonstrators and their antagonists to enliven stories. On one occasion in 1968, the managing editor of the *New York Times* told an interviewer that he had not devoted much space to a particular demonstration because it had been small and also because no violence had been expected.[71]

Because of space and time limitations, the focus in protest stories is often on the violent activity itself and not on the causes of the violence.[72] During the period when campus rallies, strikes, and sit-ins were common, editors frequently did not assign stories until the police had been called out. Even when journalists appeared on the scene before any raucous activity occurred, they tended to keep their pads in their pockets and their cameras shuttered until a confrontation took place. On one day during the 1968 Columbia University sit-ins, NBC was on the scene with its camera crew from nine in the morning until two in the afternoon. Yet the only footage that appeared on television that evening was a one-minute confrontation that marred an otherwise peaceful five hours.[73] Similarly, the producers of the nightly newscasts during this period searched for film of brief—and atypical—combat vignettes ("shooting bloody") for their nightly Vietnam story.[74] Such vignettes suggested to viewers that firefights or ambushes went on every moment of every day of a soldier's tour of duty. Interestingly, critics of this sort of coverage complained that the concentration on Americans on patrol left little time for analysis of the larger picture, either in terms of American strategy or the nature of the South Vietnamese regime. Similarly, as we shall see, when the media concentrated on the most dramatic activities during the demonstrations, they often left little space to cover the more important issues of what an antiwar activity meant (who was saying what to whom in what venue) and how it might have affected policy and the public.

According to one prominent demonstration leader, the media's "addiction to violence is matched only by its contemptuous indifference to non-violence."[75] On Easter Sunday in 1968, for example, they virtually ignored a "Yip-Out" in Central Park that drew more than ten thousand people because it was peaceful, calm, and thus, apparently, unnewsworthy.[76] This was not a new development in American journalism. Upton Sinclair complained in 1919 that the Associated Press was only interested in the violence associated with strikes during that turbulent year.[77]

Journalists in other societies behave in a similar fashion. The *Globe and Mail* (Toronto) emphasized arrests and violence in its stories of foreign and domestic demonstrations during the period.[78] Similarly, in a detailed analysis of the coverage of a London demonstration on October 27, 1968, a researcher discovered that although only three thousand among the seventy thousand in attendance behaved obstreperously, those three thousand received most of the attention from the British press.[79] That demonstration was generally peaceful, but those reading London newspapers and watching the BBC viewed coverage that led them to conclude that violence reigned supreme on the streets of London that day. The British media had apparently expected violence, because demonstrations in Paris and Chicago during that period had produced unprecedented violence. Thus, they were prepared to search out and report activities that fit their frame.

Once that frame was established and demonstrations had come to be associated with disruptions and arrests, it became difficult to alter that journalistic approach. Thus, when a demonstration produced no uncivil activities, reporters called attention to that fact in headlines or lead paragraphs. This approach reenforces the notion that demonstrations and violence go hand in hand and shifts attention away from more important aspects of the event. This is not just a phenomenon of the sixties. In that aforementioned Rush Limbaugh radio broadcast, the conservative media personality devoted an inordinate amount of attention to how peaceful his Fort Collins, Colorado, rally had been. Over and over he told his audience that no one was arrested and that local police had virtually nothing to do during the eight-hour "bake sale." Interestingly, he compared his decorous and neat followers to those unruly and messy people who turn out for liberal and environmental rallies.

The association of violent activities with political demonstrations poses serious problems for protest organizers. Demonstrations, even peaceful ones, come to be perceived negatively and thus do not aid the cause that brought the dissenters into the street. "If those are the sorts of things that happen at antiwar rallies," a reader might reason, "then I am not going to attend them," or, even more detrimental, "I am not sympathetic with the political aims of such rowdies." Lost in the thirty-second sound bite or six-paragraph story is the fact that most anti-Vietnam War activists were peaceful, and, especially during the early days of the movement, most of the violence at demonstrations was caused by right-wing hecklers who rushed the crowds to tear up Viet Cong flags and dovish placards.[80]

The perceived and real violence that came to be associated with demonstrations posed an almost insurmountable problem for antiwar leaders. The media were most interested in demonstrations when they produced violence. Yet the coverage of that violence clearly made the public less sympathetic toward the antiwar perspective. Such an outcome, as we shall see, pleased observers in the Johnson and Nixon administrations.

3

THE WHITE HOUSE
AND THE MEDIA

A lthough I am interested primarily in how the media treated the antiwar movement and the potential impact of this treatment on public opinion, I will pay attention as well to how the Johnson and Nixon administrations interpreted that impact. This is an important area of inquiry. It is quite possible for White House operatives to misinterpret media images, with dramatic consequences for policymaking.[1] Part of the problem concerns an administration's sampling procedures. In addition, misconceptions about journalistic friends and enemies and false estimations of the relative significance of various writers and columnists also skew its conclusions. As Clark Clifford commented about Lyndon Johnson: "I wish I could convince him that everyone in the country does not read the jumps on stories in the goddamn *New York Times*."[2]

LBJ and the Media

Both the Johnson and Nixon White Houses carefully monitored the print and electronic media. The chief difference between them was that Nixon developed an elaborate formal method of evaluation whereas Johnson relied on his own personal and unsystematic analyses.[3] Unlike Nixon, Johnson wanted to see the stories in the newspapers and television first hand. Before his aides arrived to wait on him each morning, he had already read the *New York Times*, *Baltimore Sun*, *Christian Science Monitor*, and *Wall Street Journal*, in addition to the *Congressional Record*. He also read the 11 P.M. first edition of the *Washington Post* as well as that day's *Washington Star* each night.[4] He looked at the news and editorials first, then the columnists and the business reports.[5]

Moreover, if possible Johnson watched each of the early evening news programs on the three networks and often the 11 P.M. news. When he was not able to watch them, they were frequently recorded.[6] A long-time owner of a television station, Johnson knew the business well. CBS anchor Dan Rather, who attests to the president's familiarity with television news operations, reports that he often called him in the middle of newscasts to either correct or applaud a segment.[7]

In the Oval Office, next to the bank of television sets, stood wire-service tickers from the Associated Press, United Press International, and Reuters. Johnson felt that "they kept [him] in touch with the outside world." Even when he left the machines in the Oval Office, he maintained his reputation as a news junkie by walking around with a transistor radio plugged into his ear (and he was not listening to rock 'n' roll).[8]

More than most presidents, Johnson was open to interviews from columnists and considered some of them, like William White, Robert Kintner (who later joined his administration), and Drew Pearson friends.[9] Such relationships were useful. On one occasion, Bill Lawrence of ABC called the White House with a "present," a preview of poll results to be announced that evening.[10]

Despite Johnson's familiarity with the business and his many friends among journalists, he may not have understood entirely how they functioned professionally. He thought that newspeople always wrote with a purpose in mind, not just to give information.[11] Moreover, he was guilty on many occasions of misinterpreting news stories.[12]

Why was Johnson driven to look at so much media reportage himself even though much of it was negative? One of his aides suggested that he was drawn to it because he had a masochistic bent and wanted to prove to himself the bias he knew was there. He also felt it important to see what voters were being told.[13]

The Johnson White House did not establish its own formal media-monitoring arrangement because the president generally would have previously read the material in any reports that could have been sent to him.[14] He and his aides also already had available to them the State Department's Bureau of Public Affairs's *American Opinion Survey*, weekly analyses of the media on foreign-relations subjects. The president was sent a copy each week, often with a comment from aides Bill Moyers, Jack Valenti, or Tom Johnson summarizing its contents, most of which concerned editorial and columnists' opinions.

The president and his staff could also glance at the Pentagon's daily exhaustive *Current News*, as well as its own informal clipping service run by Willie Day Taylor in the Executive Office Building. There appears to be no empirical rationale or sampling scheme to explain why Taylor and her aides decided to clip certain articles and columns each day from the scores of newspapers that crossed their desks. From 1967 on, however, she attempted to clip at least thirty of the most prominent columnists regularly, some of whom were of quite limited circulation.[15] White House aide Fred Panzer also clipped magazine and newspaper stories from time to time (also in an unsystematic way).[16] Occasionally, some of these were sent on to other aides for transmission to the president or for action or rebuttal, but generally they had little time to read them.[17]

In addition, political operatives often sent favorable clippings from newspapers and magazines to the president to cheer him up during times when he thought everyone was against him. On one occasion, White House aide John Roche sent a positive column from England's *Economist* with the note: "Perhaps we could trade Time, Newsweek, and two outfielders to the British for the Economist."[18] Similarly, newspaper editors and publishers sometimes sent their own material to show the president that they were backing him.[19]

The emphasis within the Johnson administration's print-media operations—and the Nixon administration's as well—was on editorials and columnists. That is, the president and his aides paid scant attention to the news stories that form the centerpiece for this study. They seemed to think that publicly expressed opinions were more important in influencing Americans than front-page news stories. It is true, of course, that both administrations paid considerable attention to the straight news on the telecasts. This is understandable considering the limited amount of air time allocated to commentary or editorials labeled as such on television.

Whatever newspapers he read from around the country, Johnson and his aides were most concerned with the *Times* and the *Post*, *Time* and *Newsweek*, and the three evening newscasts.[20] Impressed with the influence of the *Times*, George Christian noted how an error in its pages could be picked up and repeated by the networks and the wire services.[21] Knowing that others abroad thought that the *Times* was an official paper, Johnson occasionally passed stories to its reporters in order to send a message to Hanoi.[22]

Although Johnson was his own indefatigable media monitor, he did expect his aides to pay attention to the press and to watch the evening newscasts.[23] From time to time, he asked them to monitor the media for him, as in July of 1967 when a television was set up in Loyd Hackler's office because the president wanted him to watch certain news programs. For four months during the fall of 1967, Peter Benchley monitored the networks at the president's request. And Fred Panzer was asked to evaluate Evans and Novak columns from January through March, 1967, using a simple "favorable," "unfavorable," and "neutral" scoring system.[24]

In addition, aides often supplied Johnson with weekly lists of the media people they had met. For example, in one week in March of 1965, McGeorge Bundy noted eleven prominent journalists with whom he had spoken.[25] These meetings were not always initiated by the journalists. Johnson and his aides were continually speaking and writing to people in the media to correct their errors, and sometimes to flatter them. As Walt Rostow once advised Johnson before a meeting with columnist Joseph Alsop: "The more you let Joe talk, the greater will be his pleasure at the session."[26]

Johnson, like Nixon, blamed the media for many of his popularity problems. As the antiwar movement developed, Johnson linked it to media critiques of his policy. After he left the presidency, he told a biographer that the movement was started by two or three intellectuals who influenced columnists in the *Washington Post*, the *Times*, *Newsweek*, and *Life*. In a hyperbolic fit, he also told her that communists controlled all three networks and "the forty major outlets of communications."[27]

Johnson's major perceived enemies in the print media were the *Times*, *Newsweek*, and late in his administration, the *Post*. The *Times*, he felt, "plays a leading part in prejudicing people against him"; there was also "bigotry" in some *Times* reporters. Along with NBC, they "are committed to an editorial policy of making us surrender."[28]

As early as 1965, McGeorge Bundy found *Newsweek* "particularly difficult to deal with . . . because it has a vested interest in defeat" in Vietnam. Johnson was convinced the newsweekly was against him personally. Although *Newsweek* was published by the *Washington Post*, it was not until Ben Bradlee replaced Johnson's friend Russell Wiggins as editor of the paper in 1968 that the president began to see the parent newspaper as an enemy as well.[29]

Johnson also blamed the television networks for many of his political problems. He told an audience of broadcasters on April 1, 1968, the day after his speech announcing that he would not seek another term, that television had driven him to take that position. One of his aides thought that the networks were Johnson's "most visible adversary" that difficult year.[30] Whether his perception was accurate, Johnson was certain that television had become a major influence on the people who counted in Washington and throughout the country.[31]

Even before Walter Cronkite's famous report from Vietnam in February of 1968 in the wake of the Tet Offensive, CBS was singled out as the most hostile to the administration with anchor Cronkite perceived to be "out to get" the president. ABC was judged to be the fairest at that point with NBC in the middle.[32]

Finally, like all modern presidents concerned about the media, polls and mail to the White House and the executive departments served as indicators of the impact of the media on public opinion. Of course, both indicators were generally too crude to employ effectively.[33]

Nixon and the Media

President Nixon shared many of Johnson's views of the media, but he approached the problem differently. Most significantly, he generally did not read newspapers or watch television programs himself.[34] In part, this was a time-saving measure. (One exception was the *Washington Post*, a paper he considered especially important, which he read over breakfast before coming to the office.)[35] In addition, since he expected criticism from the allegedly liberal media, he preferred not to expose himself regularly to their abuse.

The fact that Nixon did not read many newspapers or magazines himself or watch many newscasts does not mean that he was not as interested in the media as was Johnson. According to one of his aides, one half of Nixon's time was spent on insubstantial matters, the majority of which was communications.[36] Even a cursory examination of the documents in the Nixon archives reveals his obsession with the media and public relations.[37] The voluminous media reports submitted to him are full of his marginalia and underlinings as well as orders to his staff to correct media misconceptions. These marginalia provide some of the most valuable insights into Nixon's daily feelings presently available in the archives. Indeed, he often ordered specific policy actions on the basis of those summaries.[38]

Unlike Johnson, early in his administration Nixon established an elaborate media monitoring system under the direction of Mort Allin. Assignments changed from time to time, but in general, Allin and his staff culled news, editorials, and columns from about fifty newspapers and forty magazines and watched the network news shows. Pat Buchanan, to whom Allin reported, also monitored the newscasts with backup from Communications Director Klein. Compiled between midnight and 5 A.M., the daily media surveys sometimes ran to thirty single-spaced pages for the print media alone.[39] Nixon did not rely on existing government sources, such as the Department of State's *American Opinion Survey*, because he felt they would be unfair to him. His perception of their biases or "disloyalty" related to his suspicion of the Democratic-dominated Washington bureaucracy.[40]

Nixon's own media surveys were supposed to be more objective. No doubt Nixon's operatives did their best to report accurately but errors and mistakes in interpretation abounded.[41] On one occasion columnist Jack Anderson, who saw several of Nixon's media summaries, complained about their biased interpretations in a column in the spring of 1971. Responding to Anderson, Charles Colson claimed that they were fair and that other journalists who had seen them agreed with him.[42]

However, either consciously or unconsciously, the media monitors fed Nixon analyses that confirmed his biases.[43] For a while, White House aide Jeb Stuart Magruder produced memos based on the news summaries entitled "Weekly Report of Little Lies Corrected and News Summary Notations." These were action memos explaining how Magruder and his staff had chastised erring journalists.[44] In addition, in the summer of 1969, Nixon cut back on the internal circulation of his media summaries because he feared leaks to journalists.[45] If they were so objective, what did he have to fear?

Moreover, his amateur social scientists made errors of judgment based upon dubious assumptions. For example, those who compiled the television summaries concentrated on the narrative and all but ignored the pictures that accompanied them.[46]

Nixon's newspaper summaries aimed for geographic balance, with, for example, the midwest covered with the *Chicago Tribune*, *Chicago Sun Times*, *Minnesota Tribune*, *Milwaukee Journal*, *St. Louis Post-Dispatch*, and *Des Moines Register*, among others. The television summaries stressed the evening newscasts, along with glimpses at the "CBS Morning News," "Today," and talk shows hosted by Merv Griffin, Dick Cavett, and Johnny Carson.[47]

Allin and others who scrutinized the media for Nixon produced long daily and weekly print-media summaries that must have overwhelmed him. In addition, the president received weekly magazine and daily television reports. As early as October of 1969, he requested only a one and one-half-page summary of "news play" covering the longer report each day since he could not always read the more detailed summary. On other occasions, he alerted his staff that he would not have much time to read anything. During the crucial period in 1969 following the Silent Majority speech and the Mobilization demonstration, Nixon told Haldeman that he had not had "the time to read the news summaries in great detail over the past few weeks and I will not be able to do so for the next month." This was a busy period but he wanted his staff to keep up with the work, particularly after the Silent Majority speech, to see if the journalists and commentators had "turned around." "While we are not going to be influenced in our policy decision on what the columnists, commentators or writers say," Nixon continued, he needed to know their comments in order "to counteract whatever effect they may be having on the public." Similarly, he warned Haldeman that he would not have time to read the summaries for a month after the Cambodia invasion in 1970, and ordered his chief of staff to flag important items for him.[48]

Aside from the monitoring operation, the Nixon White House ran several other media projects. One, instituted early in the administration, involved the dispatch of letters to the editor and to network executives from Republican loyalists whenever the administration felt it was being treated unfairly. These letters were sent most frequently after a presidential initiative or speech. This ploy was not always successful as, for example, when during the week of August 9, 1971, of fifty-one letters sent, only six were published. The emphasis in this undercover campaign was generally on the *Times* and *Post*, *Time* and *Newsweek*, and the networks.[49]

As in the Johnson administration, from time to time Allin and his aides conducted longitudinal studies of network newscast biases for Nixon. These were surprisingly amateurish productions, with Allin keeping "score" in a sloppy fashion that included crossouts and illegible tallies. Early in the administration, NBC was evaluated as the most hostile. Later, CBS began to replace NBC, with both almost always rated not as favorable to Nixon as ABC.[50] CBS hit bottom in 1971 when Nixon entertained the idea of encouraging publisher Walter Annenberg and H. Ross Perot to buy the network, fire Dan Rather, and transform the news personnel into administration cheerleaders.[51]

On several occasions, as we shall see, these evaluations led to direct high-level attacks against the networks with both Spiro Agnew and Charles Colson serving as point persons. When Colson met with network executives in September of 1970, he took pleasure in intimidating them, and noted how they ended up "almost apologetic."[52] Colson trusted his news summaries, which revealed that the administration was not "getting a fair shake," and thus he applied pressure on the networks in what he considered an entirely proper defensive tactic. While he admitted that he did not "think that anybody in government ever feels they're getting a fair shake from the news," he also used to "go up the walls" because of perceived unfair television coverage.[53]

Periodically, Nixon's aides received scorecards on network commentators with anchors and commentators rated on fairness. For example, in 1969 presidential media monitors considered Howard K. Smith, Tom Jarriel, and Herbert Kaplow friendly to the administration, Dan Rather, Walter Cronkite, Eric Sevareid, Chet Huntley, and Daniel Schorr objective, and Frank Reynolds, Sam Donaldson, David Brinkley, and Sander Vanocur unfair.[54]

Nixon speechwriter Ray Price made it a priority to see in person every major Washington demonstration. From this experience, he was convinced that the media depicted protestors "in a heroic, or at least sympathetic light, even when violent," while patriots like administration-supporting construction workers appeared as "ignorant thugs." Klein echoed this view: "Emotions ran as high within the news corps [on the war] as they did with the public."[55]

So convinced were the Nixon people of network bias that they felt that the establishment of a permanent video archive at Vanderbilt University would help them prove it, and thought of ways to support the enterprise. They reasoned that with a permanent record of newscasts available, the networks would have to change their allegedly biased reporting.[56]

As for Nixon's mail operation, the materials for which are more fragmentary than for Johnson, one study prepared by the Nixon administration shows no relationship between mail and television speech ratings, performances, and press conferences.[57] The mail counts were apparently deemed less important than in the Johnson administration because of Nixon's faith in his own commissioned polls and because those counts were often confounded by Republican operatives' unspontaneous letters.

Conclusion

In the pages that follow, I will describe the major anti-Vietnam War activities of the years from 1965 through 1971, the way those activities were covered by my seven main sources, and how the administrations evaluated print and broadcast media coverage of those activities. In so doing, I will examine the difficulties encountered by mass oppositional groups outside of the two-party system as they attempt to attract the attention of the public—and national leaders—with their messages. One source of these difficulties is institutional, relating to the way media go about their business of defining what is news. But another important source concerns the political culture and value system that influenced the way Americans assessed crowds of people exercising their constitutional rights to assemble peacefully and petition their government for an end to a disastrous policy. Those who took to the streets to oppose American military intervention in Southeast Asia began with an immense handicap—the fact that most Americans, including most journalists, simply do not approve of political activities that wander too far from the mainstream either in terms of tactics or messages.

4

THE LAUNCHING OF A MOVEMENT, 1965

> The original commitment in Vietnam was made by President Truman, a mainstream liberal. It was seconded by President Eisenhower, a moderate liberal. It was intensified by the late President Kennedy, a flaming liberal. Think of the men who now engineer that war—those who study the maps, give the commands, push the buttons and tally the dead: Bundy, McNamara, Lodge, Goldberg, the President himself.
>
> They are not moral monsters.
> They are all honorable men.
> They are all liberals.[1]

S DS president Carl Oglesby electrified a crowd of thirty-five thousand with these words at a SANE-organized antiwar demonstration in Washington on November 27, 1965. This was the last of several notable protests during the year in which the civil war in Vietnam became an American war.

The *Washington Post*'s Alfred Friendly began his analysis of the event, headlined "Anti-War Parade Lacked Virility of Rights March," with:

> The weather was more sparkling than the gathering, which tended to be earnest, good-natured and non-muscular.
>
> To contrast yesterday's March on Washington for Peace in Vietnam with the civil rights march here on Aug. 3, 1963, is perhaps unfair but unescapable. The difference was a certain virility: that one had it—this one didn't.
>
> The event two years ago was joyful, full of promise about to be realized, swirling with emotion and full-throated. The issue was less intricate and debatable and the consensus about the justice of the cause was much more nearly universal. Yesterday's convocation was of a minority, embattled, on the defensive and espousing a minority position.[2]

An antiwar movement slowly began to develop in the United States in February, 1965, in response to the Johnson administration's decision to bomb North Vietnam. No other American action in Southeast Asia so catalyzed critics of the war. The image of the United States bombing a peasant nation with which it was not at war troubled people the world over and immediately made it difficult for the administration to employ moral arguments to sell its case. "Stop the Bombing" became a central theme at antiwar demonstrations throughout Johnson's last three years in office. And his cause looked worse in late 1966 when bombs began falling closer and closer to North Vietnamese urban centers.

Although some Americans had earlier opposed other escalatory acts, particularly during the Gulf of Tonkin crisis the previous August, no groups organized effective demonstrations, marches, or other oppositional activities that attracted significant attention from the media, the public, or the administration. Even after the first round of bombing in early February, Women Strike for Peace (WSP) and the Women's International League for Peace and Freedom (WILPF) could only enlist a few hundred stalwarts to picket the White House on February 10. It took a few months of sustained bombing for the movement to reach a point where leaders could gather a critical mass of protestors who would be noticed by other Americans.

SDS Demonstration in Washington, April 17, 1965

The first major demonstration of the anti-Vietnam War movement took place in Washington on Saturday, April 17, 1965.[3] Although it was easier to gather large crowds in New York City, Washington demonstrations were important because they guaranteed attention from print and broadcast media that were read and seen by legislators and government officials. Furthermore, the symbolic value of masses of protestors at the Capitol, the White House, or the Mall was potent compared to a demonstration in Central or Golden Gate Park.

The Students for a Democratic Society (SDS), which started organizing the event in late December, had a head start on groups that slowly mobilized in February and March in response to the bombing. When its leaders began planning the then-obscure protest, they could not have predicted February's bombing decision, which immediately made their Washington weekend a focal point for all antiwarriors. In addition, when SDS leaders decided to issue their formal call for the April 17 demonstration on February 8, they did not know that day was the first of the bombing campaign against North Vietnam.

April 17 was the day before Easter Sunday, a day on which peace groups traditionally hold vigils and marches. Deferring to widespread interest among their constituents in the SDS demonstration, many of those groups shifted their activities to April 10. This gesture reflected the cooperation, on this occasion, between antiwar organizations and the more radical SDS. For its part, SDS adopted a moderate and non-exclusionary strategy in hopes of attracting as large a crowd as possible. For example, SDS-approved placards did not call for an *immediate* American withdrawal from Vietnam. As we shall see, in most of the demonstrations that followed, the language of official

slogans often set the tone for the events and even affected participation. However, organizers could not compel their foot soldiers to obey their fiats. Few in
the SDS leadership on this occasion, for example, were pleased about the
people who carried Viet Cong flags, but they had no way—and really no
inclination—to try to exclude those carrying such radical symbols from their
ranks.

Despite SDS's non-revolutionary approach, the fact that the group permitted organizations like the Progressive Labor Movement (later Party) (PL) and
the Communist Party's DuBois Clubs to participate led civil rights leader
Bayard Rustin and other liberals to threaten to withdraw their endorsements
on the eve of the rally. At the last moment, Rustin, Socialist leader Norman
Thomas, pacifist A. J. Muste, and Harvard professor H. Stuart Hughes satisfied themselves with a press release that expressed support for the demonstration, but pointed out that they welcomed only those groups opposed to
totalitarianism. The statement, which implied that subversives were involved
in the April 17 event, appeared in the print media on the morning of the
demonstration. The first major anti-Vietnam War demonstration was off to a
shaky start.

On that warm spring day in the nation's capital, busses carrying participants arrived from as far away as Maine and Mississippi. Students and faculty
from over fifty colleges were among those represented in the generally youthful and overwhelmingly white crowd of more than twenty thousand. At first
glance, this does not seem to be an especially large number considering the
size of later demonstrations. It was, nonetheless, quite impressive for a protest against a war that almost all Americans at that time supported.

The day's events transpired without serious incident. Participants first gathered at the White House where they were met by a handful of placard-carrying
counterdemonstrators, and then marched to the Sylvan Theatre on the south
slope of the Washington Monument. There they heard, among others, Yale
historian Staughton Lynd on the parallels between the French experience in
Algeria and the American experience in Vietnam, Senator Ernest Gruening
(D-AK) on the history of the war, journalist I. F. Stone on the mistakes made
by the government, and Paul Potter, the president of SDS, who disagreed with
Stone by claiming that the war was not merely a mistake, but an act fundamental to the system. Potter received the most enthusiastic reception from the
crowd. Joan Baez, Judy Collins, the Freedom Voices (a group from the Student Nonviolent Coordinating Committee), and Phil Ochs (who sang "Love
Me, I'm a Liberal"), treated those assembled to music of professional quality.
Such free concertizing, interspersed with speeches, became a drawing card at
antiwar and other New Left demonstrations.

After the musical and political presentations concluded, protestors singing
"We Shall Overcome" marched to the Capitol to present a petition to Con-

gress. The petition called for an end to the war through the employment of a variety of options including a new Geneva Conference, negotiations with the National Liberation Front, and the institution of free elections in Vietnam. The petition also noted that funds for pressing domestic problems were being drained away by the war. No one appeared at the Capitol to accept the document. For a while, three hundred people sat down on the steps hoping to produce action from the authorities. Finally, after a policeman accepted the petition, the protest came to an uneventful close.

Demonstration leaders were pleased with this event. Except for the minor glitch at the Capitol, everything went smoothly. The crowd was larger than expected, the number of counterdemonstrators and provocateurs minimal. Washington had been the scene of countless political rallies over the years. Yet this one was special because of its size and scholarly speeches, including one from a senator, and the fact that although "war" had not been declared, the demonstration took place while Americans were in combat in Southeast Asia. And its moderate petition laid out several options for U.S. policymakers well short of immediate withdrawal from Southeast Asia. The first significant anti-Vietnam War demonstration deserved serious consideration by the media because it reflected accurately the development of opposition to the course President Johnson had set for the country when he ordered the bombing of North Vietnam two months earlier.

IN THE *NEW YORK TIMES*, A SMALL, PAGE-THREE ADVANCE story on the morning of the event noted that more than ten thousand "students" were expected in the capital.[4] The implication that the crowd would be composed solely of students was unfair. On the other hand, the prediction of only ten thousand made the actual number that did show up more impressive. Of course, such a prediction may have led journalists who followed the *Times*'s lead to treat the expected small demonstration lightly.

The next day, the demonstration made the front page with a misleading picture showing scattered picketers in front of the White House along with an almost equal number of counterdemonstrators. The headline—"15,000 White House Pickets Denounce War"—underestimated the crowd and incorrectly characterized the day's events as being confined to 1600 Pennsylvania Avenue.

The accompanying story, however, described SDS accurately as "a left-leaning but non-Communist group" new to the peace movement and somewhat at odds among themselves over tactics.[5] The crowd it drew to Washington, according to the *Times*, featured a mixture of beards, blue jeans, tweeds, and clerical collars. The newspaper also presented an extended account of attempts by pro-administration Cornell students to stop busses taking students to the demonstration.

As for the speakers, the *Times* gave coverage only to Senator Gruening, and it was marginal at that. Because of this lack of attention to the overt political content of the demonstration, readers found it difficult to determine just what policies, short of opposition to the war, were being promulgated by the doves. Throughout the era, media coverage of demonstrations ignored the speakers in order to concentrate on crowd size, demographics, and behavior. Perhaps such omissions are more understandable later, when oppositional arguments had become familiar. At this juncture, the sorts of things Lynd, Stone, and the others were saying were newsworthy and represented thoughtful and rather sophisticated critiques of administration foreign policy. As one journalist noted in a discussion of how the fourth estate handles such issues in general: "The emotional vocabulary of the mass media doesn't lend itself to the discussion of complicated political issues, much less to moral ambiguity or moments of doubt."[6]

The *Times*'s story was not especially antagonistic or misleading, merely brief and incomplete; the treatment of SDS, which could have been played more radically, was fair. (The *Times* had run a balanced feature on the group in its March 15 issue.) Throughout the first half of 1965, much of the media, including the nation's chief newspaper of record, simply did not pay much attention to the developing antiwar movement.[7] With the polls overwhelmingly in support of the president and the movement composed mostly of students and young people, the media may have been correct in their assessment of the relative import of antiwar activities.

Nevertheless, sociologist Todd Gitlin, a former SDS leader, is especially disturbed by the way the *Times* trivialized the demonstration and ignored the ideas presented, the apparent black-white cooperation, and the presence of older people in the crowd. Even worse, he charges that the activities of the few right-wing counterdemonstrators were given disproportionate space, perhaps because editors were concerned that they would be attacked for being too favorable to war critics.[8]

The *Washington Post* offered a more balanced and nuanced account, a fact that should not be surprising since the march took place on its doorstep. (The venue always affected the quality and quantity of coverage accorded movement activities. This was particularly true for the way the *Times* and the *Post* dealt with demonstrations in New York and Washington, respectively.) In this case, on Sunday morning, April 18, the *Post*'s page-one headline referred to sixteen thousand marchers, slightly more than the estimate of fifteen thousand from the District police.[9] Journalists rarely accepted demonstration organizers' crowd estimates. Sometimes they were mentioned in the body of the stories but any attempt at balance was undermined when a seemingly "official" crowd size appeared in the headlines. That is, readers glancing at the figure in the headline and not reading much more of the story would have concluded that SDS drew sixteen thousand to Washington on April 17, and not the more accurate number of at least twenty thousand. It is true, of course, that the difference between the *Post*'s sixteen thousand and the march leaders' twenty-five thousand was not as dramatic as the difference between two hundred thousand and five hundred thousand in later demonstrations.

Despite the fact that the police made only four arrests, the *Post* noted them early in its coverage. On the other hand, its reporter considered the demonstration generally orderly if somewhat chaotic, attributing the confusion, in part, to tourists who mingled with demonstrators that pleasant spring day. Although the *Post* ran no front-page pictures, its editors offered four on page 18, including one of an impressive-looking throng.

The *Post*'s reporter, who did mention that SDS president Potter received the most applause, quoted from his speech. He described Senator Gruening's remarks as well but also outlined the activities of the estimated one hundred counterdemonstrators and the seven Nazis in attendance. Given their very small numbers compared to those on the other side of the political fence, the counterdemonstrators received rather handsome coverage.

How much coverage of the hawks would have been fair? Was it their numbers alone or the colorful nature of their signs and chants that determined the amount of newsprint devoted to their activities? Certainly their presence always enlivened the story for the media, especially television.

Not surprisingly, the two regional dailies in Michigan, which relied on the wire services, paid little attention to the April 17 demonstration. *The Daily Tribune*, in a small UPI story on page 1 dated the day of the event, noted that by noon, fourteen to fifteen thousand had assembled in an orderly demonstration marred by only two arrests. The account in the evening newspaper listed groups in attendance opposed to the marchers, but gave no indication of their small numbers.[10] The only sign described was one from the counterdemonstrators, "Pink Colleges Turn out Yellow Reds," a strange editorial selection given the significance of the moderate placards chosen by SDS that dominated the scene.

Neither the *Tribune* nor the *Macomb Daily* published Sunday editions. Thus, Saturday's events sometimes appeared in their Monday editions. The *Tribune* chose not to run a follow-up on Monday, while the *Macomb Daily* ignored the demonstration on April 17, and on April 19 ran only an account of a small weekend protest at Johnson's Texas ranch.

Despite the importance, in retrospect, of the April 17 demonstration, the antiwar movement was not especially newsworthy yet. Newspapers and wire services may have been surprised by the size—and respectability—of the SDS rally and did not recover in time to offer it adequate coverage. After all, this was the first major rally of its kind and it had been organized by a fringe group of young radicals, the sort who often picketed the White House on weekends. Moreover, even protest organizers were surprised by their relative success. The fact that few in the media considered the SDS demonstration important was reflected in the lack of coverage in *Time* and *Newsweek*.

CBS television did give the demonstration considerable attention that Saturday but seemed a bit unsure of how to handle it. For example, its own printed synopsis, which describes the film material in its archive, refers to demonstrators as "beatniks," although that word apparently was not used on air. But the beatniks of the late fifties had little in common with the politicos of SDS. And if newspeople referred to the SDS crowd as beatniks privately, that colored the way they dealt with them on screen.

CBS emphasized the picketing of the White House, not the speeches or mass rally. One reason may have been the presence of the counterpicketers, whose colorful signs read, "Peace Creeps" and "We Want Dead Reds." The network devoted almost as much time to the right-wingers as the left-wingers, even though the accompanying pictures revealed a great disparity between the size of the two groups. Further, the editors overused shots of beatnik types or bearded people among the dovish demonstrators. Their cameras paused as well for a glimpse at their sneaker-clad feet (it was too early in the season for sandals).[11] Viewers of CBS's account of the demonstration learned little about why the doves were in Washington, and especially, little about their political programs. They did learn to associate beards and sneakers with the movement.

Contrast the mainstream print and broadcast reportage with the *Guardian*'s description of a crowd of twenty-five thousand that constituted "The Greatest Peace Demonstration in American History."[12] The left-wing weekly had a point. This may have been the largest such demonstration (at least in recent memory) and thus deserved the special treatment its reporters and photographers accorded it. They claimed that although 75 percent of the protestors were students, the crowd came from all over the United States, included many "negroes," and certainly made up a "peaceful legion." Instead of spending much time on the few incidents of violence provoked by the counter-demonstrators, the weekly printed long excerpts from the speeches of Potter and Lynd. With those excerpts, extensive photographic display, and generally accurate, if partisan, reporting, the *Guardian* provided its limited readership with one of the most complete and professional accounts of the SDS demonstration on April 17, 1965, available in the American media.

NOT HAVING PAID ATTENTION TO THE *GUARDIAN*'S EUPHORIC coverage, the White House itself evinced little concern for the demonstration. In a note to Johnson on April 14, National Security Adviser McGeorge Bundy referred briefly to a "left-wing student protest rally" expected that weekend.

Such a casual reference could have convinced the president that the demonstration deserved little attention.[13]

The following Monday, in reaction to weekend news stories, Jack Valenti told Johnson that some newspaper editors were getting "a little edgy" about Vietnam—they were not opposed to administration policy, merely "uneasy" about where it was going. The aide suggested that Johnson meet with some of them to respond to their concerns.[14]

As for the affect of the demonstration on White House opinion indicators, mail summaries revealed not only a rise in the number of letters received on the Vietnam issue after the SDS came to Washington, but a swing in favor of the administration. Letters ran against the Vietnam policy at a ratio of more than 5 to 1 (3,276–600) for the week ending April 8; they were less than 2 to 1 (2,479–1,431) against it for the week ending April 29. That week, the White House received a total of 36,413 letters, which means that 11 percent dealt exclusively with Vietnam.[15] The 36,000 letters, which by no means reflected a random sample of 240 million Americans, seem to be an insignificant indicator of opinion. Nevertheless, Johnson's operatives kept a close watch on fluctuations in mail-flow patterns, even though professional public opinion analysts would have scoffed at such an unscientific indicator.

Considering the relative decline of dovish letters, as well as the president's overwhelming support in the polls and the positive response to his conciliatory Johns Hopkins University speech of April 7, it was easy to see why the administration could afford to take a cavalier attitude toward the first major antiwar demonstration of the era. Of course, given the relative lack of interest in that activity shown by the media, particularly the newsmagazines, the public had not yet been exposed to enough antiwar demonstrations for anyone to worry much about their impact. And even when it was covered, as in the *Times* and the *Post*, the SDS protest was framed in a way unlikely to attract middle-class readers to antiwar ranks.

National Teach-In, May 15, 1965

The SDS-led demonstration was not the only significant activity on the antiwar front in the spring of 1965. From late March through April, the teach-in phenomenon swept through scores of campuses, creating a new tool for the movement.[16] Although organizers billed them as free and open discussions that included government representatives, most speakers, faculty, and students who participated were critical of U.S. involvement in Vietnam.

The Inter-University Committee for a Public Hearing on Vietnam, a loose confederation of teach-in committees, organized a national teach-in for Saturday, May 15. The faculty-dominated committee obtained a commitment from

National Security Advisor McGeorge Bundy to participate as the chief government spokesperson at a fifteen and one-half hour teach-in during which pro and antiadministration speakers would be balanced. Organizers attempted to present equal numbers of tickets to both sides, but the vast majority of the audience was of a dovish persuasion.

The teach-in took place at the Sheraton Hotel in Washington before a live audience of three thousand. Phone lines to 122 colleges brought the debate to over one hundred thousand students and faculty. In addition, the National Educational Television Network (a forerunner of PBS, with limited facilities) covered the unprecedented event live. The commercial networks offered summaries during prime time and occasionally broke into their programming with brief live remotes.[17]

Taking the event seriously, the State Department prepared briefing papers for participants who supported the administration. Three hours before the start of the teach-in, McGeorge Bundy announced that he had to withdraw because the president had dispatched him to the civil-war-torn Dominican Republic on an emergency mission. We now know, as was suspected at the time, that Johnson did not want Bundy to participate in the teach-in and thus inflate its importance. When his absence was announced, many in the well-dressed and well-mannered crowd groaned.

Bundy's note of apology, which was read to the crowd, reminded the nation's enemies that the United States was united and strong; those enemies should not get the wrong impression from seven hundred faculty members who opposed Vietnam policy. Bundy's figure greatly underestimated the numbers of faculty and others who then opposed American involvement in the war.[18]

Arthur M. Schlesinger, Jr., became the main administration spokesperson in Bundy's absence. The distinguished historian and former Kennedy aide was the most famous participant in the teach-in. The polite audience, many of whom took notes throughout the program, remained quietly hostile to his presentation even though Schlesinger was far from a hawk. For example, while supporting Johnson in general, he called for less bombing and the dispatch of marines currently in the Dominican Republic to Vietnam for ground operations.

The teach-in was marked by civil, scholarly exchanges with few extreme positions presented either from the right or the left. The chief antiwar spokespersons were Cornell Southeast Asian expert, George McT. Kahin and University of Chicago political scientist Hans Morgenthau. One of the more unusual speakers was Isaac Deutscher, a noted Marxist (Trotskyist) historian, who discussed the origins of the Cold War. It was not often that he had the chance to speak to a non-sectarian assemblage.

A unique event, the teach-in underscored the growing concern about the war on the nation's elite campuses. With one hundred thousand participating vicariously over the phone lines, it was the largest antiwar activity to date. This first teach-in demonstrated that many of those who opposed U.S. policy in Southeast Asia were mature, fair-minded people who wanted to engage the administration in serious debate in the battle for public opinion.

The teach-in was an easy event for journalists to cover. It had been well-planned, speeches were the centerpiece, and the orderly crowd was contained in one room. Organizers expected more journalistic interest in their political ideas than had been the case during the SDS rally. They were not disappointed.

ON SUNDAY, MAY 16, THE DAY AFTER THE TEACH-IN, THE *NEW York Times* awarded the event front-page treatment along with a photograph of Schlesinger. The article led with Bundy's absence, a theme that reappeared on the jump page along with a separate piece, entitled "Bundy's Absence a Blow to the Crowd."[19] Most of that page was devoted to the teach-in with excerpts from the main speakers evenly balanced, although Schlesinger's comments were something of a mixed blessing for the administration. The next day the *Times* published two pages of excerpts from several speeches.[20]

Its reporter at the Sheraton described a crowd of mostly young students, some sporting beards, though fewer than one would find on campuses. The reporter thought that the bearded Deutscher resembled Lenin, an accurate but gratuitous comment. The interest in beards and sandals and other counter-cultural trappings appears in almost all media stories throughout the entire period, even at such a bourgeois event as the teach-in. Nevertheless, the *Times*'s coverage was full and fair, capturing the significance of the unusual activity.

The *Washington Post*'s front-page photograph on May 16 supported its description of the crowd at the Sheraton as mostly clean-cut, short-haired, and clad in coats and ties. (Photographs selected to accompany antiwar movement stories did not always reflect accurately the nature of the activity.) As in the *Times*, Bundy's absence was the lead item. In addition, the Washington daily noted prominently Schlesinger's deviations from the administration line. And even more than the *Times*, most of the *Post*'s speech excerpts were critical of official policy. Of course, one could argue that that was the news; the administration had presented its position many times before.

In a separate piece, a *Post* reporter looked suspiciously at Bundy's "abrupt withdrawal" as perhaps having been trumped up by the president.[21] An analysis on the following page noted accurately that while the doves had been strong in their critiques, they had little to offer in the way of practical alternative strategies. Indeed, the writer contended, Johnson might have fared better than expected because of that factor.

Finally, in a pleasant human-interest story on still another page, the *Post* explained how an "Aura of Classroom Surrounds Viet Debate."[22] Students took notes, scholars exchanged witty academic jibes and maintained decorum at an impressive exercise in reasoned debate in a democratic society.

The Bundy story was also the big news for the wire services that Saturday. Under its "Late News Flashes" feature that ran down the left side of its front page, *The Daily Tribune* headed its teach-in "flash," "Bundy Out of 'Teach-in' Debate."[23] The following Monday, the AP's even-handed analysis, which suggested there was no clear winner in the lengthy debate, offered a variety of comments on the impact of the event.[24] To be sure, activists thought they had won the teach-in with their superior intellectual and moral arguments. Nevertheless, at this stage in the movement, such balanced treatment from the AP had to be considered a plus.

Newsweek devoted two columns to the teach-in, along with pictures of Morgenthau and Schlesinger, "Highbrow to Highbrow."[25] Less than positive in its history of the teach-in movement ("droning diatribes," "considerable heat and occasional light"), the magazine nonetheless liked the national event a little better than the newspapers. During the "twelve [*sic*] windy hours," Bundy came in for his lumps for pulling out at the last minute and Morgenthau was labeled incorrectly "pro-withdrawal." *Newsweek* accorded Schlesinger the largest play in the eight paragraphs that described the debaters' positions. Yet since many of his statements were critical of Vietnam policy, readers received more anti- than proadministration material in a story that ultimately approved of the teach-in.

Time was not so approving in its two paragraphs on the event, which appeared within a lead article on the war.[26] The newsweekly labeled it a "platform for interacademy cattiness and pointless caterwauling." Moreover, according to its reporter, antiadministration academics did not possess enough information about Southeast Asia to be credible critics. Throughout much of 1965, *Time*, more hostile than *Newsweek*, either underplayed the movement's activities or attacked its legitimacy. This is not surprising considering founder Henry Luce's special interest in halting the spread of communism in Asia, the weekly's general conservatism, and its especially nasty and snide attitude toward America's perceived enemies.

CBS offered much more favorable treatment of the teach-in on its several telecasts that day than Luce's newsweekly. Again, the two major figures were Morgenthau and Schlesinger. The former, with a pronounced German accent, may have appeared something less than "American" when he pointed out that we were fighting a war against guerillas in Vietnam with inappropriate methods. Schlesinger, sporting a bow tie that might have struck some as an eccentricity, claimed that there were "reasonable and decent men on all sides of the debate," though he hoped that the United States would persevere in its effort to obtain a fair negotiated settlement. The cameras caught him laughing with an audience of serious-looking scholars in coats and ties. Interestingly, in a voice-over during one of the earlier stories that ran during the day of the teach-in, a CBS correspondent still expected an appearance by Bundy and maybe even a surprise appearance by Johnson. Bundy's non-appearance became the major aspect of the story on the Sunday night news.

Overall, in terms of media treatment, the teach-in was a success for the antiwar movement. Participants appeared in the print and electronic media as serious and well-behaved. The fact that the press reported dovish arguments in some detail, along with responses from administration supporters, lent legitimacy to antiwar criticism. The administration had feared such an outcome.

AS EVIDENCED BY BUNDY'S WITHDRAWAL, JOHNSON AND HIS aides took the teach-in and its coverage seriously. That move was handled clumsily because the event drew more attention than might have been the case had Bundy initially refused to participate or at least withdrawn a week earlier. The withdrawal looked even more foolhardy after Bundy did so well, according to the media, in his "make-up" televised debate on June 21.

National Security Council (NSC) aide Chester Cooper expressed concern about the impact of the teach-in, fearing it "prompted a rethinking of the adequacy of the program centering on the American Friends of Vietnam" proadministration rally that had been scheduled for June 5 at Michigan State University.[27] Writing that same day to Dean Rusk, Walt Rostow, chair of the State Department's Policy Planning Council, thought that administration involvement in the event was a good thing since it "defused quite a lot of tension on our flank." On the other hand, Rostow did not think the government had much to gain from many more such events.[28]

In the one editorial on the teach-in clipped for the White House files, *Los Angeles Times* columnist Bill Henry wrote of the "egghead revolt" that "shook up" the administration.[29] Henry may have overstated the case, but clearly the administration perceived the antiwar movement as having gained through the teach-in and its generally favorable coverage, something Johnson had been concerned about when Bundy lent his celebrity to the event.[30]

The teach-in was another indication of growing antiwar sentiment in the population, especially on the campuses. Yet judging by the White House mail flow, its impact on public opinion was marginal. Johnson's mail clerks counted 504 favorable letters and 1,317 unfavorable letters on the war during the week ending May 13. This was followed by a diminution in volume in the two weeks after the teach-in with the count at 359–753 and 111–390 against administration policy. In June, only 12 percent of those polled called for U.S. withdrawal from Vietnam.[31] That figure represented a drop in four points since April and one point since May. Perhaps Walt Rostow was correct when he suggested that the teach-in served as a harmless way for antiwar critics to blow off steam and then retire to the sidelines for a while.

Organizers of the teach-in did not expect to reach the general public. They aimed their scholarly arguments at a small attentive public and an elite audience that may not have been moved to write letters to the president.

However the White House evaluated the teach-in, the media took it seriously and generally reported the arguments presented at the Sheraton accurately and in detail. Despite the Bundy story stealing the headlines, antiwar activists had to be pleased with the way they were treated by journalists. Observers viewed the civilized forum as a wonderful tribute to the democratic system, certainly an improvement over mass demonstrations led by radical young people. Yet since the event was not followed by any dramatic opinion shift or even a noticeable growth in the antiwar movement, one must wonder about its effectiveness. The most that could be said for it is that it reenforced those who already had dovish leanings and may have planted a seed for others who recognized that challengers of administration policy were developing legitimacy.

The teach-in soon faded as a major movement activity. Considering the way most of the media admired that sort of event, one wonders why antiwar leaders did not schedule more of them periodically. Of course, editors and producers would have become bored with the format, which offered little action aside from cerebral talking heads. Here we have a great paradox of this study: The media approve of orderly middle-class oppositional activities. But they are not very newsworthy if they occur frequently. The media generally do not approve of radical and disorderly demonstrations but they make interesting stories. Unfortunately for demonstration leaders, such stories could be counterproductive. This would be the case for the next major demonstrations in 1965, the International Days of Protest.

First International Days of Protest, October 15–16, 1965

The May 15 teach-in bore little relationship to the International Days of Protest demonstrations of October 15 and 16, 1965. The organizers, their lieutenants, and the foot soldiers all came from a different sector of the fast-developing antiwar movement than those who earlier ran and participated in the Inter-University Committee for a Public Hearing on Vietnam.

Antiwar activists attending the Committee of Unrepresented People's demonstrations in Washington in early August used the occasion to form a new umbrella organization, the National Coordinating Committee to End the War in Vietnam (NCCEWVN). This loose coalition of left-of-center groups planned to meet the escalatory moves of the Johnson administration with a series of rallies and marches in the United States and around the world in the middle of October.[32] Although the NCCEWVN was the titular organizing body of the International Days of Protest, local committees were virtually autonomous.

At least one hundred thousand mostly young people in as many as eighty American cities took part in antiwar activities on Friday and Saturday, October 15–16. The International Days of Protest was the largest series of demonstrations to date. The most important actions took place in New York City and in Berkeley and Oakland.

The main happening in New York on Friday, a dramatic display of antiwar sentiment, occurred outside the Whitehall Street Army induction center. There, David J. Miller, in view of television cameras and three hundred supporters, burned his draft card. This was the first widely-publicized case of such an act of civil disobedience. It also represented an escalation in dovish tactics that would alienate mainstream, "law-abiding," antiwar critics. But it certainly was mediagenic.

The next day in Manhattan, from twenty to twenty-five thousand people marched from 94th Street to 69th Street for a rally, where they attempted to hear, among other speakers, maverick journalist I. F. Stone. (The marchers had been denied a permit to hold their event in an area of Central Park where acoustics would have been better.) As many as one thousand counterprotestors sporting proadministration banners and placards lined the parade route to jeer the doves. No other major protest produced so many counterdemonstrators, albeit at a proportion of one in twenty. Among them were egg and paint throwers who participated in the day's main lawless activities. Throughout the nation, almost all of the violence and ensuing arrests that weekend involved anti-antiwar protestors who harassed and provoked peaceful demonstrators. This proved to be the case for several years. Yet for those not reading press accounts carefully, unruly behavior appeared to be widespread at antiwar demonstrations, irrespective of its origins.

The New York crowd, which was predominantly youthful, did contain a noticeable minority of adults. Some of those who paraded carried life-size dummies caricaturing the president, children held colorful balloons, while others waved placards with the official march slogan, "Stop the War in Vietnam Now." The demonstration, like the April SDS affair, was non-exclusionary. Its leaders did, nevertheless, try to stop participants from carrying placards with more extreme slogans. Moreover, not all on the Saturday march supported the Friday draft-card burning.

The key group in the organizing coalition, the Fifth Avenue Vietnam Peace Parade Committee, was led by Norma Becker, one of the more anonymous leaders of the movement, at least in terms of media attention.[33] Among others involved were A. J. Muste and Dave Dellinger. Sponsoring associations included the Committee on Non-Violent Action (CNV), the Socialist Worker's

Party (SWP), the War Resisters League (WRL), AFL-CIO chapters, the Student Nonviolent Coordinating Committee (SNCC), SDS, PL, and the Communist Party.

On the West Coast, the Vietnam Day Committee, composed mostly of Berkeley students, planned to march to the Oakland Army Terminal to leaflet soldiers on their way to Vietnam. After a campus teach-in in the evening of October 15, as many as fifteen thousand young people began to walk to Oakland where four hundred riot police awaited them. The marchers did not have a parade permit to cross into the city. After discussions among the leadership about whether to challenge the police lines, the group returned to Berkeley without reaching its goal.

On the next afternoon, about five thousand youthful demonstrators attempted the same march only to be met again by Oakland police and this time, by marauding Hell's Angels as well. The latter waded into the crowd producing scores of injuries and arrests. After the disorder abated, protestors sat down in the street for an hour to listen to speeches and then disbanded peacefully, again without having reached their goal.

Among other activities that weekend, demonstrations outside the Selective Service office in Ann Arbor, Michigan were noteworthy. There, thirty-eight people were arrested, including the editor of the student newspaper. In a few venues, such as Cleveland, counterdemonstrators outnumbered demonstrators. Marches and other protests also took place in many European cities.

As the first nationwide—and international—series of demonstrations, the International Days of Protest deserved considerable attention. Both the New York and Berkeley actions had their dramatic moments and produced violent reactions from bikers and hawks that made for sensational stories. In almost all cases of violence that weekend, lawful demonstrators were set upon by right-wing groups.

Of course, the obvious left-wing and youthful coloration of the protestors made them less sympathetic to middle-class journalists and editors—and their audiences. Moreover, the Days of Protest were difficult for the media to cover since they took place in so many locales over two days. No single crowd was larger than twenty-five thousand although the total number of demonstrators in scores of states and foreign countries was unprecedented in the brief history of the movement. With journalists just beginning to learn how to cover such events, the International Days of Protest tested their resources as well as their objectivity.

THE *NEW YORK TIMES* MADE THE DAYS OF PROTEST ITS LEAD story on Saturday, October 16. A sub-headline called attention to unlawful behavior—police halting the Oakland march and the arrests in Ann Arbor. Further, early in the story, the reporter mentioned that an American flag had been torn. On the jump page, which included a picture of the Berkeley teach-in, the draft-card burning at the Whitehall center and the Oakland march dominated the coverage.[34]

Although the *Times* emphasized the clashes and civil disobedience, those were obviously the most colorful events of the first International Day of Protest. Moreover, given the relatively small numbers involved on Friday, the New York newspaper was generous in its attention. That attention reflected increased media interest in antiwar demonstrations since the spring, albeit concentrated on potentially violent and unlawful activities. Administration supporters contributed to that increased interest with warnings concerning the left-wing, even communist nature of the weekend's activities.[35] The fact that real communists and socialists participated in leadership positions in the Days of Protest coalitions validated their warnings. When many Americans read that leftists were involved in the protests, they found it easy to dismiss or oppose such activities, even if they were becoming skeptical about their government's involvement in Southeast Asia.

The next day, the *Times*'s coverage of Saturday's events, although generally accurate, again emphasized unlawful behavior with a front-page photograph of police seizing a counterdemonstrator. The fact that the arrestee was a hawk may have been lost on those who read the headlines: "10,000 in City Parade Join World Protest on Vietnam / Violence Breaks out in Several Communities—Pickets Arrested" and "Marchers Heckled Here—Eggs and a Can of Paint are Thrown."

The headlines were not entirely inaccurate but the figure of ten thousand was a serious underestimation that came from the police, though the reporter later offered other estimates that ran as high as twenty thousand. In addition, the emphasis on violence may have made the protestors appear to be an unruly lot, which they were not. Another picture inside the paper showed a Hell's Angels biker being subdued by the police.[36] Readers glancing at the picture might have concluded that the roughneck was an antiwar protestor.

Such coverage was not helpful to the movement. Middle-class *Times* readers, who along with their paper were beginning to express concern about the war, could have become leery about attending future mass demonstrations because of their apparently violent nature.

As for the makeup of the crowd, the *Times* noted that "Participants . . . included members of left-wing groups from many college campuses . . . [who] comprise a small fraction of the college population at schools where they have been formed." That gratuitous editorializing could have been balanced with an estimate of the percentage of students who generally supported antiwar activities.

In New York City, the *Times* noticed non-students in the crowd as well, including adults who were "well dressed." However, they and their comrades marched in a manner "jarring [to] the quiet elegance of a residential neighborhood." Further, the *Times* correspondent described in detail each of the handful of incidents that led to the arrests of four people. With so much space devoted to that aspect of the demonstration, it is not surprising that the paper could spare only a few lines for Stone's keynote address.

The *Times* was not alone in its emphasis on the most unruly aspects of what were generally decorous rallies and marches. In its Saturday issue, the *Washington Post* stressed the potential for violence in Berkeley and noted incidents of egg throwing and scuffling in other cities.[37] With no major activities planned for the capital, the *Post* did not give as much space as the *Times* to the first day of the weekend protests.

The next day, however, they took the lead position on the front page with the headline, "Protests Staged In Many Cities Over Viet Policy: Clashes Occur in New York and Berkeley, Calif."[38] The headline was a mixed blessing for the doves. On the one hand, the influential Washington daily highlighted the clashes; on the other, the "many cities" reference suggested an event of some magnitude. The accompanying photograph of the D.C. picketers, however, was unimpressive, with their numbers noted as 160.

More than half of the *Post*'s copy dealt with hecklers, paint-throwing, and scuffles in New York and California that attained "near-riot proportions." In addition, its reporters counted only ten thousand New York marchers.

Even more than the *Times*, the *Post* saw the International Days of Protest in a light unfavorable to the doves. From 1965 to 1968, the *Post*'s editorial-page director was Russell Wiggins, a friend and supporter of the president who was named ambassador to the United Nations in 1968 by a grateful Lyndon Johnson. Although there was some distance between his page and the rest of the paper, his commentaries helped to balance material favorable to the antiwar movement written by his colleagues. Its editorial page changed dramatically after Wiggins left the scene.[39]

On this occasion, the *Post*'s reportage—as well as its editorials—may have influenced government officials and readers alike to dismiss this largest protest to date as a radical affair that had been challenged by many patriotic Americans. It is true, of course, that the non-exclusionary NCCEWVN did attract left-wing sectarian protestors unpopular with establishment papers like the *Post*. Whatever the reason, its negative treatment of the International Days of Protest was an important public-relations setback for the antiwar movement in Washington.

In the Midwest, *The Daily Tribune*'s wire-service protest story on Saturday, in the lead position on the front page, concentrated on nearby Ann Arbor where it listed students who had been arrested.[40] The article noted that the draft board protest "marred the UM homecoming festivities." One of those arrested was the editor of the *Michigan Daily*, a person, the *Tribune* informed its readers, who the previous week had called for the legalization of marijuana.

Arrests nationally dominated wire-service stories in the *Tribune* on Monday.[41] Photographs showed scuffles in New York, Berkeley, and Austin. Further, a caption writer made an editorial point with: "New York City police subdue an angry man who hurled red paint at anti-war demonstrators." The writer then alerted readers to note the sign the arrested man dropped. It read: "Win the War." The story that followed stressed the violence nationwide and how police and university officials saved the day in Detroit and Ann Arbor.[42] Yet, leaders of the protest were reported as being "pleased" with their activities. Readers might have asked how protestors could be pleased by all those arrests and confrontations unless that was what they had had in mind in the first place.

A few miles down the road, Saturday's *Macomb Daily* emphasized the wire service's theme of violence with the arrests in Ann Arbor featured prominently on the front page.[43] University of Michigan protestors were said to have ripped up an American flag on a homecoming float, while, on his own campus, a Wayne State University protestor spoke unpatriotically about the flag. The caption under a picture of the Berkeley teach-in noted that only two hundred out of a student body of thirty thousand participated. That blatant editorializing was simply not true. In addition, none of the *Daily*'s wire-services excerpts mentioned the reasons that drove the demonstrators into the streets for the International Days of Protest.

The *Daily*'s UPI front-page story on Monday highlighted the arrest of David J. Miller for burning his draft card. The AP retrospective on the weekend's events referred to the demonstrators as "pacifists," a description used earlier for Miller.[44] The wire service offered a figure of seventy thousand for total participation nationwide with ten thousand in New York, numbers that were said to have pleased the organizers. China was said also to have been pleased by the demonstrations while an administration spokesperson and a GI were not. To its credit, the AP reported that the demonstrations were generally orderly and that hecklers were responsible for most of the problems.

The wire-service accounts run by the *Macomb Daily* on Monday were far more balanced than those selected by *Tribune* editors on the same day. With access to the often even-handed AP and UPI reports, editors used parts of them to form a story that confirmed their own analysis of what "really" happened. Moreover, local papers, with much less space than the *Times* and *Post* to allocate to national stories, generally highlighted the most unusual, dramatic, or violent aspects of demonstrations.

Published on the Wednesday following the weekend, the *Village Voice* decried the fact that the Sunday papers had emphasized "violence and bizarre" occurrences when the New York doves were mostly orderly and plainly dressed. On the other hand, two out of three pictures the *Voice* ran involved confrontations between demonstrators and counterdemonstrators. Though unrepresentative, such action photographs are more interesting even to readers of counter-cultural publications than simple images of people marching or listening to speeches. Sympathetic to the demonstration, the *Voice*'s correspondent Paul Cowan nevertheless estimated the New York crowd at only between fifteen and twenty thousand. In a departure from the mainstream media, he did devote one-third of his account to Stone's and Dellinger's speeches.[45]

With more extensive coverage than the *Voice*, including a front-page story headlined "The Great Protest Against the War," the *Guardian* counted thirty thousand demonstrators in New York, the largest peace parade in history. Like the *Voice*, the *Guardian* offered extensive excerpts from the speeches and pointed out the many ordinary-looking adults in the peaceful assemblage. If the FBI wanted to find out who was in this parade, the *Guardian* provided a detailed, contingent-by-contingent list of groups along the route. No other publication paid this sort of useful attention to antiwar demonstrations.[46]

The *Guardian* had a week to prepare its story. Also looking back at the International Days of Protest from the perspective of a week, *Newsweek* interpreted the one hundred thousand total turnout for "Battle of Vietnam Day" as disappointing to the movement.[47] (The *Guardian* had been ecstatic that seventy-five thousand turned out nationwide.) According to *Newsweek*, "Many students, it seemed, had either tired of protest, accepted the U.S. role in Southeast Asia or were too busy with their studies or other protests to bother." Indeed, the antiwar movement may have reached its "saturation point." To punctuate this theme, *Newsweek* reported the State Department's claim that it ignored the protests because they involved such a small percentage of the population. For his part, administration supporter Senator Thomas Dodd (D-CT) labeled the Days of Protest communist-run. Most students, according to *Newsweek*, were not radical and many supported the administration. With arrests and radicals dominating the stories, readers could easily conclude that the antiwar movement was failing and unimportant.[48]

The following week, the apparently failing movement made the newsweekly's cover with a picture of demonstrators who appeared surprisingly middle class. Photographs that accompanied the story showed an antidovish heckler, marchers wearing skull masks, a Walt Kelly cartoon-strip poking fun at long-haired young people, and an antiwar sign ("a vocal minority")·in the background at an Iowa State-Colorado football game.[49]

The long feature story began with clean-cut protestors in the offices of the WRL. Facing the draft, a "tiny but noisy minority was making newspaper headlines" with their resistance to induction.[50] *Newsweek* considered the antiwar movement in general to be larger then just the resisters, including intellectuals, pacifists, and radicals. Moreover, although most who marched the previous weekend were described as sincere and well-groomed, many of their leaders were scruffy left-wingers with ulterior motives. *Newsweek*'s several stories also emphasized the impact of the movement on the draft and, ultimately, on Hanoi and Beijing who cheered on American doves.[51]

The newsweekly described a fragmented antiwar movement with all sorts of motives, including simple draft-dodging, to be found among its adherents. The New Left was "often bearded and sandaled and nearly always verbose and earnest"; the SDS Chicago office a shabby place of "Bohemian squalor."[52] Despite these negative impressions, the magazine did devote space to SDS president Carl Oglesby and his ideas, few of which sounded revolutionary or dangerous. But the magazine reprinted an alleged movement pamphlet explaining tactics to use to dodge the draft including the feigning of homosexuality and even bed-wetting.[53]

Newsweek's unflattering cover story was not far from the mark in some respects. Many of the people involved in the International Days of Protest leadership were bohemian-looking, bearded, even sandaled. Some foot soldiers were as well although one wonders what difference this should make to anyone interested in their cause. Further, the movement was fragmented and full of radicals who joined under non-exclusionary umbrellas. In the fall of 1965, most middle-class adult liberals still supported the president. Stories like those in *Newsweek* helped Johnson to maintain their support given the unattractive sorts of young folk in leadership roles of the opposition movement. Moreover, the emphasis on draft-dodging also did not reflect well on the movement. Many Americans might have begun to feel nervous about the war, but most would never think of failing to heed their country's call to arms. Finally, the support for the movement from communist nations, noted by *Newsweek* and others, played into the hands of those in the White House who argued that antiwar demonstrations aided those who were killing American boys in Vietnam.

Characteristically, *Time* was even harder on the movement—if that were possible—in the wake of the International Days of Protest.[54] In an issue in which the optimistic cover story reported "The Turning Point in Vietnam," the magazine dismissed the demonstrators derisively as "a ragtag collection of unshaven and unscrubbed—they could be called Vietniks." *Time*'s reporters described the leaders of the NCCEWVN in unfavorable terms, and more important, alleged that the weekend's activities brought out more counter-demonstrators than demonstrators. That just was not true. Further, *Time* reported that one antiwar student hit a middle-aged mother of a soldier in the face and that the Days of Protest had confirmed the Senate Internal Security

Subcommittee's published warning about the radical nature of the movement. One of the two pictures accompanying the story showed counterdemonstrators with a large placard reading, "Victory in Vietnam / Down with Red Traitors."

For CBS, Berkeley was one of the centerpieces for its coverage of the Days of Protest because it was, as a correspondent noted, "the scene of the biggest, most disorderly student demonstration of last year." Of course, that "Free Speech" demonstration had nothing to do with the war. On the Friday, October 15, afternoon news, CBS reported a crowd of five to ten thousand likely to march to Oakland to hold a peaceful protest. A still bourgeois-appearing Jerry Rubin, described as a twenty-seven-year-old former sociology graduate student at Berkeley, explained the protestors' position in a dignified manner. Complaining about the unconstitutional denial of their rights by the Oakland police, Rubin reported that they were going to march anyway but would break no laws.

The teach-in, which began the day's events in Berkeley, appeared inaccurately on CBS to involve only a few hundred people, an interpretation reenforced by shots of students passing up the opportunity to take leaflets from organizers. Moreover, the only speaker chosen to reflect the teach-in activities was bearded. In 1965—if not the 1990s—people with beards appeared to be slightly seditious or at least outré. The impression was even more negative if the beard was combined with long and unkempt hair.

The CBS correspondent did quote university administrators who blamed right-wing politicians like Ronald Reagan and George Murphy for inflaming the situation. On the other hand, his Berkeley story closed with a snide reference to "a new academic year and a new cause," a clear diminution of the significance of the antiwar movement.[55]

On Friday night's newscast, the protest was Walter Cronkite's lead story, beginning in Berkeley where young people praised Ho Chi Minh, while others called the war immoral because "Americans [were] murdering innocent people." Despite the lack of a permit, the march to Oakland was ready to go, with six hundred National Guardsmen prepared to keep order if needed.

CBS accurately described the Harvard turnout as light, perhaps no more than one hundred protestors. One graduate student, who was rooting for a Viet Cong victory, had words of praise for communists in the antiwar movement because they understood American society. An interview with the editor of the *Harvard Crimson* made a better impression when he pointed out that although some in the movement were not students, the students in the movement tended to be among the brightest in their classes. Overall, the articulate editor felt that 10 percent of his classmates opposed the war and at least half were disturbed by American policy in Vietnam.

CBS's coverage at the Whitehall induction center was briefer on Friday evening, showing a small crowd and a speaker talking about Vietnamese children being bombed in schoolyards by Americans. In addition, viewers saw glimpses of picketers in Chicago numbering fewer than one hundred, who were met by counterpicketers carrying signs reading "No Compromise in Vietnam." There was little difference in the respectable clothing worn by doves and hawks in Chicago in the pre-hippie fall of 1965. The CBS correspondent noted that the University of Chicago was able to turn out only one hundred marchers opposing the war out of an enrollment of seven thousand. (This frequent disclaimer from both the print and broadcast media is akin to a sports reporter noting that while the Detroit Tigers attracted a sell-out crowd of fifty-one thousand, that represents only a very small percentage of the people who live in the Detroit metropolitan area.) Whatever the significance of the one hundred marchers, CBS's microphones picked up exchanges between them and counterdemonstrators with a dove calling the war genocide and a hawk responding that the United States would get out as soon as the communists did.

Another protest story that evening came from Madison, Wisconsin, where, in front of the student union, according to the reporter and the supporting visuals, few students were paying attention to the speakers. The student union, he noted ironically, had been erected to honor University of Wisconsin men who had fought in America's wars.

As if to punctuate that thought, Senators Dodd and John Stennis (D-MS) then appeared on the program to rail about communists and draft dodgers who were protesting. Anchor Walter Cronkite concluded the lengthy coverage by noting that, apparently by coincidence, small demonstrations in London, Paris, and Bonn also took place that day. He seemed not to understand that these were "international" days of protest.

Among the stories on Saturday's CBS newscast was one concerning another small protest in Chicago, this time involving a handful of Roosevelt University students confronted by counterdemonstrators. Both groups were unattractive with the doves shouting, "LBJ, LBJ, How many kids did you kill today" (perhaps the first time a national audience heard that chant), and the hawks carrying American flags, signs that proclaimed "Better Dead than Red," and pictures of doves with hammers and sickles on their breasts. Given more air time than the demonstrators, the counterdemonstrators explained that though the Roosevelt protests were a flop, they did encourage Hanoi.

As for California, "The biggest demonstration held yesterday was in Berkeley but it did not lead to any violence." That loaded statement clearly linked the expectation of violence with demonstrations. The correspondent did point out that most of the violence of the day was caused by counterdemonstrators but he also noted that North Vietnam approved of the rallies.

CBS's coverage on Sunday night was again rather extensive, despite the fact that the protests had all but ended on Saturday.[56] That night, a Wisconsin antiwar leader was shown expressing satisfaction with the success of his demonstration outside an army base while Vice President Humphrey referred to the weekend's actions as "feeble, futile, and unnecessary."

This first weekend-long antiwar activity was the lead story on Monday night's news with White House aide Bill Moyers commenting that the president worried about its impact on Hanoi. Walter Cronkite reenforced the White House's concern by quoting from Russian and Chinese newspapers that were encouraged by the demonstrations. David J. Miller was then given a chance to explain his actions, which he said were a reflection of his Christian faith. His comments were followed by Senators Everett Dirksen (R-IL) and Gale McGhee (D-WY), both vigorous opponents of the International Days of Protest. During the early period of American escalation in Vietnam, it was difficult for editors to find dovish senators willing to appear on national television. Part of the problem was that most of the doves came from Democratic ranks, and few were willing to incur Lyndon Johnson's wrath.

Overall, CBS news paid a good deal of attention to the protests. In almost all accounts, the network balanced dovish presentations with those of their opponents. Moreover, seeking out the most provocative and dramatic activities, camera operators and directors left the impression that the demonstrations often led to clashes between two equally divided camps of demonstrators. Yet, the antiwar movement was getting its message on the air, with some of its spokespersons (even on a weekend sponsored by the left-leaning NCCEWVN), appearing as mature and reasonable adults. At this point, most viewers preferred the messages from administration spokespersons. CBS, however, forced them to share the limelight with antiwar critics, and in so doing treated the movement more favorably than most of the print media.

The networks usually tried to offer equal time to doves and hawks, or Republicans and Democrats for that matter. In 1965 and 1966, this approach favored the doves who were still a small minority of the population. Later, during the period from 1969 through 1971, equal time tended to work against the antiwar movement since a majority of the population had by then accepted the general outlines of its critique.

WITH GOOD REASON, THE JOHNSON ADMINISTRATION BEGAN to worry about the demonstrations. As early as September 16, its interdepartmental Public Affairs Planning Committee for Vietnam called for the release of some peaceful announcement during the "Berkeley-sponsored Days of Protest."[57] At the time, the memo writer thought that this was solely a Berkeley operation.

The State Department's weekly news roundup, *American Opinion Survey*, had begun running selections from editorials and columns on the war in the fall of 1965. For the week ending November 3, its collators noted widespread support for administration policies everywhere with only a small percentage of students in opposition. Editorially that week, the administration could take comfort in support from the *Chicago Sun Times*, *Denver Post*, *Washington Star*, the Scripps-Howard chain, the *Chicago Tribune*, *U.S. News*, and the Hearst publications. The *Nation*, not unsurprisingly, was one of the few publications to support the demonstrations. The following week, with only the *St. Louis Post-Dispatch* seen as unfavorable to Vietnam policy, the *Survey* added the *Philadelphia Inquirer*, *Washington Post*, and *Los Angeles Times* to the president's side. And a Harris poll revealed that two-thirds of those queried supported the policy in Vietnam. The newspaper clippings collected by the White House generally reflected the same line with emphasis on communist support and infiltration of the movement and draft dodging.[58]

The mailbag also brought the White House good news.[59] The week before the demonstration, monitors had tallied over 1,000 letters opposing the administration on Vietnam and only 59 supporting. The next week, after the Days of Protest, that count had changed to 444 in support and 1,289 against. Moreover, on the specific issue of the Days of Protest, the White House received only 7 letters from supporters of the antiwar activities compared to 135 that opposed them. The following week (ending October 28), the administration received more letters supporting Vietnam policy (921–807) than opposing it. It is impossible to explain just what led to this situation but negative depictions of the protests might have activated "patriotic" Americans to demonstrate their support for the president.

Nevertheless, movement leaders, along with the president, could take some comfort in their treatment by the media. The leaders were at least getting their stories in the papers and on the air, even if violence and rowdiness overshadowed their political message and growing strength. On television, especially, they received time to explain their positions. The president, on the other hand, had to be pleased by the negative images of protestors, editorial support from the press, and the fact that the International Days of Protest involved mostly unknown young people.

SANE Rally in Washington, November 27, 1965

The media had been suspicious about the political orientations of people involved in the International Days of Protest. Six weeks later they had the opportunity to cover a more decorous demonstration that involved respectable adults. The way they treated it offered clues to movement leaders—and to the White House—about the relative effectiveness of different dissenting strategies.

On Saturday, November 27, Washington was again the scene for a major antiwar activity.[60] This one, organized by the National Committee for a Sane Nuclear Policy (SANE), a respected and effective peace group, drew as many as thirty-five thousand participants. Although the final speaker, Carl Oglesby of SDS, delivered the most memorable address ("They are all honorable men. They are all liberals"), most who preceded him were moderates like author Saul Bellow and entertainer Tony Randall. SANE did not permit several noted radicals to speak, urged demonstrators to carry moderate placards and American flags, and issued a dress code. Not everyone adhered to the "rules"—several people insisted on carrying Viet Cong flags, a gesture that Dave Dellinger considered to be "senseless" and "inflammatory." (On one of his later trips to Hanoi, Vietnamese communists told him that American anti-warriors should carry American and not Viet Cong flags.)[61]

Despite the occasional Viet Cong flag and the fact that one thousand counterdemonstrators showed up to heckle, the November 27 activity in Washington produced little in terms of fiery rhetoric (except for the little-known Oglesby), civil disobedience, or peculiar costumes to engage the sensation-seeking media. Their sound bites and photographs of the characteristic activities of the day did not make for dramatic reportage.

The *Times* and the *Post* placed the SANE story on the front pages of their Sunday editions, but underestimated the crowd size, overestimated the importance of the counterdemonstrators and a handful of arrests, and all but ignored the many interesting and reasoned speeches.[62] In a rather anachronistic reference, both noted that few "beatniks" participated. Most important of all, the two influential dailies thought that the protest lacked spirit. What they meant was that it was dignified, serious, middle-class—and quite boring to people trying to sell papers.

CBS television's oral coverage that weekend was relatively accurate and fair to the protestors. But the network also offered enough scenes of violence and Viet Cong flags to produce a negative impression. Thus, viewers could have easily concluded that SANE people were the radicals and rowdies who provided the colorful action sequences on which the newscasts dwelled. Throughout the period, television consistently relied on the most extreme—and exciting—actions for their protest stories. After all, an antiwar talking head with short hair made for a dull sequence.

The *Guardian* again saw things differently than most other media. Not enthusiastic about SANE's moderation or the relative lack of "negroes" in the crowd, its correspondent nonetheless hailed the rally of forty thousand (a figure only five thousand more than most estimates), as the largest peace demonstration to date. We have seen how the radical newsweekly emphasized that each succeeding peace demonstration from April through November broke earlier records. In addition, as expected, it paid attention to the speeches and perceptively explained the political origins of the "mighty march for peace."[63]

In general, despite the *Guardian*'s suggestion that the antiwar movement was taking off, the Johnson administration did not consider the SANE demonstration to be of much importance, even though it attracted middle-class people and was the largest one-city antiwar activity to date.[64] In part, the lukewarm press coverage reenforced its confidence as 1965 came to a close with less than 25 percent of the population thinking that American entry into the war was a mistake and with fewer than 10 percent calling for withdrawal. Further, about half of those polled approved of Johnson's handling of the war against 30 percent who opposed his policies. And that 30 percent was split between doves and hawks.

No doubt, as NSC aide Chester Cooper pointed out on the day of the SANE demonstration (for which he was administration point person), the problem posed by the antiwar movement was still a "cloud no-bigger-than on the horizon."[65] He was confident that with good public relations and a sensitivity toward those who were beginning to lean toward the doves, the president could ride out the storm. Of course, a lot depended on how the media covered the movement in the future. Up to this point, except for the teach-in and the expected favorable—and accurate—coverage from countercultural publications, the president and his allies had done quite well indeed.

5

FROM FULBRIGHT TO THE PENTAGON, 1966–1967

Slowly the wedge began to move in on people. With bayonets and rifle butts, they moved first on the girls in the front line, kicking them, jabbing at them again and again with the guns, busting their heads and arms to break the chain of locked arms. The crowd appealed to the paratroopers to back off, to join them, to just act human. They sang the 'Star Spangled Banner' and other songs: but the troops at this point were non-men, the appeals were futile. . . . Some individuals left, but most remained. To leave was to leave one's brothers and sisters to get clubbed, yet to passively remain in the locked chain was to participate in the senseless brutality. . . . one cannot articulate the agony of those who sat and watched this go on slowly for hours amidst the songs, the pleas, the tears, and the impotent curses of 'Motherfucker!' and 'Bastards!' from those who could not leave yet could not resist.[1]

Early in the morning of Sunday, October 22, 1967, after many of the demonstrators—and the press—had left the Siege of the Pentagon, government forces waded into the crowd of remaining, non-resisting doves with astonishing brutality, according to participant-observers from the Washington *Free Press*. Although not the largest antiwar protest during the Johnson presidency, the Siege of the Pentagon was the most turbulent since the 1965 escalations.

On Monday, October 23, the influential *New York Times* columnist James Reston ignored the bloody event described by the Washington *Free Press* in his front-page analysis titled "Everyone Is a Loser":

This was a sad and brooding city tonight because everybody seems to have lost in the anti-war siege of the Pentagon this weekend.

The majority of the demonstrators who marched peaceably and solemnly to the banks of the Potomac were unhappy because the event was taken over by the militant minority. The leading officials of the Government were troubled by the spectacle of so tumultuous a protest against their policy in Vietnam.

Even the pugnacious young activists who battled the marshals and the soldiers at the Pentagon were not satisfied at the end, for they had not won support for ending the war . . . but may very well have done the opposite.[2]

Compared to 1965, 1966 was a year of slow, almost imperceptible growth for the antiwar movement. No demonstrations that year matched the relative success of the three main demonstrations of the previous year. Moreover, at the end of the year, the percentage of Americans who told pollsters they felt the war was a mistake had increased only slightly, from 24 to 31 percent, with those favoring immediate withdrawal holding at about 10 percent.

On the other hand, during 1966, almost as many of those polled disapproved as approved of Johnson's handling of the war.[3] In addition, given the way that antiwar opinion slowly developed from 1965 through 1968, the movement's varied activities during 1966 added cumulatively in many ways to the arguments against the war. The successes the movement experienced in 1967 had much to do with the groundwork laid during the previous twelve months. Obviously, those successes were related as well to the intensification of the bombing, the escalation of the American combat role in Vietnam, increased draft calls, and, of course, a growing casualty list. However, the way the press covered the movement in 1966 proved to be a mixed blessing.

Senate Foreign Relations Committee Hearings, Winter 1966

Senator J. William Fulbright (D-AR) was never a leader of the movement. In fact, like most politicians, he was deeply suspicious of mass actions in the streets led by people unknown to him. All the same, his speeches in the Senate and around the country and his direction of the Senate Foreign Relations Committee contributed to the respectability of an antiwar position.

On January 26, 1966, Fulbright's Foreign Relations Committee began a routine hearing on a supplemental aid bill for South Vietnam. Under the Arkansas senator's shrewd direction, the sessions were transformed into a general investigation of American policy in Southeast Asia.[4] After Secretary of State Dean Rusk and several senators clashed dramatically early in the hearings, the media became interested, particularly the television networks, which began covering the sessions live.

General Maxwell Taylor and Dean Rusk defended administration policy vigorously against strong criticism from skeptical senators and gentler critiques from General James M. Gavin and diplomat-historian George F. Kennan. The challenge to administration policy from a ribbon-bedecked general and the architect of containment made dissent legitimate for many observers for the first time since the bombing began a year earlier.[5] The hearings made news for three weeks. By the time they concluded, 71 percent of Americans polled had heard about them, and almost 60 percent had seen segments on television.[6]

Both the *Times* and the *Post* approved of the hearings and generally devoted more space to the arguments of the doves than the hawks.[7] *Newsweek* described them as the "most searching public review of U.S. wartime policy" since the MacArthur hearings of 1951, highlighted by the comments of General Gavin, a "soft-spoken, cerebral . . . paratroop hero."[8]

Unlike demonstrations or even the national teach-in the previous May, the elite media reported the Fulbright hearings fairly, fully, and prominently. It helped, of course, for the hawk-dove debate to take place in a congressional hearing room. In addition, the antiadministration witnesses were moderates who supported capitalism and containment. No other antiwar activity, if one can call it that, was treated so well by the press.

Johnson worried so much about the hearings that he hastily called a conference in Honolulu to take the media spotlight away from Washington. This may have been overkill. At the least, in the hearings' aftermath, he and his aides received much encouragement from their friends. They were buoyed by the strong performances of Rusk and Taylor and White House mail flows showed renewed support for administration policies in Southeast Asia.[9]

Not everyone in the White House was so sanguine. Former press secretary George Reedy advised the president that Gavin and Kennan were really on his side and that the doves were using them. He suggested the president meet with them to eliminate a "rallying point" for the opposition.[10]

Johnson considered such a genuflection to the opposition unnecessary. Nevertheless, although the Fulbright hearings did not produce an immediate decline in support for the president, they did offer doves their most important platform to date. Above all, the attention the media lavished on Kennan and Gavin made the questioning of Vietnam strategies, if not the entire commitment, more legitimate than it had been before. Indeed, one wonders how rapidly antiwar opinion might have developed had Fulbright-style hearings been televised periodically through 1966 and 1967. Of course, like the 1965 national teach-in, they might have lost their novelty by the second or third iteration and thus lost the attention of the media—and the public. In any event, the media chose not to cover live any more Foreign Relations Committee hearings until 1968. And there was no C-Span or CNN to fill the gap.

Second International Days of Protest, March 25–27, 1966

Predictably, the media were not as impressed with the activities of the NC-CEWVN's Second International Days of Protest that took place in eighty cities in 1966.[11] Hailed by its organizers as the largest antiwar demonstration to date, it was not much larger than the first Days of Protest the previous fall.

But the somewhat disappointing turnout was not the main reason the media judged the series of demonstrations a relative failure. With communists and other radicals again welcome in the loose coalition that formed the NC-

CEWVN, even liberal journalists marginalized the event. In addition, the Johnson administration had momentarily gained the initiative with its peace offensive at the end of 1965, widely accepted reports of progress in the land war, and the impressive showings of Rusk and Taylor at the Fulbright hearings. Finally, demonstrations were beginning to become boring. Unless the crowds grew larger or their activities became more unusual, they did not impress. Journalists paid less attention to the antiwar movement during the spring of 1966 than they had during the fall of 1965 when it was more novel.[12]

Both the *Times* and the *Post* emphasized violence in their coverage, much of which was provoked, as usual, by counterdemonstrators, even though the Second Days of Protest were more peaceful than the First.[13] The New York daily's front-page treatment on Sunday offered an interesting juxtaposition when the editors placed the demonstration story next to the lead headlined "U.S. Marines Land to Protect Ships on Saigon River," which described a successful operation by young men who were not protesting that day.

Newsweek took a similar tack by beginning with, "As US troops score a succession of fresh victories in Vietnam, peace groups in the U.S. doggedly cranked up" demonstrations full of "strident marchers." In another feature story on the draft in its next issue, the magazine judged the "tiny minority" of antiwar activists to be motivated more by a selfish interest in avoiding combat than political or moral issues.[14] With coverage like this in *Newsweek*, for once the movement did better in *Time*, which simply ignored the Days of Protest.[15]

Boredom enlivened by an occasional scuffle dominated the mood at the Central Park rally that drew twenty thousand in New York on Saturday March 26, according to "CBS Evening News." Nevertheless, the shots selected by the director suggested a massive and enthusiastic crowd. From the appropriate camera angles, a crowd of twenty thousand could look quite large indeed. When the reporter noted that the protestors were not chanters, he ignored the widespread use of the "Hey, Hey, LBJ, How Many Kids Did You Kill Today" chant. He also did not notice that the handful of black marchers were carrying signs that read "The Vietcong Never Called Me a Nigger," perhaps the first time that soon-to-be-famous slogan had been seen nationally.

As might have been expected, publications friendly to the movement portrayed these activities a bit differently. The *Village Voice*, which accepted the official 20,080 count for New York City, described a friendly demonstration, full of people from all walks of life and from political perspectives ranging from the center to the left to pacifism and even anarchism. Its correspondent was pleased that the heckling from counterdemonstrators was more restrained than had been the case the previous fall.[16]

The *Guardian* was even more upbeat, claiming a crowd of 50,000 in New York, the largest ever, and 125,000 nationwide, a figure that surpassed the

100,000 of the First International Days of Protest. Like the *Voice*, the weekly viewed the demonstrations as successful, particularly when it catalogued the growth of the movement from 20,000 the previous April in Washington, 25,000 the previous October in New York, and the 35,000 in Washington in November. The numbers were not overwhelming but the *Guardian* was correct in emphasizing the ever-increasing crowds, a fact skimmed over by mainstream media.[17] Of course, in order to accept this growth, one had to accept its "enumerators'" 50,000 count for the New York event.

If anyone read the *Guardian* at the White House, no one took it seriously. Johnson and his aides were not as concerned about the Second Days of Protest as they had been about the Fulbright hearings. After all, the NCCEWVN was dominated by young radicals without a following among liberal and moderate Democrats and without much support in the media. The State Department analysis of public opinion for the week of March 24–30 correctly characterized most print media as not only critical of the demonstrations editorially, but also much less interested in them compared to those of the previous fall.[18]

With the administration holding the upper hand in the battle for opinion, and the antiwar movement, particularly the soon-to-disband NCCEWVN, in disarray, no other major national demonstrations occurred in 1966. Some antiwar activists devoted their efforts to generally unsuccessful attempts to elect dovish senators and representatives in the November election.

McNamara Confronts Harvard Radicals, November 7, 1966

The day before election day, 1966, the movement made the front pages with a story that did not serve it well. On November 7, Secretary of Defense Robert S. McNamara traveled to Harvard to discuss international politics in a private seminar with fifty hand-picked students.[19] Although he tried to leave the seminar through a back door to evade SDS-led protestors, they discovered his escape route, surrounded his car, and began rocking it, threatening bodily harm if he did not emerge to give them a "seminar" as well. He did answer a few questions and then left remarking that he had been "tougher and . . . more courteous" when he was a student.

The sensational story had to compete for space with election-day reportage on November 8. The mainstream media depicted McNamara as the brave hero of the affair, the student radicals as reckless and irresponsible. They saluted his statement about toughness and generally ignored the main reason for the protest: the secretary's unwillingness to appear in a public forum at Harvard.[20] "CBS Evening News" that night was characteristic, with viewers seeing an earnest and polite McNamara in a dangerous situation confronted by what the reporter labeled "an unruly pack of anti-Vietnam demonstrators." The brief and superficial story certainly gave the antiwar movement a black eye and influenced viewers to sympathize with McNamara. On the other hand, Americans might have been concerned that this unpleasant and unprecedented incident took place in the safe confines of that bastion of the establishment, Harvard University. Even though many Americans did not like antiwar protests because of the perceived disorder that came in their wake, they might have reasoned that if the war ended, Harvard students—and those at Michigan, Stanford, Columbia, and so forth—would return to their books or maybe at worst, panty raids.

Whatever their impact, nasty verbal, and even attempted physical, assaults against administration officials occurred periodically throughout the era. Camera crews were often standing by to capture colorful images of irreverent and profane antiwar protestors that must have alienated most viewers.

Salisbury Visits Hanoi, December 1966

The movement received a boost at the end of 1966 with the publication during the last week of December of *New York Times* journalist Harrison Salisbury's reports from Hanoi, which highlighted civilian deaths and injuries and damage to non-military structures caused by American bombing.[21] A "national disaster" according to former assistant secretary of defense Phil G. Goulding, Salisbury's stories and photographs belied earlier administration assertions that only military structures had been attacked by air force and navy pilots.[22] Salisbury later traveled around the country speaking to antiwar groups about what he had seen in North Vietnam.

His original dispatches did not hurt the administration as severely as was at first feared. Government aides raised the issue of the propriety of an American journalist reporting from an enemy capital during wartime. Moreover, when Salisbury was forced to admit that some of his data came from Hanoi's "official" casualty figures, his credibility was weakened. Finally, rival journalists and editors were jealous of the power of the *Times* and the way its correspondent obtained his sensational scoop. (Critics raised all of these issues again in 1991 when CNN's Peter Arnett broadcast from Bagdad during the Gulf War.)

The *Washington Post*, in a story headlined "Hanoi Seen Exploiting Civilian Casualties," began to support the administration in its conflict with Salisbury a few days after he filed his first story.[23] Salisbury thought that the *Post* wrote "nasty stories" about him not only because it still supported the Vietnam War effort in its editorial columns but also because of its rivalry with the *Times*.[24] Yet only three days after the initial story, the *Times* itself began covering the growing opposition to the alleged traitor on its staff.[25] The daily's distinguished military analyst, Hanson Baldwin, was especially hostile to his colleague. So too was *Time* magazine, which referred to Salisbury's reportage as "strictly one dimensional" in a lead story in early January.[26]

The *Guardian* did not agree with *Time*. It preened in a story, titled "Salisbury and the Stranageloves," pointing out that for two years its correspondent in Hanoi, Wilfred Burchett, had been reporting civilian damage caused by American bombing. The Salisbury story demonstrated that Burchett and the *Guardian* had been correct all the time.[27]

Despite the occasional defense of Salisbury from the likes of the *Guardian*, the State Department's *American Opinion Survey* accurately noted that the majority of the press was more anti-Salisbury than anti-bombing but that the administration had taken a hit for its lack of credibility. These reports, analyzed by Johnson's aides, cheered him during a difficult period.[28] As the flap began to fade from the front pages, Walt Rostow told the president that the *Times* had the secretary of defense "under the gun" on the civilian-bombing issue and was treating the administration unfairly, but the *Times* "is not the country." Such heavyweight journalists as Chalmers Roberts, Crosby Noyes, Joseph Alsop, Howard K. Smith, and William Randolph Hearst, Jr., as well as much of the Pentagon press corps, supported Johnson in the affair.[29]

What is missing in these analyses is the way that the bombing stories energized and reenforced those already committed to the antiwar movement and added to the president's growing "credibility" problem. At the least, Salisbury's stories may have contributed to the renewed newsworthy activism of the doves in 1967.

THE LONGER THE WAR WENT ON WITHOUT VICTORY IN SIGHT, the more administration supporters began to have second thoughts. No doubt those second thoughts were affected, in part, by critics' arguments presented in a variety of locales in 1967. By the time that year drew to a close, 45 percent of the population considered intervention in Southeast Asia a mistake, and more important, support for Johnson's handling of the war dipped to 30 percent. Indeed, the president found this rapid decline in support disconcerting enough in the late fall to mount his most energetic sell-the-war campaign.[30]

King Speaks Out, April 4, 1967

The bad news for Johnson on the antiwar front in 1967 began on April 4 when Dr. Martin Luther King, Jr., spoke out forcefully against the war for the first time and immediately became one of the leaders of the movement.[31] In a lecture at New York's Riverside Church, King told an audience of three thousand that the war was "madness" and that the United States was "the greatest purveyor of violence in the world today." At a press conference preceding the speech, he called upon young people to resist the draft and announced that he had joined the leadership of the Clergy and Laymen Concerned about Vietnam (CALCAV) and Negotiation Now!, two important liberal antiwar groups.

King's break with the civil-rights-friendly administration was major news. The strong language that he used to announce his opposition to the war made him at once one of the most outspoken and passionate of antiwar leaders. Indeed, the language was so strong that moderately dovish Americans reacted negatively to his assault, which opposed not just the war but American foreign policy in general. King himself was aware of his apparent rhetorical excesses; when he keynoted the April 15 demonstration in New York, his critique of American policy was much less inflammatory. This is another example of how the media affected movement strategies.

The *New York Times* and the *Washington Post* covered the King story on their front pages, emphasizing his more radical suggestions for ending the war, with the *Post* noting gratuitously that some of his proposals resembled Hanoi's recent peace plan. King's denunciation of the United States as the world's greatest "purveyor of violence" appeared prominently in both stories.[32] The newsweeklies gave the speech much less attention.[33]

King did receive generous, if not lead coverage, on the CBS Evening News on April 4, with the only sour note struck by the feature that followed, dealing with a draft-dodging scheme. As we have seen, the networks tended to lump Vietnam stories together. In this case, King's call for draft resistance looked less noble because of the draft-dodging story in the succeeding time slot.

Once again, the president could take solace in the fact, as the State Department's *American Opinion Survey* reported, that the vast majority of newspapers and magazines found King's rhetoric too strident and that he had done the civil rights movement a disservice by shifting its focus. No doubt the department's media monitors were correct. Even during the height of opposition to the war, from 1969 through 1971, few newspapers or television journalists—or many doves for that matter—endorsed King's radical perspective on American foreign policy. Throughout the war, doves discredited the movement in the eyes of most observers when they linked Vietnam to American imperialism everywhere, from the treatment of native Americans in the seventeenth century to the treatment of African-Americans in urban ghettoes in the 1960s. (Revolutionary rhetoric also made for colorful sound bites for the telecasters.) No doubt, more people would have listened to the antiwarriors had they concentrated on the nuts and bolts of what was going wrong in Vietnam. Of course, many doves, including King, believed in the need for a wholesale change in the way the United States related to people of color.

This was an insoluble problem for the doves. Many in the audience at rallies demanded fiery, antiimperialist rhetoric.[34] Many viewing those rallies through a media filter were appalled by the suggestion that their nation was guilty of imperialism. How was an antiwar speaker to appeal to both audiences at the same time?

The Spring Mobilization, April 15, 1967

Despite rhetoric that distressed the media, King's break with the administration cheered activists who were pleased to have such a respected moral leader in their van. His presence as keynoter of the New York antiwar demonstration on April 15 helped make it by far the largest demonstration to date.

A new umbrella organization, somewhat more moderate than the NCCEWVN, the Spring Mobilization to End the War in Vietnam (Mobe), brought more than two hundred thousand participants of every political stripe to march from Central Park to the United Nations building. There, they listened to Harry Belafonte, Pete Seeger, Linus Pauling, Benjamin Spock, and Stokely Carmichael, among others.[35] King may have irritated nationalistic observers when he presented a petition to U.N. Undersecretary Ralph Bunche complaining about American policy in Vietnam.

That same day, in Central Park's Sheep Meadow, albeit some distance from the official demonstration, more than one hundred protestors claim to have burned their draft cards. In addition, in a coordinated event at San Francisco's Kezar Stadium, Coretta Scott King addressed a crowd of at least fifty thousand.

The April 15 demonstrations were peaceful, massive, and projected relatively moderate political views.[36] The draft-card burning at the Sheep Meadow, although providing a sensational sound bite, was not characteristic of the day's events. After several seasons of relative quiescence, the mass antiwar movement was reenergized with this impressive turnout.

The *Guardian* was characteristically ecstatic. Its correspondents counted a crowd ranging from three hundred to five hundred thousand, so immense that participants were "stunned." Moreover, aside from the absence of SANE, they saluted the fact that once again the movement had turned out a broad coalition of peaceful and earnest demonstrators.[37] The *Guardian*'s West Coast correspondent noted how the mainstream media "played down crowd size, displayed photographs of 'way-out' types, emphasized the youthfulness of the majority of marchers" and red-baited.[38] That critique, which most likely struck mainstream journalists as paranoid, was not far from the mark.

The *Times* with 100,000 in its headlines and the *Post* with 125,000 underestimated the New York crowd. Moreover, although both papers offered extensive and generally accurate coverage, the vast majority of demonstrators, who were rather genteel, had to vie for space with the relative handful of Viet Cong flagwavers, obscene chanters, and the usual assortment of New York crazies. The *Times* also saw fit to run a separate story on counterdemonstrators who numbered 1,000 at most.[39] For its part, *The Daily Tribune*'s wire-service round-up story on the following Monday, tucked away on page 14, contained a disproportionate amount of material relating to Dean Rusk's denunciation of the demonstration.[40]

Although *Newsweek* reported that the demonstrations were the largest to date, its editors were niggardly with space for such an important event. *Time*, adopting a more derisive tone, thought that the large New York crowd was "about as damaging as a blow from the daffodils" for the administration, although it probably did result in "delighting Ho Chi Minh."[41]

CBS was impressed with the turnout in New York on the April 15 evening news, even though its reporter contended erroneously that fewer than expected had shown up. More important, King's speech received less attention than the remarks of the fiery Stokely Carmichael who called the president of the United States a "buffoon" and a "fool." Such epithets, which were not employed by other speakers, were certain to anger most viewers.

All the media undercounted the crowds at both rallies, an important issue since Mobe organizers hoped to impress observers with a massive outpouring. Further, radical and potentially violent young people received too much attention; as countercultural grooming and sartorial styles began to dominate almost all youth gatherings irrespective of the political context, descriptions of hippie-dominated crowds alienated much of adult America. The distortion of and relative lack of attention to the largest peace march in American history was surprising, especially from the *Times* and the *Post*, both of which had become skeptical about the war by the spring of 1967. Perhaps they felt that demonstrations were not the way to extract the United States from Vietnam. Of course, their coverage of those demonstrations helped to create an unfavorable impression of the movement among many citizens.

The administration viewed the Mobe correctly as a left-wing antiwar coalition, especially after the FBI informed Johnson of the alleged communist and radical tinge of its leadership.[42] Analysts in the *American Opinion Survey* for the week ending April 19 concluded that the administration came out ahead, especially when the media spent a good deal of time on the "relatively small proportion of demonstrators who burned the flag or their draft cards." This was not a case of the *Survey* fearing to bring bad news to the administration. It captured rather accurately the surprisingly bad press accorded the New York demonstration. Moreover, the White House mail flows produced a small boomlet of support for the president after the event. That boomlet disappeared by the beginning of May.[43] In general, as we have seen, demonstrations were often followed by an increased number of letters and telegrams to the White House that approved of the president's policies in Southeast Asia. This was no coincidence. Correspondents were most likely moved to write to Johnson because of the unfavorable impressions they received, through the media, of antiwar demonstrations.

However the media undercounted and miscovered the Spring Mobilization and whether or not there had been an immediate turnaround in public opinion, movement leaders were pleased with the turnout at the Spring Mobilization. They looked forward with confidence to an even larger outpouring at a fall demonstration in Washington. What would happen, they wondered, if three hundred or four hundred thousand people came to the capital? By bringing their protests to the warmakers' home turf that October, the doves hoped that they would attract considerable media attention. Those hopes were fulfilled but not necessarily in the manner expected.

The Siege of the Pentagon, October 21–22, 1967

Not as massive as the Spring Mobilization, the antiwar activities in Washington on the weekend of October 21–22 were nevertheless the most dramatic and most important of the Johnson presidency.[44] They ended with violent confrontations and mass arrests in front of a besieged Pentagon, and through the media, in front of the world. It was the first in a chain of events that led to Lyndon Johnson's decision on March 31, 1968 to deescalate in Vietnam and to drop out of the presidential race.[45] (It also led Daniel Ellsberg, a Pentagon official who watched the siege from inside the Pentagon, to rethink his views on the war.)[46]

On the heels of its successful New York march, the National Mobilization Committee (which had changed its name from the Spring Mobilization at a meeting in Chicago in May), expected an even greater gathering of antiwar foot soldiers for a fall demonstration in Washington to "Confront the Warmakers." Optimists talked about attracting a cadre of one million.

Several factors combined to limit the crowd to numbers significantly lower than that of the April 15 march. First, the organizing coalition spent weeks wrangling over the format. With militant pacifist Dave Dellinger and flamboyant Jerry Rubin taking leadership roles, moderate groups were nervous about sponsorship or even participating. SANE, for one, refused to serve as a sponsor. On the left, SDS, among others, opposed mass demonstrations for tactical reasons, although some of its members ultimately joined in the activities.

The Johnson administration contributed to the relatively small turnout by denouncing march leaders as communists and radicals. Its propaganda barrage was reenforced inadvertently during National Draft Disruption Week (October 16 through 21), when militants and police fought with one another on the West Coast. Finally, the logistics of gathering a large crowd in New

York are far simpler than transporting thousands of people to the less popu-
lous area surrounding the District of Columbia. Nevertheless, in the case of
the Pentagon demonstration, the numbers were less important than the activity
itself and the attention that it drew from the world's media.

A crowd that ultimately totaled between fifty and seventy-five thousand
began gathering in Washington on Friday, October 20. Antiwar actions
started that day with a draft-card turn-in at the Justice Department and an
evening of speeches at the Ambassador Theatre. There Norman Mailer, carrying a coffee cup full of bourbon, spoke incoherently and intemperately, litter-
ing his speech with expletives, and generally making a shambles of what
started out as a dignified event.

The next day, protestors met at the Lincoln Memorial to listen to speeches
and music at the first and largest rally of the weekend.[47] As planned, that
activity was entirely peaceful and conventional. The rhetoric at the Memorial
was more militant than that at the U.N. the previous spring, however. Black
leader John Lewis called for a moment of silence for the recently killed revolutionary Che Guevara and led a "Hell No, We Won't Go" chant, SDS leader
Carl Davidson advocated draft-card burning, and Benjamin Spock announced
that the real enemy was Lyndon Johnson, not the communist Vietnamese. The
crowd was so large and the sound system so feeble that many toward the rear
had difficulty hearing the speeches and even the folk songs of Phil Ochs and
Peter, Paul, and Mary. Journalists later ignored much of the speechmaking,
perhaps because many people could not hear what was being said. Thus, the
messages from Spock and the others could have been legitimately judged
unnewsworthy since they had only a minimal impact on the audience. Of
course, those on the platform hoped that their messages would reach well
beyond the Lincoln Memorial through the media. After all, how many
speeches at national party conventions covered by the television cameras are
heard by the gossiping, politicking, and partying delegates?

As the program continued at the Memorial, marshals collected money to
help defray legal and other costs for those who might be arrested at the Pentagon. Over thirty thousand dollars was deposited in buckets passed through the
crowd, an indication of the number of middle-class adults at the rally. Whatever the crowd size, and irrespective of movement expectations, this part of
the event, the largest antiwar demonstration in Washington to that point, had
to be considered a success.

At its conclusion, Dellinger announced that peaceful protest was over—
anyone was free to join him for civil disobedience and "confrontation" at the
Pentagon. During previous weeks, demonstration organizers had negotiated
painstakingly with Harry Van Cleve of the General Services Administration
what they could and could not do on Pentagon property. While negotiations
had been going on, various individuals announced that whatever was decided,

they planned to levitate the Pentagon through the chanting of mantras or even to enter it illegally by any means possible. Mobe organizers warned the administration that once the marchers reached the Pentagon, many would do their own thing, despite legal agreements.

Whereas the Lincoln Memorial crowd included many middle-aged people, young people made up most of the estimated thirty-five thousand who began marching toward Arlington over the agreed-upon parade route. Hippie-looking free-lancers, taking direction from no one, set out ahead of the march leadership and celebrities like Spock, Mailer, and literary critic Dwight McDonald. Those on the official front line walked under a huge banner that read "Support our GIs, Bring Them Home Now!" That front line and the banner made the cover of *Time*. The media rarely gave that slogan such prominence, perhaps because demonstrators did not emphasize it enough. That may have been a tactical blunder since many opponents of the movement contended that antiwarriors did not "support" the boys in the field.

The original plan called for the marchers to leave the Memorial at 1:30 and meet up at 3 P.M. at the north parking area of the Pentagon, which was across the highway and down the embankment from a grassy mall in front of the complex's north entrance. After a two-hour rally, the group was then to cross the highway to the mall and climb the steps in front of the Pentagon. Anyone trying to proceed further into the small parking area or the building itself would be arrested. Over eight thousand five hundred members of the 82nd Airborne joined local police and federal marshals to defend the structure. This was the first time since 1932 that federal troops had been called out to protect the capital. Inside, Pentagon aides Daniel Henkin, Richard Fryklund, and Phil Goulding, among others, participated in a round-the-clock vigil that ended at 4 A.M. Sunday morning. The Pentagon had prepared for a siege.

The legal rally at the Pentagon aborted when at least one thousand militants bypassed the north parking area venue and charged up the embankment to the steps and beyond. Scores tried to break into the complex, perhaps as many as twenty-five did penetrate its defenses. This initial vanguard was led by a "Revolutionary Contingent" that included SDS members.

Because of the extensive terrain in question and the rapid movements of protestors and soldiers, observers found it difficult to record accurately the events of the next twelve hours. Eyewitness chronicler Norman Mailer doubts whether an "accurate history is conceivable."[48] By 4 P.M., most of the marchers reached the mall area and the steps below it. At least five thousand staked out spaces on the plaza in front of the building. According to the official agreement, that group had gone beyond legal demarcation lines. There, at the major point of confrontation, a demonstrator attached an NLF flag to a Pentagon flagpole and young people challenged soldiers with flowers, obscenities, eggs, bottles, bags of excrement, and even with love-making under their rifle butts. One photograph of a young man placing a flower in the barrel of a gun made front pages around the world.[49] Among the few formal presentations was one by Vietnam veteran Gary Rader, who delivered a moving speech to the soldiers explaining why he and his fellow demonstrators were there and that they were not protesting against GIs.

Some participants had come to get arrested. That feat was not so easy to accomplish given the number of people violating parts of the original agreement and the relative handful of marshals present to make the arrests. Benjamin Spock, for example, who entered a forbidden area, was not arrested. Norman Mailer was—to his great relief. Many of those arrested were clubbed despite the fact that they offered no resistance.

After the initial flurry of arrests, neither side engaged in significant acts of violence, although militants opposite the line of troops were provocative and abusive. When it became dark, much of the by-then-leaderless crowd drifted away, in part because of the cold evening. Indeed, it was so chilly that one wag commented that draft cards had been burned for warmth as well as for symbolic protest.

After midnight, and after almost all the media had left the Pentagon, soldiers advanced without warning on the remaining hundreds of demonstrators. Committing the major violent action of the weekend, they beat young people in their way, some of whom claimed later that paratroopers selected women for particularly harsh treatment. Observers later judged the clearing operation illegal since many of those set upon were in areas to which they had been granted access in the Van Cleve negotiations. By early morning, only a few hundred remained at the Pentagon although their numbers increased to two thousand when the sun came up. There were some speeches and chants that morning, mostly led by an SDS contingent, but eventually everyone drifted away without further confrontation.

According to the Justice Department, 667 people were arrested over the roughly twenty-hour period at the Pentagon, the largest group ever arrested at a peace demonstration.[50] Over 80 percent of those arrested were under twenty-five. Despite the brutality of the early-morning clearing operation, few protestors or soldiers suffered serious injuries. The government estimated that the defense of the Pentagon cost one million dollars.[51]

The fact that the army had gone into action to defend the Pentagon from American citizens made this a most significant demonstration indeed. Undoubtedly, its size disappointed organizers who hoped to improve upon the numbers in New York on April 15. Some were also upset about the confrontational tactics employed by militants who were permitted by a loose, and sometimes invisible, leadership to "do their own thing." Yet crowds of more than fifty thousand peaceful demonstrators at the Lincoln Memorial and thirty-five thousand mostly peaceful demonstrators at the Pentagon reflected the growing antiwar sentiment in the country. The events in Washington on the weekend of October 21–22, 1967 deserved careful attention from the media.

According to critics like Norman Mailer, the media had "created a forest of inaccuracy which would blind the efforts of an historian."[52] The administration did its best to present the demonstration in an unfavorable light, or better, no light at all. Television did not cover the protest live, a result, Todd Gitlin suggests, of government pressure.[53] Network executives explained they ruled out live coverage because they feared that their presence would lead demonstrators to perform for the cameras.[54] In addition, they were concerned that they would have to give equal live time to proadministration demonstrations the following weekend.[55] Finally, they reasoned that with Johnson still enjoying support in the polls, the movement did not yet deserve the special treatment that live coverage would signify.

CBS'S COVERAGE OF THE COLORFUL DEMONSTRATION IN ITS nightly telecasts began on October 20, with an extensive interview with Dellinger, a middle-aged, soft-spoken man. He warned that Americans were angry about the war and that the next day's action would be more than a "polite registering of disapproval." Although his organization had received a permit for some activities, he predicted civil disobedience beyond the permit conditions. The war itself was "uncivil disobedience." According to Dellinger, some of the actions that might be taken had to be put in the context of an illegal war and a restrictive or even unconstitutional permit. His carefully reasoned presentation, despite the rhetoric, belied the notion that this was a radical hippie event. On the other hand, many viewers would not have responded positively to Dellinger's strong charges against the administration.

CBS's Sunday night roundup generally presented favorable images of the protestors, even the ones who were provocative at the Pentagon. For example, viewers saw clips of marshals arresting people and even clubbing young women, with the precipitating provocation, except for a peaceful sit-in, absent on film. Viewers could also hear shouts and shrieks coming from apparently defenseless protestors. The early morning violence occurred too late for most Sunday morning newspapers but not for the Sunday evening newscast.

At a postmortem press conference, covered in part by CBS, Dellinger calmly promised "more militant," "persistent," and "insistent" demonstrations in the months to come. Terming the March on the Pentagon a success, he exuded optimism. Finally, the cameras flashed back to an impressive-looking crowd at the Lincoln Memorial listening to Dr. Spock say that the enemy was not the North Vietnamese but LBJ, and then panned to several Viet Cong flags along with placards reading "Support Our Boys, Bring Them Home." The former symbol weakened the potential attractiveness of the latter slogan.

Print journalists were not as flattering to the doves as CBS. One problem may have been the length and complexity of the almost twenty-four hours of antiwar action that frustrated Norman Mailer when he tried to put it all together in his famous history as novel, novel as history, *The Armies of the Night.* Those who covered the weekend for the movement-friendly *Village Voice* and *Guardian* admitted a similar frustration. Jack Newfield, who went to Washington for the *Voice*, wrote about how "reality and fantasy, truth and untruth were lost in the chaos," while the *Guardian*'s correspondent tried to be accurate but found the "situation truly confusing." Publishing a week after the dust had settled, the latter suggested that the conventional press accounts "had to be entirely discarded." Among other distortions, several major newspapers not only denied that the authorities had used tear gas on the demonstrators, which they did, but claimed that the demonstrators were the ones to use that weapon. Moreover, according to Newfield, perhaps because so many things were happening at so many places, journalists and their informants simply did not see the "sudden, savage and accidental" outbursts of violence, mostly committed by poorly organized authorities. As usual, the *Guardian*, something of a newspaper of record for the left, devoted attention to the speeches at the Memorial, which were "conventional and lacking in fire," but the *Voice* virtually ignored them in its story—"Pentagon Day: Flight Over the Cuckoo's Nest." In addition, the former thought that 100,000 had turned up at the Memorial with only 30,000 at the Pentagon while Newfield insisted that an improbable 100,000 besieged the Pentagon.[56]

Needless to say, the mainstream media did not cover the demonstrations in the same fashion. The *New York Times* Saturday morning edition featured a page-one story about the arrival of the doves in Washington, most of whom were young but "many [were] in middle life." The *Times* described the National Mobilization Committee as a coalition of as many as 150 organizations that ranged from church groups to the Communist Chinese supporters of the PLP. Dave Dellinger was described as a "cool" leader, a conscientious objector, not a leftist.[57] He did tell the paper that some at the Pentagon, who were not pacifists, would try to reach the forbidden steps using force.

The *Times* reported as well that "2,200 flower children" would surround the Pentagon crying "Love, Love, Love." The advance story captured the somewhat bizarre nature of the event. However, in an indicator of things to come, on Saturday morning, the editors displayed little interest in the major rally at the Lincoln Memorial that turned out to be the largest to date in the capital.

On Sunday, violence at the Pentagon dominated the *Times*'s reportage as may be seen in the caption for the pictures of conflict, the only front-page pictures: "Scuffles at Pentagon Follow Rally and March by Opponents of Policy in Vietnam." The lead story, headed "Guards Repulse War Protestors at the Pentagon," began: "Thousands of demonstrators stormed the Pentagon today after a calm rally and march by some 50,000 persons opposed to the war in Vietnam." "Thousands" had not "stormed" the Pentagon.

Working against a deadline that occurred before its reporters could discover the administration-produced violence of the post-midnight hours, the *Times* noted that although members of the "surging disorderly crowd" that taunted the troops and threw eggs and bottles were arrested, no serious injuries were incurred. On the jump page, the paper offered three more pictures of the Pentagon action.[58] There, for the first time, the *Times* alluded to the Lincoln Memorial event where from fifty to fifty-five thousand people had rallied.

Overall, the coverage of the Pentagon events, "Beards, Bayonets and Bonfires," offered fodder for both doves and hawks.[59] As the *Times* pointed out, the siege was indeed at times "Halloween-like," most of those at the Pentagon tried to keep things orderly, and the enemy of the young protestors was not the contingent of young men guarding the Pentagon but those inside the building itself.

Another front-page story on Sunday covered a New York City proadministration vigil attended by only one thousand people. The small vigil was a newsworthy event to be sure, but it did not merit front-page treatment.

On Monday, the arrests of Sunday morning framed the story, with the left lead, "War Protestors Defying Deadline Seized in Capital."[60] The account suggested that the protestors were arrested for violating the rules established in negotiations with the government, an interpretation that was only partially correct. More important, the newspaper again paid little attention to the bloody military sweep of early Sunday morning.

However, it also reported Dellinger's exaggerated crowd estimate of 150,000 at the Memorial.[61] As for the Pentagon siege, reporters, who tried to count everyone who crossed the Memorial Bridge to Arlington, concluded that fifty-four thousand was a reasonable number, while the Defense Department claimed that only thirty-five thousand eventually surrounded its headquarters.

Sunday was also the day for a major New York march to support the GIs. That story made page 32 on Monday with the evenhanded *Times* challenging the organizers' one hundred thousand crowd estimate with its own figure of fifty thousand.

In a front-page column sympathetic to the protestors' purposes, James Reston declared that "Everyone Is a Loser / Washington a Sad and Brooding City in the Wake of Antiwar Demonstration."[62] He pointed out that militants, only a small minority at the Pentagon, had been opposed by their less radical colleagues. Reston congratulated the police for how well they handled the lawless few who were planning "ugly and vulgar provocation."

Like the rest of his colleagues, the columnist devoted little attention to the political arguments of the demonstrators, even those clearly articulated at the

Lincoln Memorial. This omission was understandable. It was difficult to distinguish between the many motives and programs of the diverse participants that weekend in Washington. Who did speak for those who showed up at the Memorial or even for those who were at the Pentagon? In addition, the arrests and the spectacle of the siege of the Pentagon were clearly the most newsworthy and unique activities of the weekend.

With the demonstrations on its doorstep, the *Washington Post* lavished even more attention on them, and because of the virtually unlimited space allocated, did a somewhat better job in covering its permutations. Indeed, at a November 2 meeting of the Wise Men, Johnson's informal advisory group, General Omar Bradley complained about the paper's extensive coverage. He noted that the *Post* used three pages to describe the thirty-five thousand or so peace marchers at the Pentagon. "However, there were 180,000 [sic] in New York and New Jersey who demonstrated in support of our men in Vietnam and this was played on page 17 of the *Post*."[63] Nevertheless, Bradley and his colleagues had to approve of the general line taken by the paper, which stressed the activists' violence at the Pentagon and all but ignored the excessive force used by the military in the post-midnight confrontation.

On Sunday, October 22, a banner headline dominated the *Post*'s front page—"GI's Repel Pentagon Charge: 55,000 Rally Against War / 152 arrested as violence takes over." Pictures included Secretary of Defense McNamara observing the proceedings and marshals swinging clubs at protestors. The main story started by noting that the day began peacefully but then, "In many isolated incidents, military police and U.S. marshals clubbed the jeering, rushing demonstrators who invaded forbidden spots or pushed against defensive lines." The authorities denied using tear gas even though *Post* reporters witnessed its employment. Like their colleagues at the *Times*, they briefly mentioned the Lincoln Memorial event halfway through the lead story and then readers were taken back to the Pentagon where a "self-styled radical" was one of the organizers.

On the jump page, the *Post* did offer two columns of excerpts from speeches at the Memorial from Spock, Dellinger, David Dowd, and Black Muslims.[64] The speeches were characterized as "a mixture of angry militance threatening civil disobedience and agonizing expressions of concern for war." Included also was a picture of black radical Charles Kenyatta of the New York Mau Mau organization whose appearance at a major antiwar rally was unprecedented.

Back on the front page, Jimmy Breslin, like the *Times*'s Reston, offered his analysis of "Bloodied Heads, Bloodied Cause: Quiet Rally Turns Vicious." The popular columnist thought that the Pentagon action, precipitated primarily by militants, hurt the Memorial rally, which had had "the structure of taste and human respect." One wonders what sort of coverage that somewhat routine rally would have received had the doves simply left Washington at its conclusion.

A third story showed how the army's "flexible response" led to no shots being fired and admirable restraint in the face of extreme provocation. Like the *Times*'s reporters, the *Post*'s analysts underplayed the late-evening sweep at the Pentagon where there were fifteen thousand protestors, most of whom were "youngsters and many of them in hippie dress and hairstyles."

Another story, on page 10, accompanied by five more pictures of violent exchanges, predicted that most Americans would be upset by what happened at the Pentagon and that, consequently, the antiwar movement had suffered a setback. That page was dominated by another huge picture of the confrontation on the steps of the Pentagon where police resisted a "surging band" of demonstrators.

The next day, when the smoke had cleared, the *Post* continued to emphasize the violence of the protestors, not the defenders of the Pentagon. Its front page featured an account of the arrests and the ending of the protest with a picture, this time, merely of a peaceful crowd, which, however, did leave much "debris" behind.[65] Comments about messy demonstrators and the incidental environmental damage left in their wake appeared frequently in the media. Finally understanding the importance of this negative image, leaders of later protests devoted a good deal of time to organizing clean-up crews to police their areas. This was one tactical change produced by media criticism that all could applaud.

Other *Post* items covered those protestors taken to jail, with Norman Mailer appearing in the lead, and a detailed chronology of the siege. The narrative accompanying the chronology saluted the restraint shown at the Pentagon by the military; justified force had been used to push the demonstrators back behind the agreed-upon demarcation lines. Dr. Spock disagreed with that analysis on the jump page while Dave Dellinger claimed the event was "a tremendous victory" for the movement.[66] Perhaps, but Dellinger might not have taken into consideration the impact of the *Times*'s and *Post*'s coverage on American opinion leaders and their constituents.

The Daily Tribune's Saturday afternoon UPI coverage offered a picture of a rather small crowd at the Memorial and another of a sign in a shop window in the District warning demonstrators to stay out.[67] At noon, UPI counted twenty-five thousand at the Lincoln Memorial, though Dellinger claimed that one hundred thousand had already arrived. The only minor incident at the rally had been precipitated by a handful of Nazis. In addition, the UPI devoted attention to Spock's speech.

By Monday, the *Tribune*'s coverage had lost its evenhandedness. On page 1, the demonstration story centered around a Johnson speech attacking the doves. Inside the paper, UPI's Merriman Smith, who thought that at most fifty thousand were in Washington over the weekend, criticized the press for being too harsh on police and soldiers who behaved with admirable restraint. He was "depressed" by what he saw at the Pentagon—the hippie garb, poor manners, and Viet Cong flags. Accompanying his long column were three pictures, one of the litter left behind by the protestors, another of a violent clash, and a third of a protestor carrying a picture of Johnson with the words "war criminal."[68]

On Saturday, the *Macomb Daily* ran a headline across the first page, "Barbed Wire Rings Pentagon." The AP, which expected a crowd of seventy thousand, linked the earlier violent Oakland antidraft clashes to the confrontation. Readers in the Detroit suburbs also saw a photograph of an attempt by protestors to "physically disrupt" induction in Oakland and a warning from Dellinger that not all at the Pentagon would be pacifists.[69]

The eight-paragraph lead story from UPI on Monday, October 23, in the *Macomb Daily* concerned the arrests and the injuries, with the latter said to be distributed evenly on both sides. The lead sentence, which described the event as the largest antiwar demonstration in history, ignored the huge April New York march.[70]

Time magazine made the march its lead and cover story on October 27 with the banner, "Protest! Protest! Protest! A Week of Antiwar Demonstrations." The eight-page story, illustrated profusely, included two full pages of photographs.[71] Among those events depicted were the MPs repulsing the demonstrators at the Pentagon, McNamara looking out of his office window, a woman with a baby in a backpack at the Lincoln Memorial, "Mailer and Mug" at the Ambassador Theatre, thirty-five hundred demonstrators "defying court injunction" at Oakland, violence at Madison, Wisconsin and, for *Time*, an uncharacteristically peaceful candlelight demonstration in Claremont, California. "Mob Leader Dellinger" also appeared; the famous picture of the flower in the barrel of the gun was paired with one of a Che Guevara poster with a caption under both: "On the attack with water pistols, marbles, and bubble-gum wrappers, plus swamis, warlocks and speed freaks." As can be seen from this catalog, almost all of the photographic images and captions offered unfavorable impressions of the movement.

As for its lengthy copy, *Time* began with a description of the scene at the Pentagon with "35,000 ranting, chanting, protestors" who were the losers in the affair. A mixed group of doves at the Memorial, full of "acid and acrimony," heard "Baby Doctor" Spock speak and others who "caterwauled in competition with blues and rock bands as the demonstrators jostled across the lawn." (Jostled is a peculiar verb for this sedate gathering.)

At least ten demonstrators were said to have breached the defenses at the Pentagon and made it inside. Norman Mailer was arrested "after a wild buildup of booze and obscenity." It was, however, the biggest "peace" demonstration in capital history. *Time*'s quotes around peace suggested irony, of course.

A biography of Dellinger ("an uncompromising radical") revealed his close ties to the left, his visit to Hanoi, and implicit endorsement of violent actions at the Pentagon. In fact, according to *Time*, his position on this issue led SANE and other moderate groups to drop out of the protest. Overall, the antiwar activists in Washington, reflected in *Time*'s photos and prose, appeared to be left-wing radicals, hippies, acid heads, and people with painted faces in bizarre costumes. On the other hand, the magazine applauded the government for its restraint.[72] Fearful of a new McCarthyism, *Time* described a patient Johnson who had protected the right to dissent even though Dean Rusk and others worried about the communist leadership in the movement.

As in April, *Newsweek* offered briefer coverage than *Time*. This could be attributed in part to different deadlines, with *Newsweek*'s edition appearing three days later when the demonstration was older news. The newsweekly's cover photograph featured two hippies and the headline, "Trouble in Hippie Land." This long story about Haight-Ashbury had nothing to do with the siege but, appearing when it did, readers might have thought about the antiwar demonstration when they saw hippies staring out at them from *Newsweek*'s cover.[73]

The Washington protest was, however, the magazine's lead story that week.[74] Three of the four accompanying pictures documented violent confrontations in Wisconsin, Oakland, and Portland. A fourth was an impressive shot of a large number of peaceful marchers in Washington. Forty thousand were said to have gathered at the Pentagon, which had been "prepared for the worst." *Newsweek* reported Dellinger and Rubin's ties to North Vietnam and the Progressive Labor Party and described "bloody encounters elsewhere" and Norman Mailer's "freak out." On the other hand, compared to most mainstream media, *Newsweek* was one of the few to suggest that the discipline of the troops at the Pentagon cracked a bit.

Further, the newsweekly did think the protest was important.[75] Its disorderly nature was blamed on its leftist leadership but also on the "hardening of the whole protest movement," which was angry and frustrated. *Newsweek*'s reporters concluded that although most of the public would not be affected by Pentagon activities, young people might.

With few exceptions, the media concentrated on the violent and the sensational, seeking out the most colorful sound bites or photographs, and virtually ignoring the peaceful aspects of the largest Washington antiwar protest to date. They ignored as well the major violence of the weekend, the early Sunday morning military sweep. On the other hand, as was the case with the assault against McNamara the previous year, images of instability and disruption, which included more than just a symbolic attack on the Pentagon, made many Americans uneasy. They may not have become dovish activists by accepting the media's view of the demonstrations but they may have become more convinced than ever that the way to return their increasingly crazed society to "normalcy" would be to end the war.

THE MARCH ON THE PENTAGON TOOK PLACE AT A TIME WHEN the administration was beginning to accelerate its campaign to drum up support for its policies.[76] No other antiwar demonstration up to this point had been so carefully monitored by government agencies. This caution and planning was understandable since hundreds of thousands of protestors could have shown up in the capital, some of whom would be prepared to engage in violent activities. In fact, although the FBI thought as early as September 20 that only forty to fifty thousand would appear, the organizers were still hopeful about attracting two hundred thousand. The bureau feared that the protesters would "move against the White House, the Capitol, and very likely other government buildings."[77]

At a cabinet meeting on October 4, Attorney General Ramsey Clark still expected as many as one hundred thousand protestors, and described the demonstration's sponsors as "extreme left-wing groups with long lines of Communist affiliations. . . . They are doing all they can do to encourage the March."[78] Clark and others had leaked those alleged and real communist affiliations to the press to help keep the crowds down.[79] However radical the leadership of the demonstration may have been, the government's early intelligence about who was in control and what was expected to occur was accurate.[80] Nevertheless, as aide Roger Wilkins told Clark, the government was in little position to influence what was going to happen at the planned rally.[81] Many casualties were expected with one hospital preparing up to two hundred beds.[82] Orders went out to the Army to be fair but firm and to avoid force if at all possible.[83]

On October 16, Joseph Califano told Johnson that the one hundred thousand crowd estimate was too high; twenty to fifty thousand was more likely. Much depended on how many local activists joined those who were coming in from other parts of the country.[84] Two days later, at another cabinet meeting, Clark concluded that the number was "undeterminable" although he thought something under thirty thousand was possible. One reason for his optimistic prediction of a relatively small turnout was the media's approach to the event—"We have been pleased by the low-key coverage of this."[85] With such underestimations, when at least fifty thousand protestors did show up, the White House had to be impressed.

On the eve of the march, Ramsey Clark offered the president details of the October 20 draft-card turn-in at the Justice Department. Including a UPI story with his memo, which claimed that over nine hundred draft cards and photocopies of others had been turned in, Clark's department tabulated only 185 bona fide cards and 172 classification notices.[86] When Johnson met with congressional Democrats a week after the demonstration, he told them about his more accurate numbers and embellished the account with the assertion that many of those who did turn in some sort of draft documents were mentally unbalanced. The media apparently had not yet picked up the truth of the story—"Someone has to uncover this information."[87]

On the day of the demonstration, Johnson received frequent reports, roughly every hour in the late morning and early afternoon, most of which had to do with the numbers of people arriving on busses. For example, at 11:55 that morning, administration monitors had counted 32,300 demonstrators gathered at the Memorial. A few minutes later, this number was downgraded to either 22 or 28,000.[88] That same day, Marvin Watson sent LBJ a letter he had received from Senator Everett Dirksen (R-IL) in which a black in Watts claimed that black power groups and the Communist Party were going to kill Johnson and start a revolution in the capital using weapons from Cuba. Watson did not take the letter seriously, but added "You never can be sure just what is nut mail."[89]

Another fear of black militant activity dissipated when Califano reported to Johnson at 1:55 that "'Black Power' People who were marching towards the White House apparently went to a movie on 14th Street."[90] Two hours earlier, Johnson had received other good news—Jim Evans on radio station WMAL was playing patriotic music and saying supportive things about the administration in a one-person answer to the antiwar activists.[91]

The first administration postmortems on the demonstration were not positive. An aide told Ramsey Clark that despite all the planning, the defending forces were poorly organized and did not communicate well. Moreover, there was excessive violence, with the marshals more undisciplined in general than the MPs.[92] A week later, Harry Van Cleve was not as pessimistic although he too was distressed by the violence perpetrated by people about whom they had little intelligence—the leaders of the demonstration generally had kept their word about what they planned to do. More interesting, Van Cleve was concerned about the many pictures of conflict in the media between the soldiers or marshals and the demonstrators that he felt were "wholly out of context."[93] Van Cleve was not looking at those photos from a political perspective. No doubt they helped the administration, even when they depicted soldiers striking protestors.

Johnson also received an accounting of certain activities that occurred during the demonstration that were not reported by the media.[94] Joseph Califano sent him an "Obscene Report" for "night reading" that told of placards that read "LBJ Sucks" and "LBJ pull out like your father should have done." In addition, Califano reported that three boys had had intercourse with two girls in the Pentagon parking lot at 5:30 A.M., people carried placards with slogans proclaiming that they would "rather fuck than fight," many of the protestors urinated in public, the debris on the steps included sanitary napkins, and "motherfucker" was a common expression used on the bullhorns.

Had journalists reported these X-rated items, the demonstrators would have made an even worse impression on the general public. But, as we have seen, they did not receive good press for the weekend's activities in any case. Nevertheless, the White House was not entirely pleased with the media's performance. For example, Califano informed Johnson that two UPI reporters probably planned their Pentagon arrest in order to have a story on arrest and incarceration procedures.[95] Moreover, Johnson heard that David Brinkley's October 23 radio commentary divided the protestors into a large group of civil people and a small group of rowdy militants. White House aide Fred Panzer thought that the movement was trying to make "a strategic withdrawal from the great boomerang at the Pentagon." In a memo entitled "Keeping the Doves on the Hook," Panzer concluded that the movement had suffered a defeat at the Pentagon.[96]

James Reston, who, as we have seen, thought that both the government and the demonstrators were losers in the affair, came in for censure from the president who noted at a meeting on November 2: "When Mac Bundy walked out of Washington, so did Scotty Reston and he doesn't know what is going on."[97] At that same meeting, Bundy himself asserted that although the communications people in New York could not be won over, the administration should not allow them to set the tone of the debate. A few days earlier, an aide suggested that someone should talk with officials at CBS in an off-the-record session, "since these people are the immediate source of so many of our troubles."[98] When Johnson met with ABC's Howard K. Smith on November 25, the president offered more criticism of the *Times*, pointing out that he had not seen James Reston in three years.[99]

Another indication of the concern evidenced by the administration, even after pictures of the "hippies" at the Pentagon were seen around the world, is that it continued its communist-link propaganda after the event. On October 26, Walt Rostow sent House Republican leader Gerald Ford a report on the alleged communist role in the protests.[100]

In general, however, much of the news coming into the White House about the impact of the demonstration was favorable. Rhea Howard of the *Wichita Falls Times*, for example, sent in her editorials, which were very critical of the demonstrators.[101] Operatives in the White House's clipping service, concentrating as usual on opinion and columnists, not the straight news stories, filed a supportive editorial from the *Hartford Courant*—the march achieved little and encouraged Hanoi—James Reston's comments on October 22 that the demonstrators will be hurt by television images of the violence, the *Philadelphia Inquirer*'s "Carrying the Enemy's Flag," a "Sickening Spectacle of

Support for an Alien Tyranny," as well as critical editorials from the *Beaumont Journal*, *Daily News*, *St. Louis Globe-Democrat*, *Baltimore Sun*, *Wall Street Journal*, and *Dallas Times Herald*.[102] All the clipped editorials blamed the violence on the demonstrators. The White House's only concern was the growing feeling that the extreme actions taken by the protestors suggested that time might be running out for the United States in Vietnam. But Johnson's stock had risen compared to that of the movement as symbolized by the Pentagon besiegers. He and his aides had to agree with Marine Corps General Lewis Walt that the demonstration "has helped to open the eyes of responsible American people."[103]

The White House mailbags brought support for that view.[104] Before the march, during the week ending October 19, letters opposing the policy in Vietnam outnumbered supporting ones at a ratio of 3–1, though an additional 135 letters supported the bombing of North Vietnam to 108 that opposed it. For the week ending October 26, the bombers still outnumbered the anti-bombers as the ratio of doves to hawks dropped to less than 2–1, and 200 letters arrived that opposed the demonstration to only 91 in support of it. The following week, the administration did even better in all categories. Once again, it appeared that a violent demonstration compelled administration supporters to send letters to the White House.

Finally, although a majority of Americans polled still disapproved of Johnson's handling of the war, the numbers improved after the demonstration. In early September, only 28 percent approved of his war policy. That number rose to 40 percent in November only to fall back again in subsequent months.[105] It is possible that the temporary rise in the polls, which might have also been affected by his conciliatory speech in San Antonio in September, reflected the rallying of some Americans around the president and the Defense Department who were under attack from the wild and dangerous hippies and radicals they saw in the media.

Yet even though the media helped the administration to survive the unprecedented confrontation at the Pentagon in pretty good shape, there is no doubt that Johnson and his aides were shocked by the spectacle. The media's lack of sympathy for the demonstrators could not hide the fact from friends and foes alike that the United States was coming apart over the war.

The antiwar movement, never very cohesive, was coming apart as well. In the wake of the Pentagon action and especially the perceived brutality of the authorities, many doves threatened even greater militance in the future. Others, who were frightened by the government's response and the reaction of the public to media reports, vowed to continue the struggle using traditional means and also to work to nominate an antiwar candidate in the 1968 presidential election. Both the administration and the antiwar movement were at a crossroads.

6

EXIT JOHNSON, ENTER NIXON, APRIL 1968–OCTOBER 1969

> We didn't want the demonstrations to center in Washington. We wanted them to be all over. We wanted marching on the green in small towns in New England, silent vigils in Iowa; church bells rung all over. It was symbolic: you didn't have to say anything. People would know what the church bells were ringing for. And people could do it anywhere.
>
> There was a terrific outpouring. There were mayors all over the country. Mayor Lindsay in New York, senators and congressmen. An awful lot of people who had not come out against the war before took the occasion to come out against it. There was even a demonstration on Wall Street.
>
> By the morning of the Moratorium, it was clear that we had achieved what we had hoped to do in another six, seven, or eight months. We had made our contribution and had shot our wad. We had accomplished it all at the very first go-around, and demonstrated the depths of antiwar sentiment.[1]

Looking back at the nationwide Moratorium of October 15, 1969, that he had helped organize, David Hawk was pleased with his astounding accomplishment. In the largest and most impressive demonstration in the history of the American peace movement, Hawk and his young colleagues had clearly caught the attention of the Nixon administration, an administration that was considering a dramatic escalation in the war.

The *New York Times*'s John Herbers was nowhere as ebullient as Hawk. He found far more general support for the war on "M-Day" than movement leaders. His front-page account on October 16 began:

> Protests ranging from noisy street rallies to silent prayer vigils and involving a broad spectrum of the population were held across the nation yesterday.
>
> The Vietnam Moratorium . . . was termed an overwhelming success by its planners.
>
> But it also demonstrated the great divisions in American society created by the prolonged American involvement in Southeast Asia. The demonstrations generated counter protests in some areas, and some supporters of the war who had been quiet for months spoke out in anger.
>
> It was the largest public protest of the many that have been held against the Vietnam war.[2]

The March on the Pentagon had a long-range effect on domestic and foreign politics that no one could have predicted at the time. According to former attorney general Ramsey Clark, it was "the moment that the fever broke in the whole antiwar movement."[3] It exemplified the antiwar sentiment that had been growing exponentially throughout 1967. Clark was not just talking about poll numbers or demonstrations. Each week brought new defections from the establishment—the *Wall Street Journal* one week, a prominent senator the next, a corporate executive the next.

With no end to the war in sight and shaken by the Pentagon siege, a nervous Johnson launched a public-relations campaign in November to keep more supporters from falling off his bandwagon. When he, Ambassador to South Vietnam Ellsworth Bunker, and General William Westmoreland toured the country that month, they oversold the progress being made in Vietnam in order to shore up the domestic front. The campaign contributed to the shock Americans experienced when they saw on television Viet Cong sappers inside the Saigon embassy compound during the massive communist Tet Offensive that began on January 31, 1968. From that point on, despite the ultimate American and South Vietnamese military victory against the National Liberation Front and the North Vietnamese's offensive, American leaders realized that further escalation was impossible. By March 31, when Johnson announced that he was going to restrict bombing in an attempt to bring Hanoi to the peace table, that he was not going to escalate the ground war, and that he was not going to seek reelection, half of those polled believed that the war was a mistake. One wonders whether more Americans would have come to such a conclusion earlier had it not been for the media's often negative portrayal of the antiwar movement.

By 1968, antiwar criticism, if not the movement itself, had become mainstream. This development made positive coverage of protests more likely. In addition, the defeat of the Democrats in the November election permitted pro-Johnson journalists and editors, as well as Democrats in Congress, to express their opposition to the war more openly. For the first time, the war in Vietnam was to become a partisan issue.

Most of the members of the fourth estate, like most Americans, accepted the fact that war in Vietnam was a lost cause—the sooner the United States withdrew the better. But, as we shall see, to adopt a dovish perspective and to embrace increasingly radical antiwar activists were two different things. Despite the media's growing criticism of administration polices, the movement did not always receive fair treatment from journalists who covered its activities.

Mobe Demonstrations, April 26–27, 1968

Many doves thought that they had won a major victory when Lyndon Johnson announced his decisions on March 31. Yet the war against the war was not over. For the fourth spring in a row, antiwar forces gathered in large numbers to demonstrate their opposition to the American presence in Vietnam. These protests came only a few weeks after the nationwide disturbances that erupted after the assassination of Dr. Martin Luther King, Jr. No doubt many of those who viewed the antiwar activities at the end of April remembered the extremely violent activities during the days following the assassination on April 4. They were in no mood for more demonstrations.

On the weekend of April 26–27, Mobe and Student Mobe protests took place throughout the nation.[4] These included student strikes in high schools and colleges on Friday, marches in New York and San Francisco on Saturday that drew as many as one hundred thousand and twenty thousand respectively, and a Chicago rally of more than seven thousand marked by police assaults against those who marched without a permit. The Chicago action was an augury of things to come that summer.

The fact that spring antiwar demonstrations had become routine contributed to the manner in which the media chose to cover the event. Moreover, they, as well as most Americans, could easily have concluded that the antiwar movement had become irrelevant or not worthy of special attention now that the United States was apparently withdrawing from Southeast Asia.

Such sentiments were reflected in the *New York Times*'s speculation that the successful student strike ("200,000 Cut Classes in War Protest in Metro Area") represented "spring euphoria," the *Washington Post*'s observation that a New York crowd listening to Coretta Scott King seemed "strangely lifeless," *Time*'s conclusion that the weekend events "fizzled," and *Newsweek*'s decision not to run a story on the protests.[5]

The *Guardian* disagreed with such evaluations. Its correspondent counted 120,000 in New York, was struck by the moderation of the crowd of which 30 percent sported Eugene McCarthy buttons, and attributed the "rather sluggish pace" of the rally to a faulty public address system.[6]

The *Guardian* aside, the press again emphasized the violent confrontations and language even though, as had generally been the case in the past, most of the demonstrations were peaceful. Indeed, even the *Village Voice*, after acknowledging that violence was a minor aspect of the activities, devoted considerable space to its manifestations.[7] It is true, of course, that the left was in disarray, with a small violence-prone minority becoming increasingly impatient with the pace of deescalation, and even more important, with what it perceived to be the growth of repression in the United States. Journalists and camera operators no longer had to look on the fringes of demonstrations to find Viet Cong flags, revolutionary rhetoric, and especially, challenges to the police. On the other hand, both *Times* and *Post* reporters were impressed with the number of demonstrators the movement was still able to attract, even after

Johnson's "valedictory," especially when compared to the feeble turnout for rival Loyalty Day demonstrations the same day.[8]

Democratic National Convention Riots, August 25–30, 1968

The demonstrations at the Democratic Party's national convention during the last week of August in 1968 were the most tumultuous of the Johnson administration. Because of the presence of thousands of journalists on hand to cover the convention, they also received more attention than any previous movement activity.

The major antiwar organizations did not participate formally in the Chicago protests against Democratic electoral and foreign policies.[9] Leaders feared a repetition of the tactics used by the tough Chicago police during the melee on April 26. Only about ten thousand protestors showed up for the convention, with as few as five thousand coming from outside the Chicago area.

Mayor Richard J. Daley had made it clear he would not tolerate protests at "his" convention. Aside from the threat from his police force, he made it virtually impossible for organizers to obtain march and overnight-camping permits, and declared the convention site off-limits to picketers. He also manipulated an electrical workers's strike and erected barriers at crucial assembly points to make it difficult for the broadcast media to cover events in the streets.[10]

The violence was the only movement story here. The unprecedented series of bloody confrontations between police and demonstrators in Lincoln and Grant Parks and in front of convention hotels overshadowed the speeches, marches, songs, and vigils. By the end of the convention, 688 people had been arrested, over 100 people—mostly demonstrators—were hospitalized with injuries, and another 625 suffered minor injuries. One person was shot to death. And despite the electrical strike and Daley's other obstructions, an astonished nation saw much of what happened on television.

At first glance, the Chicago riots might have helped the antiwar cause in much the same way that police beatings of civil rights marchers helped that cause a decade earlier. Observers should have sympathized with the young people, who were in most cases the victims of police brutality.[11] Things did not turn out that way.

Despite the *Guardian*'s assertion that "Millions of Americans were repelled by the official violence,"[12] surveys reported that a majority supported the police actions. Many viewers, according to two television analysts, apparently "adjusted the television images to fit their own preconceived beliefs."[13] Even a majority of the people who labeled themselves doves supported the police.[14] No doubt, the media offered confusing and sometimes out-of-context views of the protests. Mayor Daley saw no such confusion as he accused the media of presenting unfair pictures and stories about his police. Nevertheless, considering that the Walker Commission later clearly labeled much of what happened a "police riot," the public's reaction to the Chicago disturbances raises serious questions about the power of the media to influence their audience.

Part of the problem in the Chicago case was the fact that many of the protestors were relatively militant youngsters in hippie garb. Of all the major demonstrations, this one contained the smallest percentage of non-students. Many television viewers witnessing violence between "hippies" and police instinctively sided with the police, no matter what they saw on their screens. The country had become polarized and protestors of all stripes were perceived as violent and unpatriotic by the majority of those influenced by media portrayals of dissent. Richard Nixon successfully played to this sentiment in his presidential campaign that fall.

The coverage of the riots may have been affected by the police assault against print and broadcast reporters—*Newsweek* headed its story, "Beat the Press."[15] Journalists were often singled out during demonstrations for special treatment by club-wielding police and several were even mugged on the floor of the convention hall. NBC anchor Chet Huntley was convinced that the attack on the media, and particularly on photographers, was part of a premeditated attempt by Daley to make it impossible for them to cover repressive police actions.[16]

Although few were as furious as the *Village Voice*, most of the media, even the generally anti-dove *Time* magazine, concluded that though the protestors had been provocative and rude, the blame for the bloodshed rested with the police. For example, *Newsweek* referred to Daley's "overkill" in a story called "Lots of Law, Little Order"; *Time* referred to the "sanctioned mayhem" from a "Chinese warlord."[17] Reports from the scene to the *New York Times* were so critical that editor A. M. Rosenthal excised several unfavorable references to Daley and his police that he considered editorializing.[18]

Lyndon Johnson at his ranch during the convention was monitoring events both inside the amphitheater and outside in the parks and streets. Like Mayor Daley, he and his aides had been planning the defense of the convention for several months.[19] Two weeks after the convention ended, Johnson saw a Gallup Poll that revealed that Americans supported the Chicago police 56 to 31 percent. White House aide Fred Panzer thought it would have been interesting to determine what difference there was, if any, between respondents who saw the convention events on television, which he thought were skewed against the police, and those who had not.[20] Not much it turns out.

On the other hand, a week after the convention, Panzer told the president that his latest job-approval rating in the Gallup Poll had declined, perhaps because of the unpopularity of the continuing war.[21] Although the White House received far more mail in support of the protestors than the police in

Chicago, the mail to the networks told another story.[22] In the tens of thousands, letters ran 11–1 against the broadcasters for their allegedly biased coverage of the convention. In fact, CBS newscaster Harry Reasoner was so affected by those letters that he worried about the press's future in the United States.[23] Thus, while some in the White House thought that television had depicted Humphrey and his majority as the "villains" in Chicago and the dissidents as "heroes," a majority of the public disagreed with such analyses.[24]

The fact that many Americans did not accept what they saw with their own eyes suggests that one can never predict with certainty the impact of stories in the print and broadcast media on popular attitudes and public opinion. By the time of the convention, political demonstrations involving young people from the New Left and the counterculture had become so unpopular that images of police beating protestors either were not believed or, more frightening for the movement, may have been countenanced by many viewers who felt that the young people—and the journalists for that matter—deserved the beatings. In part, the media had only themselves to blame since they had dwelled on the violent and destabilizing aspects of antiwar protests ever since they first made headlines in 1965.

By the summer of 1968, it was difficult for many Americans to separate the concept "demonstration" from "violence."[25] And Richard Nixon, elected on a law-and-order platform to fight crimes in the streets, especially those allegedly perpetrated by protestors, took advantage of that development.

Resistance and Renewal Demonstrations, April 5–6, 1969

When Nixon took office in January, 1969, after a raucous and unprecedented counter-inaugural demonstration that irritated many Americans, the media, which had discovered a "new Nixon," were prepared to give him time to present a plan to end the war with dispatch. Leaders of the Student Mobilization Committee and the newly-formed National Action Group (NAG) were not as patient as they organized the fifth consecutive series of spring rallies.[26]

The 150,000 protestors who turned out on April 5 and 6 in more than forty cities constituted the second largest antiwar action to date. As many as 50,000 participated in Central Park on a wet and raw Saturday, while Chicago organizers drew 30,000, their largest antiwar crowd, and 4,000 people showed up in Atlanta. In contrast to the Chicago Convention riots and the increasing acts of violence committed by disaffected members of the New Left, these nationwide demonstrations were generally peaceful, including the one which took place in Mayor Daley's Chicago.

The April, 1969, protests reflected the slow renewal of antiwar forces in order to confront the new president who had not yet ended the war. The prominent place given to Vietnam veterans in several demonstrations was a

Protests Staged In Many Cities Over Viet Policy

Clashes Occur In New York and Berkeley, Calif.

Organized protests against this country's military involvement in Vietnam taxed police facilities across the country and abroad yesterday, attaining near-riot proportions in New York and California.

In nearly every instance, the demonstrations met counter-demonstrations. In some cities wholesale arrestes were made as police lines broke and fighting began. Locally, a protest march and its counterpart were conducted almost without incident.

In New York, about 10,000 demonstrators plodded e i g h t abreast down Fifth Avenue, beset by hecklers who hurled red paint and eggs and invective.

Trouble in Berkeley, Calif.

In Berkeley, Calif., some 35 members of the notorious Hell's Angels motorcycle club burst through police barricades to mount an attack on students demonstrating against the fighting in the Far East.

Around the world, protests sponsored by various pacifist and ban-the-bomb groups were organized to coincide with the demonstrations in this country. Typically, a small girl toddled in the van of a group of British marchers, carrying a lighted candle and leading their \chant of "Stop the slaughter in Vietnam!"

Another section of that parade sang out "Wilson is Johnson's poodle," a reference to British Prime Minister Harold Wilson's open support of President Johnson's Vietnamese policy.

1. The *Washington Post*'s account on October 17, 1965, of the previous day's activities of the First International Days of Protest not only underestimated the size of the New York City crowd but, more importantly, framed the first sections of the lead story around violent activities of "near-riot proportions." In almost all cases, the violence had been precipitated by unruly counterdemonstrators. Reprinted with permission of the *Washington Post*.

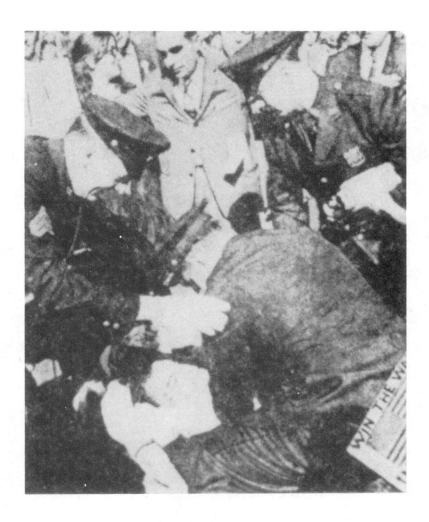

2. The seemingly innocuous captions that newspaper editors choose to explain their photographs often reflect their biases. Here, for example, in its coverage of the First International Days of Protest activities, The *Daily Tribune* for October 18, 1965, included this UPI photograph with the caption, "New York City police subdued an angry man who hurled red paint on anti-war demonstrators. Note sign he dropped." The sign, visible at the bottom right, reads "Win the War." Reprinted with permission of the Bettmann Archive and the *Daily Tribune*.

3. *Newsweek* reprinted this Walt Kelly cartoon that originally appeared in the *Herald Tribune* to accompany a feature story on the draft (see also fig. 4). Here we see an early humorous assault against the longhaired unisex look. As we moved through the second half of the sixties, more and more urban young people adopted countercultural styles to a point where it was impossible to distinguish between doves and hippies. Whether in cartoons or in photographs, such images distressed many middle-class Americans. Reprinted with permission of Whitcom.

THE ABC'S OF DRAFT DODGING

Serious or satirical? That is the question about a little pamphlet entitled "Ways and Means of 'Beating' and Defeating the Draft." Poorly mimeographed, the two-page broadsheet fluttered out of Berkeley, Calif., the protest capital of America, during the recent demonstrations protesting the war in Southeast Asia. At first, no one paid it much heed, but then Sen. Thomas Kuchel read it and called it "a dirty and contemptible little sheet." Its authors hastily insisted that the compilation of draft-dodging advice was facetious. Some excerpts:

■ Be a C.O. Write your local draft board requesting the special conscientious objector form SSS 150. Now if you don't have religious or philosophical reasons that cause you to be against war "in any form," don't let it bother you. It's fairly certain that your local board will turn you down. However, you can then appeal their decision, be investigated, appeal again and so on. The whole process takes about a year, and by that time we'll have stopped the war in Vietnam (we hope).

■ Have a "demonstration" during your pre-induction physical. This is a way for political objectors to get a 4-F and cause the military a lot of trouble. Arrive at the examining center wearing signs. Leaflet your fellow prospective inductees. Be determined and the officers will be only too glad to be rid of you.

■ Refuse to sign the loyalty oath. They'll investigate you and if you've been fairly active in any of the "subversive" campus movements, they won't want you.

■ Be "gay." Play the homosexual bit. Mark 'yes' or don't mark the "Homosexual Tendencies" line on the form. Psychiatrist may give you the runaround but stick with it. Besides flicking your wrist, move your body like chicks do—hold cigarette delicately, talk melodically, act embarrassed in front of the other guys when you undress. Ask your girl friend to give you lessons.

■ Note from doctor. If you have a "friendly" family doctor or can buy one, you'll find he's extremely handy. Get a signed note from him attesting to an allergy, a trick knee or elbow or shoulder or back trouble, or asthma. Without a doctor's note, you'll have to do a pretty good job of faking these things. Certain

chemicals will temporarily induce allergies—see your chemist.

■ Jail record. Most of us aren't lucky enough to have a felony record, but if you've got one—use it. They insist on it; you'll see signs all over the place telling you what a crime you'll be committing if you don't tell them. Misdemeanors—if you've got enough of them—are a good deal.

■ Play psycho. If you've ever been to see a "head shrinker"—even once —by all means mark so on forms. A note from him and a little bit of acting with this will go a long way. Chew your fingernails. Talk about the Viet Cong being out to get you. Tell them you're a secret agent for God Johnson.

■ Arrive drunk. Being late here really helps. They may send you

Draft card: Burning question

away to come back another day, but it'll look good to have it on your record. If you do this bit enough times, they'll probably run you back to the head shrinker to find out why.

■ Arrive high. They'll smell it, and you won't have to admit it. If you want to go about the addiction scene in a really big way, use a common pin on your arm for a few weeks in advance.

■ Be an undesirable. Go for a couple of weeks without a shower. Really look dirty. Stink. Long hair helps. Go in barefoot with your sandals tied around your neck.

■ Be a troublemaker. Refuse to follow orders. (You don't have to, you're not in the Army). Let them know exactly what you think of them. Be antagonistic; smoke where the signs say NO SMOKING.

■ Bed-wetting. Tell them you wet the bed when you're away from home. If they don't defer you, prove it when you're inducted.

4. Interest in the First International Days of Protest led *Newsweek* to run a long feature on the antiwar movement in its November 1, 1965, edition. Among other issues, the magazine emphasized draft avoidance as a major reason for the growth of opposition to American policies in Southeast Asia. To illustrate the point, it included the draft-dodging manual reproduced above. Considering its contents, readers were certain to share Senator Thomas Kuchel's (R-CA) views of that "dirty and contemptible little sheet." From *Newsweek*, November 1, 1965, © Newsweek, Inc. All rights reserved. Reprinted with permission.

Throng of 20,000 Marches In Protest of Vietnam War

PEACE IS THEIR PLEA—Anti-Vietnam war marchers fill 15th Street, en route to Sylvan Theater.

More Pictures on Vietnam War Marchers, Pages A6 and D39.

Only 8 Arrests Mar Mild Tone Of Peace Appeal

A throng estimated by police at 20,000 to 25,000 persons marched around the White House and then massed on the Washington Monument grounds yesterday in an orderly and strangely silent appeal for peace in Vietnam.

The day-long demonstration was remarkable for its mild mannered tone. Marchers were surprisingly neat for the most part, many of them middle-aged and middle-class in appearance.

Isolated scuffles and alleged refusals to move along resulted in eight arrests, unnoticed by most of the demonstrators.

Some of the trouble came from the Vietcong flags unfurled by members of the Committee to Aid the National Liberation Front of South Vietnam. A few of the flags were hoisted, but only one survived marchers' appeals to put them down, and it was surrounded by American banners.

'Of Higher Caliber'

One of the Vietcong flags was grabbed by a man in a group of counter-demonstrators across Pennsylvania Avenue from the White House, but attempts to burn the wet flag failed. The counter-demonstrators in Lafayette Park, including spectators as well as opposition pickets, numbered 1000 to 1500 at one time.

Deputy Police Chief Thomas Rasmussen was impressed by the orderliness of the White House marchers, who strung all the way around the Executive Mansion, down 15th and 17th Streets to Constitution Avenue and around the Ellipse.

The demonstrators were of higher caliber than the people

See MARCH, A6, Col. 2

"Monitors" credited by police for maintaining order during demonstration.
Page A6.

Neo-Nazis, Ku Klux Klan and Hell's Angels stage all-day counter-demonstration.
Page A6.

2 GI Captives To Be Freed By Viet Reds

SAIGON, Nov. 27 (UPI)—The Vietcong radio said today that two U.S. Army war prisoners captured two years ago were being released in honor of anti-Vietcong demonstrations in the United States.

The broadcast identified the two as Sgt. George E. Smith and Spc. Claude E. McClure. It said they were captured Nov. 24, 1963, at the Special Forces camp at Hiephoa.

American military records show that Smith, of Chester W. Va., and McClure, of Chattanooga, Tenn., were captured when the Communists overran Hiephoa. Authorities added that they had no indication that the two soldiers actually had been freed.

The rebels' clandestine "Liberation Radio" announced this afternoon that the Vietcong "have decided to release" the two men. Later it broadcast the text of an open letter saying they were "just released." The radio did not say when or where. It said in part:

"Expressing the certainty that there are many people who will struggle against the U.S. Government policy," and "in response to the Nov. 27 American movement, and to mark both the fifth anniversary of the Liberation Front and Christmas, the Liberation Front has ordered the release of two U.S. soldiers."

Index, Page A2

Second class postage paid at Washington, D. C. Printed at 1515 L St. N.W. Washington 5.

Balmy, Pleasant Outing

Anti-War Parade Lacked Virility of Rights March

By Alfred Friendly
Washington Post Staff Writer

The weather was more sparkling than the gathering, which tended to be earnest, good-natured and non-muscular.

To contrast yesterday's March on Washington for Peace in Vietnam with the civil rights march here on Aug. 3, 1963, is perhaps unfair, but inescapable. The difference was a certain virility: than one had it—this one didn't.

The event two years ago was joyful, full of promise about to be realized, swirling with emotion and full-throated. The issue was less intricate and debatable and the consensus about the justice of the cause was much more nearly universal. Yesterday's convocation was of a minority, embattled, on the defensive and espousing a minority position.

For the most part, the Vietnam protesters were young and obviously dedicated. There was little to suggest that more than a few came for the kicks, or for exhibitionistic reasons, or to find "identity" or escape "alienation" or the other much-advertised ailments of the youth of our times.

A Different Day

Rather, they seemed resolute, sincere and convinced that their presence would have some impact in changing a national policy that they view, in the literal sense of the word, as terrible.

Had he been on the White House porch, President Johnson would not have been pleased with the sentiments, but he might have enjoyed the view. It was surely a change from most weekday Pennsylvania Avenue.

Some thousands, predominantly collegians, sauntered in pleasantly unsystematic oval patterns, a dozen of the formations occupying all the sidewalk space from the Treasury to 17th Street. For the most part, their placards spoke the "authorized" words, the relatively moderate exhortations to stop the bombing, negotiate, permit self-determination, respect the 1954 Geneva agreements.

Stronger Views Heard

The tougher, angrier anti-Administration views of the more radical left groups intruded only occasionally: "Impeach Johnson," "McNamara Be Human," "Support the National Liberation Front."

The first impression of the crowd was of beatniks, but

See MOOD, A7, Col. 2

Marines Land South of Saigon—Marchers Protest Policy on Vietnam

In South Vietnam, United States marines wade toward shore after leaving boats. Aim is to safeguard Saigon River.

On Fifth Avenue here, opponents of United States action in Vietnam march down Fifth Avenue. Later they held rally.

Thousands on Fifth Ave.
March in Vietnam Protest

6. Quite often the media linked stories about the war in Vietnam with stories about demonstrations at home—to the detriment of the antiwarriors. Glancing at the *New York Times* front page on March 27, 1966, readers might compare the lead article about the brave soldiers fighting in Vietnam to the adjacent story about the Second International Days of Protest march in New York City. Copyright © 1966 by The New York Times Company. Reprinted by permission.

UPI

APOCALYPTIC PROTEST: As U.S. troops scored a succession of fresh victories in Vietnam, peace groups in the U.S. doggedly cranked up another weekend of protest demonstrations. On the Berkeley, Calif., campus, some 1,000 of the faithful trudged with apocalyptic placards and standards (above) while U.N. Ambassador Arthur Goldberg was defending the U.S. commitment at university ceremonies. There were similar strident marches and rallies across the nation—Boston, Chicago and Baraboo, Wis., site of an ordnance firm—in the weekend's soft spring weather. Most were marked, as is becoming a custom, by wispily smoking draft cards and a few scuffles.

7. *Newsweek* devoted little attention to the Second International Days of Protest in its April 4, 1966, issue, despite the impressive size of the worldwide demonstrations. In its only reference to them, the caption below a UPI photograph of an antiwar crowd denigrated the relevance of the movement. Beginning "As U.S. troops scored a succession of fresh victories," it appeared that the enemy was on the ropes. In addition, as seen in the last line of the caption, antiwar protests had apparently become routine and predictable events offering little to interest the media. Reprinted with permission, the Bettmann Archive.

Rusk, King Disagree on Red Involvement

8. The antiwar protest in New York City on Saturday, April 15, 1967, was the largest to date, drawing an impressive crowd most likely in excess of 250,000. Yet the *Daily Tribune*, which did not have a Sunday edition, ran its account on page 14 in its Monday, April 17, issue. Moreover, the emphasis in the accompanying story was on the degree of radicalism in the crowd and the caption certainly would not have pleased the doves, especially the suggestion that the burning of draft boards was on their agenda. The media's frames were influenced by the Johnson administration's attempt to depict the antiwar movement as dominated by violent radicals. Reprinted with permission of United Press International, Inc., the *Daily Tribune*, and the Bettmann Archive.

9. On October 22, 1969, the Sunday morning after the Siege of the Pentagon, the *Washington Post* stressed the activities of "a surging band of about 30 demonstrators," missed the story of the brutal early-morning military assault against passive doves, and skimmed over the larger peaceful rally at the Memorial that preceded the Pentagon activities. Similar photographs dominated the coverage nationwide. Reprinted with permission of the *Washington Post*.

The caption reads: "The confrontation: Compact mass of armed military policemen resist a surging band of demonstrators on the Pentagon steps."

ABC   :07:00   NOV 14 69

ANTONIO PONCE   CAREY BEST

10. From Thursday, November 13, to Friday, November 14, 1969, Moratorium participants marched from Arlington to the Capitol carrying over forty thousand placards with the names of American soldiers who had died in Vietnam or villages destroyed in the war. As they passed the White House, they called out the names on the placards. ABC television cameras captured the dignity and solemnity of the March Against Death for the evening news on November 14. Most of the placard carriers were as clean-cut and genteel as those shown above. Despite the drama of the event, the network spent more time on two small but quite raucous rallies at the Justice Department that occurred the same day, which, of course, provided more "action" than the march. Copyright © 1969, Capital Cities/ABC, Inc.

A police officer with drawn revolver confronts a group of demonstrators near the Embassy of South Vietnam Friday during a night of violence in Washington, D.C.

Police use tear gas to hold back the militant war protesters. It was the first violence of the three-day peace march. More pictures on Page 37. (Unifax)

Notables Present

Thousands Marching for Peace

WASHINGTON (UPI) – Tens of thousands of young Americans, chanting "p e a c e now", marched down Pennsylvania Avenue t o d a y to dramatize their conviction that the United States should withdraw from Vietnam immediately.

In the vanguard of the orderly, mass march walked

Sens. Eugene J. McCarthy, D-Minn., George McGovern, D-S.D., and Charles E. Goodell, R-N.Y.; Mrs. Coretta King; folk singers Pete Seeger and Arlo Guthrie; composer Leonard Bernstein; and a group of clergymen.

But, people over 30 were scarce — and black people

11. The *Daily Tribune*'s front-page lead on November 15, 1969, the day of the massive Mobilization demonstration in Washington, employed the word "Peace" in the headline. However, the UPI pictures accompanying the story of the previous day's violent activities, including a reference in the caption to "a night of violence," did not look at all peaceful. The most important event of the previous day was the dramatic March Against Death, not the minor and extracurricular incident at the Republic of Vietnam embassy. Reprinted with permission of United Press International, Inc., the *Daily Tribune*, and the Bettmann Archive.

The captions read (*left*): "A police officer with drawn revolver confronts a group of demonstrators near the Embassy of South Vietnam Friday during a night of violence in Washington, D.C." and (*right*): "Police use tear gas to hold back the militant war protesters. It was the first violence of the three-day peace march."

Moratorium Leaders Plan More Protests; Plan Action on Local Levels

12. In another indication that Nixon's campaign against the antiwar movment was succeeding, the *Daily Tribune*'s Monday, November 17, 1969, coverage of the Moratorium and Mobilization events included two UPI photographs, one of uncharacteristic violence in San Francisco and another of a disabled World War II veteran who supported the president. In addition, the caption writer confused the Moratorium with the Mobilization. Reprinted with permission of United Press International, Inc., the *Daily Tribune*, and the Bettmann Archive.

The captions read (*left*): "ESCAPED—San Francisco mounted policemen galloped toward an antiwar demonstrator Saturday, who stole a billy club from one of the officers during gathering of Moratorium Day marchers at Golden Gate Park's Polo Field. The man escaped into the bushes with his prize." and (*right*): "'THE SILENT MAJORITY'—Disabled World War II veteran Lee Hyatt raised his uninjured left arm to salute U.S. flag after placing a wreath on Veterans' Memorial Saturday in Walden, N.Y. Larger than usual Veterans Day observers were a major highlight in a week full of demonstrations in towns and cities throughout the country, as antiwar protesters vied with President Nixon's 'silent majority' to make their feelings known."

Protest and the President: Rally at the monument and Mr. Nixon at Capitol

THE BIG MARCH: ON A TREADMILL

Down Washington's Pennsylvania Avenue, the "path of Presidents," they marched in the morning chill, some 250,000 Americans come to their Capital to tell their President he was wrong. They bore the flags of the United States and the Viet Cong—and some waved banners hailing Che Guevara. They were led by the men and women who have come to embody the several strains of American protest—Eugene McCarthy, Coretta King, Arlo Guthrie, Benjamin Spock—and by twelve wooden coffins containing the names of U.S. servicemen killed in Vietnam. This was the 1969 March on Washington, the largest antiwar demonstration ever held in the Capi-

—"for an enemy agreement on the shape of the bargaining table" in Paris, where he was chief U.S. negotiator with the North Vietnamese. The antiwar side, too, had its hotheads, notably SDS's Weathermen, warriors of violent revolution who leave no bridge unburnt and no battlement unstormed.

In the end, however, the extremists were well contained. Mayor Walter Washington persuaded the President to overrule the Justice Department's initial opposition to granting a Pennsylvania Avenue parade permit, and thus the demonstrators' main event was channeled inside legal boundaries rather than encouraged into outlawry. When the ultra-

ernment, except for its law-enfor authorities and a few maverick w seemed entirely unrelated to the of marchers in its midst. The Pr had vowed to pay absolutely no tion to the show in the streets, no how massive or how orderly. And one highlight of Mr. Nixon's week surprise trip to Capitol Hill to tr lidify the very Vietnam policy t demonstrators had come to ridic

Solidarity: The visit was ocasi a House resolution endorsing his to negotiate a just peace in Vi With the help of a crash lobbyin by the Administration, it attrac signatures of no fewer than 3

13. On November 15, 1969, the more than 300,000 demonstrators organized by the Moratorium and the Mobilization who gathered in Washington constituted the largest demonstration in American history. This massive protest represented an effective response to the president's vigorous offensive against the antiwar movement. Nevertheless, most of the media, responding in part to Nixon's Silent Majority speech and Agnew's direct assault against them, portrayed the event as a standoff, with the antiwar movement seen to have lost momentum since the previous month's Moratorium. *Newsweek*'s approach was characteristic. From *Newsweek*, November 24, 1969, © Newsweek, Inc. All rights reserved. Reprinted with permission. Photographs reprinted with permission of the Bettmann Archive.

Veterans Discard Medals to Protest Viet War

Their week of protest at an end, these antiwar veterans show solidarity as they walk away from the Mall near Capitol.

14. The Vietnam Veterans Against the War activities in Washington from April 19 through April 23, 1970, provided many poignant photo opportunities for the media. Of all the demonstrations of the era, the VVAW's Operation Dewey Canyon III, which included protests at the Supreme Court, appearances before congressional committees, street guerilla theatre, and most spectacularly, the returning of battle ribbons and medals, received the most generous treatment from the media. The Nixon administration was furious at the quality and quantity of press coverage of the VVAW. Reprinted with permission of the *Washington Post*.

15. Howard K. Smith appeared in front of a map of Washington on ABC's May 3, 1971, evening news as he began a lengthy sequence on the Mayday Tribe's attempt to shut down the government through civil disobedience. The map in the background, along with the revolutionary clenched fist, evoked military images of a battle raging through the streets of the capital. Smith announced correctly that the demonstration "failed of its main purposes" but "the confrontations were lively enough to ensure maximum publicity." The confrontations ABC then selected to air did not produce the sort of publicity that doves appreciated. Copyright © 1971 Capital Cities/ABC, Inc.

16. ABC's coverage of the first day of the Mayday Tribe's civil disobedience actions emphasized uncharacteristically offensive—albeit colorful—attempts to shut Washington down. This "guerilla warfare" looked at times like a game of "cowboys and indians" with the police on motorcycles playing the role of the cowboys. For example, in the shot above, a man pulled the distributor cap from a Volkswagon whose driver happened to linger too long in his vicinity, an action that reporter Virginia Sherwood considered to be "one favorite trick" of the demonstrators. Few viewers would sympathize with a protestor disabling a car in such a fashion in order to "make it part of the roadblock." More important, this action was not a common tactic used by the Mayday Tribe. Copyright © 1971 Capital Cities/ABC, Inc.

noteworthy development as was the appearance of many middle-class demonstrators, including elected politicians. With Nixon in office, it had become easier for Democrats to appear at such forums.

Our two left-wing weeklies caught the significance of the April event that was missed, to some degree, by the other sources. The movement was clearly at a crossroads—the *Guardian* talked of the "incredible boredom of ritual parade" and the *Voice* of the "annual rite of righteous indignation." To be sure, the demonstrations were peaceful and large but they featured more clenched fists, more NLF flags, more militant rhetoric, and enthusiastic chants of "Fuck the Pigs." More ominous, many formerly compliant foot soldiers refused to accept orders from organizers.[27]

Like Johnson and his advisors, Nixon and his media monitors paid scant attention to the *Village Voice* and the *Guardian*. Less than four months into his first term, the new president was still on a honeymoon with the mainstream media. The *New York Times*, for example, which counted only 26,600 people in Central Park, ran its demonstration story next to one headlined, "Nixon Has Begun to End the War in Vietnam." The *Washington Post* discerned a "heavy and grim" mood among the New York doves, less festive than in 1967 and less militant than in 1968. *Newsweek* ignored the event, *Time* offered a paragraph and a picture, and the networks undercovered it.[28]

The media should have done more with the story of the rebirth of the antiwar movement that April weekend, if only because of the magnitude of some of the protests. Organizers had demonstrated that their activities could still be nonviolent, that more than students and radicals were involved, and that even members of the military were becoming restive with the pace of withdrawal. Yet, aside from the military issue, the demonstrations offered little that was new to attract attention. Neither the size of the demonstrations—respectable, but not the largest ever—nor the nature of the protests were novel or unusual. The mass antiwar demonstration had become too routine to be interesting. Media uninterest, as well as the increasing uninterest of antiwarriors in protests as usual, caused leaders to consider new tactics to keep their movement on the front pages and to maintain enthusiasm in the ranks.

Media uninterest in the movement was matched by uninterest shown by the Nixon administration's media monitors. In their summary of Sunday, April 6 newspaper coverage, aside from a brief mention of the demonstrations as one of the five major stories of the day, analysts made no other comment in their three-page review.[29] Such indifference suggests they did not consider the demonstrations very important. Further, they applauded ABC commentator Howard K. Smith's remark on April 7 that Nixon had been responding to the doves with his policies.[30]

On this occasion the White House operatives read their sources accurately, although one might have expected a bit more interest in the GI-protestor angle. By not paying much attention to the April protests, both the media and Nixon's media monitors contributed to the sensation caused by the wildly successful October Moratorium.

The Moratorium, October 15, 1969

The relative failure of the April demonstrations to attract interest compelled antiwar leaders to develop new and imaginative tactics for their next round of protests. As the months went by, it became apparent that the light at the end of the tunnel in Vietnam was as imperceptible under Nixon as it had been under Johnson. Indeed, the first six months of his administration were the second bloodiest for American soldiers. The situation was apparently getting worse, and that is why so many people decided to return to the streets.

By the fall of 1969, many Americans had begun to doubt that Nixon was going to withdraw from Vietnam with any speed. Of course, they did not know that Nixon had given Ho Chi Minh an ultimatum to become more forthcoming at the peace table by November 1 or face a major escalation. But that sort of information would have made doves, who desired a swift and bloodless termination of the war, even more distressed with administration policy.

Leaders of the antiwar movement needed a new tactic to compel Nixon to recognize that they were a force that reflected significant opinion in the United States. Just another large rally or series of marches would not be effective in the face of the president's resolve to ignore the minority in the streets. More of the same would also fail to attract the attention of the media—the only way the movement could attract Nixon's attention. And given the fact that many doves seemed to be merely going through the motions at the annual spring rallies, short of being guaranteed free dope or performances by the Rolling Stones, many would not show up in the fall in large enough numbers to affect the course of the war in Vietnam. Organizers were trapped into the numbers game in which each of the by-now annual spring and fall events had to be larger than the preceding ones or they would be considered failures.

The novel idea for a Moratorium solved all of these problems, at least temporarily. The chair of the Moratorium Day Committee, Sam Brown, a non-sectarian antiwar activist, began planning the event in April. His committee proposed that instead of holding massive demonstrations in one or two cities on a fall weekend, it would declare a weekday, Wednesday, October 15, Moratorium Day. On that day, citizens would take off minutes or hours from their work or classes to join others to record their opposition to the pace at which the United States was withdrawing from Vietnam. Additionally, the committee planned one such activity each month until the war ended, with each succeeding month's moratorium expanding by one day. For example, if the war continued through December, the moratorium that month would take place over three days. The longer the war went on, the more days each month that Americans would refuse to carry on business as usual.

Among the manifestations of dissent, organizers recommended traditional rallies and marches, vigils in cemeteries, prayer services, the tolling of bells, and moments of silence. Each community would organize its own activity. The Moratorium message was a simple one, and may be summarized as follows: We who are gathered here pausing in our daily routines think that the president is not doing enough to extricate the United States from the war. Although the press was somewhat slow to grasp the potential of this new sort of protest,[31] the advertisement in the *New York Times* calling for a Moratorium was the most successful fund-raiser of its kind. As the Moratorium approached, the media began to legitimize it with favorable advance stories about its responsible leadership and unique concept.[32]

At least nine members of Congress endorsed the protest, as did former U.N. ambassador Arthur Goldberg, U.A.W. president Walter Reuther, and W. Averell Harriman, Johnson's chief negotiator at Paris. On the other hand, Nixon's opponent in the election of 1968, Hubert Humphrey, announced his support for the president's policies in Vietnam on the eve of the Moratorium and did not participate in its activities on the Macalester College campus where he was teaching.

The Moratorium succeeded in attracting numbers far in excess of what its organizers expected. The lowest estimates suggest that one million Americans joined in, the highest an improbable ten million; three million seems plausible. Given the thousands of events and the fact that so many took place on busy city streets during lunch hour, the Moratorium posed the most difficult problem for crowd enumerators of any antiwar demonstration.[33]

Estimates for some cities were relatively precise because of the nature of their events. Bostonians produced the largest single-event crowd of the day, with one hundred thousand gathering on the Common to listen to George McGovern, among other luminaries.[34] Boston's M Day constituted the largest political demonstration in that city's long history. In New York, an estimated 250,000 citizens took part in several events including a rally that drew between 50 and 100,000 people into relatively small Bryant Park behind the New York Public Library to hear Shirley MacLaine, Tony Randall, and Janis Joplin. Four local television stations devoted programming to special Moratorium events during the day. In the city in which Republican Mayor John V. Lindsay declared a day of mourning and ordered flags flown at half mast, former Johnson aide Bill Moyers addressed 20,000 on Wall Street at a lunch-hour service with former Air Force Secretary Roswell Gilpatric and CBS president Michael Burke at his side. Many Broadway shows darkened for the day, including Woody Allen's *Play It Again Sam*. Other M Day turnouts included 100,000 in Chicago, 50,000 in Philadelphia, 40,000 in New Haven, 30,000 who heard Coretta Scott King in Washington as well as a sizeable number of government employees who demonstrated on the Capitol steps, 10,000 in Minneapolis, 5,000 in Salt Lake City, 8,000 who heard Republican Senator Charles Goodell lecture at Cornell University, and 12,000 at a rally in Pittsburgh endorsed by the city council.

In all venues, many more American flags appeared than Viet Cong flags, many more traditional prayers were intoned than conventional political chants, and there was almost a total absence of violence and arrests. The major "violence" of the day took place in front of the White House, where several hundred black picketers, whose agenda was broader than that of the Moratorium, advanced toward the front gate after their demonstration was broken up by District police; pushing and shoving marked this encounter. The remarkable lack of violence on October 15 was surprising given the fact that the Weathermen's Days of Rage took place in Chicago on October 8 and 11, only a week before the Moratorium. On that occasion, for the first time, an organized group of left-wing youths purposefully set out to destroy property and to battle the police. Yet, a week later, peace vigils, candlelight processions, and moments of silence characterized Moratorium activities.

On the eve of the event, Premier Pham Van Dong of North Vietnam sent greetings to peace demonstrators in the United States. The North Vietnamese had not yet learned that such support was counterproductive.[35] The administration gleefully called attention to the message that was also read into the *Congressional Record*.

Although no nationwide counter-Moratoriums developed, in scores of cities, people organized activities to support the president, which ranged from flag flying to driving with headlights on during the daylight hours. However, the number of citizens who turned out in a formal way for proadministration rallies was minuscule. On the other hand, although the Moratorium attracted participants in many unlikely cities and towns, many cities in the midwest, south, and southwest were virtually untouched by its activities. Finally, there were countless instances of individual challenges to picketers and leafletters.

The varied responses to M Day posed a problem for the media. More Americans protested against their government's policies on October 15 than had ever done so before. All the same, the vast majority either opposed the Moratorium or was indifferent to it. How much of that sentiment should one capture in the coverage? In few cases did the national media pay an equal amount of attention to both positions. The "news" was those who turned out for the Moratorium, not those who did not. That was a sensible editorial decision. (The media do not normally note after the coverage of an earthquake in California that there were no earthquakes in the rest of the nation.) Further, they were generally careful to intersperse Moratorium coverage with remarks from administration spokespersons.

However the press tried to achieve balance, the Moratorium was not only the most successful demonstration of the Vietnam War period, it was also the most popular. And why not, considering the sorts of people who were protesting, the methods of their protest, and the moderation of their message?

THE MORATORIUM WAS ESPECIALLY TELEGENIC. MOREOVER, this was the sort of protest most middle-class producers, reporters, and camerapeople preferred—adult, dignified, non-radical, yet still full of opportunities for colorful sound bites. To illustrate the point, the independent Marxist *Guardian*, which approved of the Moratorium, was nevertheless concerned about the "doubtful politics" of its leadership.[36]

ABC devoted virtually its entire evening newscast on October 15 to M Day. With more time allocated overall, the network also devoted more time than its rivals to proadministration activities.[37] The newscast opened with shots of masses of humanity at the Chicago Civic Center and in front of Trinity Church on Wall Street, clean-cut students singing "America the Beautiful" at Catholic University in Washington, bells tolling at bucolic Bethel College in Newton, Kansas, a march across the Golden Gate Bridge in San Francisco, and a group of Los Angeles City College students reading the names of war dead. Most of those scenes appeared in one form or another on all three networks. Interestingly, all three picked up the Bethel College story but none noted that Bethel had a special academic interest in conflict resolution programs. Those who saw the scene without that knowledge must have been impressed by the fact that the Moratorium had reached rural Kansas, deep in the heartland. Like the other two networks, ABC shied away from announcing a total number of participants but crowd scenes in so many places suggested a mass movement of unprecedented proportions.

After this two-minute montage, the editors cut to the scuffle outside the White House, assigning it an inappropriate position in the news budget considering the peaceful nature of M Day. ABC then moved on to interview the gentle Sam Brown balanced with Nixon's director of communications, Herbert G. Klein, who suggested in a non-confrontational manner that others out there did not agree with Brown and his cohorts. This was a hint of the Silent Majority to come.

After a brief look at the silent vigil held by several hundred Congressional staffers during the lunch hour on the Capitol steps, ABC offered perspectives from dovish Senator Mike Mansfield (D-MT) and hawkish Senator Barry Goldwater (R-AZ), and reported, as well, that fourteen congressmen had called upon Nixon to escalate. News of Senator Edward F. Kennedy's (D-MA) plan for withdrawal from Vietnam balanced that item. Curiously, it was well into the program before ABC shifted to Boston Common where the largest crowd of the day gathered and where "despite their numbers, their marches were peaceful." That loaded comment suggested that numbers themselves may produce disorder.

ABC also aired a gathering at Whittier College, Nixon's alma mater, noting that it was the largest political demonstration at that college in thirty years. All the networks recorded the Whittier events.

Viewers of the ABC newscast received a generally accurate portrayal of the day's events. The fact that almost all of the program was devoted to the Moratorium underscored its importance. Rarely do newscasts devote so much time to one story. Of course, if it was such an unprecedented event, why did not ABC and the other networks cover it live during the day? CBS and NBC did run ninety-minute specials out of prime time (at 11:30 P.M.) and all three broke into normal programming from time to time with remotes and bulletins. Nevertheless, the Moratorium justified even more attention than that, with the sort of coverage networks devote to presidential nominating conventions, natural disasters, or Super Bowls.

CBS allocated its first eighteen minutes to the "historic day" of "dramatic protest." With a background shot of the huge crowd at the Washington Monument, Walter Cronkite began the show cautiously, talking of nationwide crowds of "hundreds of thousands," but there was no way to obtain an accurate estimate. Moreover, the respected anchor pointed out that some of the people on the streets that day were supporters of the administration.

CBS interspersed favorable coverage of the day's events with unfavorable assessments. One minute of Eugene McCarthy speaking at Rutgers was followed by Humphrey's dissent and Goldwater's concern that the Moratorium encouraged Hanoi. CBS then went around the country to look at mostly responsible and dignified protestors. Brief scuffles took place in Detroit and in front of the White House where black militants tried to sit in. (ABC had described them as rushing the White House.) CBS did note that one person in front of the president's home was carrying a Viet Cong flag. This was an unfair jab at the Moratorium considering the preponderance of American flags and patriotic singing evident throughout the country.

As for the president and his supporters, CBS found him tending to "business as usual" while fourteen Republican legislators called for victory, not withdrawal, from Vietnam. The scene then shifted to Boston and its "sea of humanity," Wall Street and Moyers and Lindsay, and even peace activism at Fort Benning, Georgia. The South was least affected by the Moratorium, with Georgia Governor Lester Maddox opposing the flying of the flag at half-mast at the Atlanta City Hall, and the absence of any activity in Savannah, where the mayor warned that M Day was dangerous because it aided the enemy.

After showing the Whittier College ceremonies, which involved the wife of the president of the college, the correspondent noted that only four hundred of the two thousand one hundred students attended and that a campus poll revealed that 52 percent of the students supported Nixon. CBS also took its cameras to Los Angeles, San Francisco, Bethel College, and empty classrooms in Ann Arbor where the Moratorium looked successful and to Indianapolis and Des Moines for pro-Nixon demonstrations.

Despite Coretta Scott King's appearance in Washington and Ralph Abernathy's in Los Angeles, CBS accurately noted that blacks were not involved in any great numbers in M Day. Such a comment might have gained rather than lost support for the Moratorium among those who were concerned about protests that included Black Panthers and black nationalists. Indeed, one wonders about the impact in general when the media noted in pictures, as well as in narration, the absence of black participation in most antiwar activities. What they presented as an implicit critique might have redounded to the benefit of the movement.

CBS's coverage of the Moratorium offered another accurate portrayal of the day's events with many moving visuals of the demonstrators. However, the network's critical comments from its own analysts and administration supporters diluted some of the positive impact.

Of the three television networks, NBC devoted the fewest number of minutes (sixteen) to the Moratorium but offered the most dramatic visuals. In his opening statements, David Brinkley mentioned counterdemonstrations and the fact that Pham Van Dong had endorsed M Day. Although he did not offer crowd estimates, he did refer to a "substantial display" but not "enormous" demonstrations to which Nixon paid no attention. The lead did not prepare one for what was to follow, almost nine minutes of vignettes from the day's activities without a word of narration from the anchors or their correspondents. And what a dramatic nine minutes it was.

NBC's M Day coverage began with a morning prayer service in Lincoln, Massachusetts, and then moved on to a bell-ringing ceremony in nearby Newton, which featured shots of somber demonstrators crying for American boys killed in Vietnam. From the East Coast, with only captions to guide the viewers, the cameras shifted to Lake Forest, Illinois and young people leafletting commuters with gentle refrains of "Give Peace a Chance" in the background, a similar leafletting in Palo Alto in the rain, a rain that drenched protestors in nearby San Francisco, elementary school children in Cleveland talking about peace, students in Illinois singing "We Shall Overcome" who were met by a few opponents carrying pictures of John Wayne, Professor George Wald addressing a clean-cut crowd at Harvard, a conflict between two students at Louisiana State University, earnest young people singing "Give Peace a Chance" at Case Western University in Cleveland, government workers offering the peace sign on the Capitol steps, a person reading the names of war dead at Trinity Church in New York to a huge, mostly adult crowd on Wall Street, another impressive group in Chicago listening to "Let the Sunshine In," George McGovern in Boston telling a mass of humanity about the "politics of reconciliation," and the demonstration in front of the White House.

Only at this point, after a narration-less sequence of shots that captured the coast-to-coast, orderly nature of the event, did John Chancellor break in for some comments. With the candlelight procession beginning in the nation's capital, he noted that an end was coming to what was probably the largest demonstration in American history. It had been "free of violence . . . but the night lies ahead." That comment was a low blow, but few antiwar activists could complain about the astounding coverage, full of emotional vignettes of serious people demonstrating in a dignified manner. Chancellor noted that few blacks were involved but opined that the mostly middle-class crowds were important politically. Moreover, confronted by this unprecedented protest, the White House seems to "have lost its poise." NBC was the only one of the three networks to suggest that the demonstrations might be having an impact on Nixon.

The network devoted the final three and one-half minutes of Moratorium coverage to counterdemonstrations and pronouncements of Nixon supporters. These included comments from Governor Ronald Reagan of California, Goldwater, the fourteen congressional hawks, headlight-burning for Nixon in Indianapolis, Patriotism Day in Oklahoma, wounded Vietnam veterans in a Cleveland hospital, and Maddox standing in front of the Georgia State Capitol leading the singing of "God Bless America."

Of the three networks, NBC's coverage was the fairest in terms of maintaining the proper balance between pro and antiwar groups, with the majority of the coverage going to the Moratorium, the major story of the day. Moreover, the tactic of letting the pictures speak for themselves permitted viewers to think that they were receiving a more objective view than they would have received had some narrator interpreted the images. This approach suggests objectivity though there was not much—NBC liked the Moratorium and was impressed with the breadth and dignity of the protests.

No other demonstration before or after received so much attention on the nightly newscasts. No other demonstration looked so impressive to neutral viewers, with the emphasis in the visuals on well-dressed American adults, patriotic songs, prayer services, and silent vigils in cemeteries. These were the sorts of activities many in the media could personally support. The organizers of the Moratorium had engineered a brilliant public-relations coup. This new, interesting, and dignified way to oppose government policy captivated the cameras. Viewers had to be impressed with the sight of such a reasonable group of adults who, like all patriotic Americans, wanted to hasten the end to the war. Although newscasters devoted too much time to M Day opponents, their depictions of the demonstrations were overwhelmingly positive for the first—and as we shall see—only time since the movement began in 1965.

The print media devoted considerable attention to the spectacular Moratorium as well and they liked it almost as much as the broadcast media.[38] M Day dominated the *Times*'s front page on the morning of October 16.[39] A picture of Eugene McCarthy addressing the Bryant Park throng appeared over the first three columns and a headline covering four front-page stories read "Vietnam Moratorium Observed Nationally by Foes of War: Rallies Here Crowded, Orderly." Along with the reference to the absence of violence was a failure to highlight the magnitude of the event, perhaps because an accurate count, even within a million or two, was problematic. One subhead referred to the Day's opponents— "Many show support for Nixon." In the absence of hard numbers for the doves, the objective "many" used to describe the hawks is misleading.

The *Times*'s lead story did refer to the "unique" character of the Moratorium, the "largest protest so far," which involved millions, though not many blue-collar people or blacks. The account highlighted the Boston rally, along with rallies in unlikely places like that bastion of conservatism, Orange County, California. The newspaper's three other page-one stories dealt with Humphrey's statement of support for Nixon, the Washington activities, and the conflict in New York City between pro-Moratorium Mayor Lindsay and unions and other groups that refused to lower flags in front of city offices to half-staff.

Aside from the continuation of the front-page stories, the *Times* presented two more pages of Moratorium stories and pictures.[40] These included a favorable profile of Sam Brown, a roundup of activities on college campuses full of moving descriptions of memorials to slain GIs, the impact on the city schools ("Most Students and Teachers Stay out of School"), a survey of local events, especially the way Broadway casts cancelled matinees to take to the streets, and limited coverage of venues untouched by the Moratorium.

Although the World Series featuring the miraculous New York Mets took lead position on October 17, the *Times* again covered the Moratorium in detail with a major front-page analysis of its impact as well as two interior pages crammed with diverse related items.[41] Overall, the *Times* presented a favorable rendering of M Day, with pictures that enhanced accounts underscoring the large numbers of orderly citizens expressing their displeasure with the Nixon policy while paying tribute to those who had died in the war. Establishment and show business figures who took part received considerable attention along with human-interest stories of ordinary concerned citizens gathering to petition their government to bring the war to a swift end.

Like the *Times*, the *Washington Post* concentrated on events in its own region. The front page was dominated by a picture of another massive Moratorium crowd, this time listening to Dr. Spock at George Washington University.[42] And like its New York competitor, the *Post*'s headlines underscored the gentle nature of the protest—"Massive Rallies Peaceful." Its analysts could not give an accurate overall count of participants nationwide but did mention crowds of one hundred thousand in Boston, thirty thousand in Washington, and thirty thousand in New Haven. In a separate story on Washington, the daily described the solemnity of the day's last event at Sylvan Glen, attended mostly by young people. Although business was off in downtown Washington all day, almost as if it had been a Sunday, *Post* reporters noted that Rotary Club luncheons took place, along with topless dancing in the bars.

Another front-page report looked at Nashua, New Hampshire, where only three hundred people showed up to mark the Moratorium. Yet the small size of the crowd, according to the correspondent, did not reflect the true feeling of concern about the course of the war in that conservative community. Closer to the capital, a final page-one story described the Moratorium at the University of Maryland, where another relatively small crowd of two thousand gathered. But as the article noted, for a conservative campus, this was a respectable turnout.

The *Post*'s extensive coverage continued over more than five pages with only a limited amount of space devoted to opponents of the Moratorium. Many pictures depicted well-dressed demonstrators. Somewhat jarring amid the decorous photographs was one of former University of California president Clark Kerr as the recipient of a pie in the face at the University of Indiana.

Not surprisingly, the two local, conservative, Michigan newspapers, which carried wire-service reports, were less favorable to M Day participants than the *Times* and the *Post*. The *Daily Tribune* and the *Macomb Daily*, both of which devoted most of their attention to activities in Michigan, noted Pham Van Dong's blessing and Spiro T. Agnew's warning to demonstrators in page-one stories on October 15. The *Daily* spent at least half of its story on Agnew and comments from President Nguyen Van Thieu of South Vietnam and his representative at the United Nations. Its AP account covered the protest of soldiers in Vietnam on patrol who were wearing black armbands, but noted, correctly, that there were only a "few" of them. Pictures showed Americans protesting in Tokyo and in Saigon *against* the Moratorium. Another AP advance story on the same page told of the wife of a soldier who was marching in an anti-Moratorium parade in North Carolina.[43]

On the day after the Moratorium, the *Macomb Daily*'s banner headline blared, "M-Days Record Protest for Peace," but the UPI story that ran under it began with President Nixon's remark that he would not be affected by it, or, as the *Tribune* noted in its head: "Moratorium Fails to Change Nixon's Stand on Vietnam."[44] Naturally, the fact that Nixon said he was unmoved did not mean that M Day did not affect him. We now know that Nixon and his advisors canceled plans to escalate after the November 1 deadline given to Ho Chi Minh in part because of M Day.

Both Michigan papers reported on the crowd of one hundred thousand in Boston with the last three paragraphs in the Macomb paper devoted to "untoward incidents." The *Tribune* did offer a UPI story on the impressive Wall Street crowd and the way the Moratorium was observed in so many places in New York in general. With Bill Moyers described as "eloquent" in the pulpit at Trinity Church, it was "A day of commemoration. A day of high emotion. And a day of ambivalence." With the latter phrase, the wire service hedged its bets.[45] As usual, the AP and UPI had provided subscribers with a balanced variety of material from which they could pick and choose.

Both newsweeklies covered the Moratorium over several issues. *Time*'s October 17 number featured a cover with the headline: "Moratorium: At War with War." The misleading pictures of scruffy, young demonstrators making the peace sign, taken from an earlier rally, illustrates the problem in running a story about an event before it happens.

However, *Time*'s five-page lead story, generally favorable to the Moratorium, emphasized that the movement was not dominated by hippies, longhairs, or radicals.[46] Some M Day protestors had never demonstrated before and some of their protests would take place in venues that had never witnessed such activities. The dedication of the people who followed moderate Moratorium leader Sam Brown was "awesome."[47] *Time* felt that the White House was concerned, with Nixon's popularity declining in the polls as dovish sentiment rose. The Moratorium had put the ball in Nixon's court—what was he going to do to end the war?—"Nixon cannot escape the effects of the antiwar movement."[48] *Time* had obviously changed its position on the effectiveness of the protests.

The following week, the editors at *Time* again made the Moratorium the lead with another five pages devoted to its activities and impact.[49] The accompanying pictures were especially impressive, with a large crowd at the Washington Monument, followed, however, by a picture of a larger crowd watching the World Series, pictures of Moratorium participants Eugene McCarthy, Coretta Scott King, and Helen Hayes, the Boston Common multitude, a candlelight procession in Miami, and ceremonies in St. Patrick's Cathedral. One page of photos covered Moratorium opponents.

The Moratorium was "without precedent," but the numbers that took part, *Time* estimated, were "not overwhelming," perhaps not more than one million nationwide. What was impressive was its middle-class nature, a "sedate Woodstock Festival of peace," a cute phrase that damned with faint praise.[50] The magazine concluded that a majority of Americans was touched by the

Moratorium, which, after all, did not call for immediate withdrawal, merely for Nixon to speed things up. In this extensive analysis, reporters presented plans for speeding things up from Moratorium supporters, Edward Kennedy, Arthur Goldberg, Edmund Muskie, and Kingman Brewster of Yale University. Anti-Moratorium activities received only one-half page of prose in the newsweekly.

Newsweek also devoted a generous amount of space to M Day in two issues. The lead and cover story in the October 13 number was "Nixon in Trouble." Part of that trouble was the Moratorium.[51] Featuring a photograph of matronly women carrying flowers and polite signs in front of the White House, the newsweekly described the leadership of the Moratorium, an impressive group of seven thousand five hundred activists nationwide. With more than one thousand campuses expected to participate, *Newsweek* thought the protest might be the "most spectacular in history." Although some university administrators were not supportive of the activity and its intrusion into campus life, in a Columbia University Senate debate, not one of the one hundred professors present spoke out in favor of the Nixon administration's policy. *Newsweek*'s concentration on universities suggests that its editors may have underestimated, at first, the appeal of the Moratorium to adults.

Its staff rectified that misperception in its six pages of coverage in the October 27 issue.[52] According to the headline writers, the demonstration was "A Day to Remember." Most of the photo coverage was flattering to the Moratorium, with two shots of the massive Boston Common crowd, Coretta Scott King and the candlelight vigil in Washington, doves on Wall Street (along with one anti-Moratorium protestor whom the caption writers noted was not alone), the St. Patrick's Cathedral ceremony, well-scrubbed young women at a candle-lighting ceremony, a GI with a Moratorium arm band, photos of Lindsay, Kennedy, and McCarthy, and a huge crowd at Berkeley. Representing the opposition, there was Clark Kerr getting the pie in the face, Nixon and Mamie Eisenhower, and some administration supporters.

Newsweek's often spectacular color photographs reenforced its reporter's judgment that "There had never been a phenomenon quite like it . . . before."[53] Like others, its correspondents underscored how the Moratorium had reached everywhere, with mostly young, mostly white, mostly moderate people turning out in crowds of as many as 250,000 in New York and 100,000 in Boston. Nixon allegedly ignored the events, while his vice president assailed the demonstrators for accepting Pham Van Dong's support. Agnew received backing from Gerald Ford and Hubert Humphrey among others. Nevertheless, *Newsweek* saw the doves as gaining popularity nationwide.

The magazine compared the demonstration, which took place in all fifty states and even Vietnam, to Coxey's Army of 1894 and the 1963 civil rights march on Washington in terms of its potential impact and historical significance. Criss-crossing the country, *Newsweek*'s balanced account pointed out places where crowds were small and where patriotic groups challenged anti-warriors. And one reporter did note marijuana and wine in evidence at the Boston Common. The president, meanwhile, was in "semi-isolation" while his advisors met with doves.[54] The latter were reported as disappointed—their meetings with Kissinger, Ehrlichman, Undersecretary of State Elliot Richardson, and members of the NSC staff led them to believe that the administration had no plan to end the war in the near future. By concluding on that somber note, and by emphasizing the growing impatience with Nixon's Vietnam policy as reflected in a truly amazing demonstration, *Newsweek* served the antiwar movement well.

Indeed, all of the major print and electronic sources examined here served the movement well with regard to coverage of M Day. This appeared to be a major disaster for the Nixon administration.

IT IS DIFFICULT TO DISCERN WITH PRECISION HOW THE NIXON administration perceived the Moratorium as it played in American media. On the one hand, the president went on the offensive immediately after M Day, a reflection of the seriousness with which he and his aides took the protest. Jeb Magruder sent Haldeman an important memo outlining his strategy to defeat the allegedly biased media, "The Rifle and the Shotgun," on October 17, in the wake of the Moratorium.[55] On the other hand, the media offensive had begun earlier (albeit in a shotgun mode), and Nixon claimed that his Silent Majority speech of November 3 was in the works before the Moratorium and was not meant to be an answer to it.[56] Further, in a preliminary analysis of the event, Haldeman was not especially impressed with the numbers of participants—the Moratorium was "not successful across [the] country."[57]

Although shaken by M Day, White House aides nonetheless concluded that they had done better than could have been expected in the media. For example, on the eve of the Moratorium, with antiwar demonstrations dominating the news, they perceived the administration as coming off reasonably well. Nixon's and Agnew's statements had received prominent attention, particularly the latter's warnings on the morning of M Day.[58] As for television newscasts on October 14, Nixon's media monitors were pleased to note that David Brinkley began with Hanoi's endorsement of the demonstration and followed that item with a lengthy story that Pat Buchanan judged to be neutral with good administration coverage. They saw ABC as having given the counterdemonstrators significant attention while CBS had "our side coming out on top again."[59]

The next day, Nixon's television analysts again found much to cheer them in the newscasts, with all reporters except John Chancellor viewed as maintaining neutrality.[60] The coverage was "enormous" but balanced. The networks' themes, according to the staff, were that the Moratorium was "massive and peaceful," predominantly middle-class, and that the president had to be affected by it. With some pleasure, other monitors noted that the small bit of scuffling outside the White House received good play. However, the Johnny Carson show, guest-hosted by Alan King, apparently offered too much time to doves George McGovern and Robert Ryan according to one telewatcher.[61]

Specifically, CBS earned high marks for balance, with its comment that Whittier's dovish students were unrepresentative of the student body, as did ABC for its glimpse of hawks in Newton, Kansas. Moreover, the monitors picked up Brinkley's remark that crowds were "big but not enormous," a comment that is repeated in several places in the analyses. Whoever monitored NBC that day failed to note the most spectacular aspect of the coverage, the nine minutes of film without narration that presented a sensitive and supportive picture of the demonstrators. Nixon's television analysts spent more time on the narration than the possible impact of the pictures, a curious way to analyze a visual medium. That might explain why they underplayed NBC's powerful nine-minute narration-less sequence.

Exaggerating the networks' attention to administration supporters, Nixon aides concluded that television coverage was "admirably two-sided." As one noted, the media appeared to "be getting wise to the fact that they had been had for the past few years."[62] This inaccurate evaluation would certainly have surprised antiwar leaders. One reason for the upbeat analysis may have been the prior expectation of far worse coverage—it was not a total disaster since some Nixon loyalists did receive air time. Or it may simply have been a case of the messengers fearing to bring the bad news, searching for positives in a sea of negatives for a president who vowed not to be moved by the demonstration. Mary McGrory in the *Washington Star* on October 16 reenforced the White House's relative optimism when she noted that Moratorium leaders were upset by the evening news programs because their numbers were underplayed and the approach too evenhanded.[63]

Not all columnists pleased the president. After reading that *New York Times* reporters who appeared on an NET show felt that the Moratorium was successful, he scribbled, "Surprise?!" He also noted that in a generally unfavorable column, *Life*'s Hugh Sidey had written that Nixon sympathized with the young idealistic demonstrators though no one knew it, a line that the president recommended to Haldeman, Ehrlichman, and Kissinger as "a good lesson for the future."[64]

As for newspaper coverage in general, the AP and UPI concluded that editorials and columns were divided nationally with a slight majority opposing the Moratorium.[65] Characteristic of other good news identified for Nixon were comments by Jack Anderson on radicals in the movement, the *Washington Star* and *Washington News* reports that the majority of students and adults wanted the president to hang tough, and a Nick Thimmesch column in the

Newsweek syndicate that revealed that the left was in control of the Mobilization. Nixon liked the piece so much that he had it sent to members of Congress, governors, and newspaper editors.[66]

Analysts also noted *Time*'s and *Newsweek*'s handsome treatments of M Day, especially the photographs, but noted *Time*'s comment that the turnout was "not overwhelming." More than *Newsweek*, however, they saw *Time* as suggesting that the president would have to do something to meet the outpouring of antiwar sentiment. In this analysis, the monitors underplayed the damage done by the massive reporting in both newsweeklies, dominated by often poignant pictures of vigils and dignified protesters, to find the few items that would make the Moratorium look less successful than it was.[67]

Some, like Daniel Patrick Moynihan, advised the president that the "Moratorium was a success" and that the demonstrations were full of "radiant" people, but most of what the president and his people saw underplayed its significance.[68] Nixon's analysts interpreted the coverage of the counter-demonstrators as showing considerable anti-Moratorium activity and, in any event, it was clear that the majority of Americans were still with the administration, despite what happened on October 15.

Nixon's evaluation of the limited impact of the Moratorium was reenforced by a Sindlinger Poll he received on November 10 that showed support for his job performance rising from 60.4 to 66.3 percent, and on Vietnam from 55.4 to 69.4 after the Moratorium. He was so pleased with those results that he asked Haldeman, "Have we any further dope on Sindlinger? He may turn out to be a good asset."[69] Other polls that arrived at the White House were not as comforting. The large and positive change in public opinion came only in the weeks after the Silent Majority speech and the second Moratorium in November.[70] Perhaps that is why the president was so pleased with Sindlinger's results.

Overall, White House operatives claimed to be comforted by what they saw in the media on this latest protest. Yet, undoubtedly, the Moratorium was a major demonstration that merited attention, with even the business community, as seen in *Business Week* and the *Economist*, giving it favorable play.[71] Nixon's offensive against the movement and the media that began in late October and continued through the first half of November, 1969, is one tribute to the effectiveness of the Moratorium and its generally favorable treatment by the networks, the newspapers, and the newsweeklies. Another, and even more important tribute, was its effect on Nixon's decision not to hit North Vietnam with a massive blow after Hanoi failed to alter its negotiating posture by the November 1 deadline.

All the same, the way the administration viewed the Moratorium and, more particularly, the way that President Nixon heard and read about it, posed problems for activists. He did not read or see much about it first-hand and relied, as had been the case in the past, on his media monitors for their analyses. They skewed their analyses to make the best of a bad situation. That they were inaccurate and unperceptive is not important—the president relied upon them for his "objective" perspective on the Moratorium. Unless M Day had an immediate impact on the public opinion polls, which it apparently did not, it had less of an impact on Nixon than one would judge from the positive media blitz it received.

It is true, however, that the president and his advisors worried that Hanoi received the wrong impression from such large-scale manifestations of dissent. The communists would not read the media the way that he did, Nixon feared. From that perspective, he could not afford many more M Days. Thus, in that sense at least, the Moratorium—and its coverage—shook the Nixon administration.

7

NIXON VERSUS THE MEDIA, NOVEMBER 1969

A million and a half? A million? Half a million?

Only one man in America has accurate estimates of the number of people who demonstrated in Washington and San Francisco Nov. 15 for immediate withdrawal of U.S. troops from Vietnam and he's not talking—presumably because he does not intend to be affected by the activities of such 'noisy minorities.'

The exact number (probably a million on both coasts) doesn't really matter. It is obvious the majority has spoken, louder and clearer than ever before. For every person who has traveled many miles under difficult circumstances, experienced the cold winds of Washington and the rains of San Francisco, marched and then listened for hours to speeches condemning the war and to antiwar music, finally returning home again, exhausted, there were dozens, scores, who for one reason or another were unable to attend the massive demonstrations.

It was not a 'noisy minority,' Vice President Spiro Agnew notwithstanding. And no President can remain unaffected, regardless of Richard Nixon's pretensions.[1]

So exulted a report from UCLA's Young Socialist Alliance on the massive Moratorium-Mobilization protests of November 15, 1969, which followed on the heels of the Nixon administration's attempt to rally an alleged silent majority of Americans to do battle with antiwarriors who promised to escalate their protests each month until the United States left Southeast Asia.

Time magazine was less impressed with the demonstrations as its reporters saw the administration's counter-attack beginning to succeed:

Once again on main streets and Broadway, in village halls, statehouses and the national capital, at coliseums, campuses and churches, Americans turned out to march, argue and declaim over Vietnam. This time, answering Richard Nixon's call, the opponents of dissent also demonstrated in force, making a counterattack and purposeful counterpoint to the antiwar protestors.

. . . . The massive demonstration in Washington showed the continuing momentum of dissent. Nonetheless, the week's activity nationwide served to emphasize that those who want an immediate end to the war, regardless of consequences, still represent a minority.[2]

Although this study concerns the media's treatment of demonstrations and not the administrations' treatment of the media, the two subjects intersect in a dramatic way in the attempt by the Nixon administration to deflect attention from the joint Mobilization and Moratorium protests planned for November 13–15, 1969.

Nixon Launches an Offensive, November 3, 1969

However well Nixon and his aides felt they appeared in the media on M Day, at least in a relative sense, it was not good enough. The time had come, they decided, to take off the gloves so that Hanoi would not get the wrong idea about American resolve in Vietnam.

Before moving into the White House, they had received conflicting advice from the media-battered Lyndon Johnson. Johnson told Spiro Agnew that Nixon should be leery about taking on the powerful media, lest they turn on him.[3] On the other hand, Herbert Klein reports that Johnson told him to tell Nixon not to be "bullied by that God-damned *New York Times.*"[4]

Nixon hardly needed advice about the American press. He and his colleagues came into the White House with a deep-seated hostility toward the most influential media.[5] After a brief honeymoon, when journalists and their editors gave the "New Nixon" the benefit of the doubt and after the antiwar movement began to react to the slow pace of withdrawal from Vietnam, the press became more of a perceived problem for the White House. After listing in his memoirs a variety of antiwar activities from July through September, 1969, Henry Kissinger noted that "All of this was conspicuously and generally approvingly covered by the media." According to the national security advisor's reading of the accounts in the newspapers, magazines, and on television, the movement "dominated the media and made full use of them."[6]

Such a reaction would have come as quite a surprise to antiwar leaders in September, 1969, who felt that they were not getting the sort of attention their activities merited. Of course, the next month, the Moratorium did receive much favorable publicity, and Kissinger remembered particularly the "vivid pictures" in *Time* and *Newsweek.*[7]

The newsweeklies and the television networks, according to Herbert Klein, had written off the Nixon administration before he took up the cudgels against them.[8] Yet Klein's colleagues had begun their assault even before the Moratorium. One scholar found twenty-one separate requests from Nixon to his aides to challenge the media from September 16 to October 17.[9] In their defense, Nixon loyalists point to *The News Twisters*, Edith Efron's controversial study of the television networks from September 16 through November 4, 1969, in which she found a pervasive anti-Nixon bias. Nixon liked the book so much that he tried to promote it onto the best-seller lists.[10]

Whatever may have come before, the coverage of the Moratorium was the last straw. Indeed, despite his media analysts' view through rose-colored glasses, Nixon was more upset by the media coverage than by the protestors themselves.[11] The targets for his anger were the networks and the major East Coast magazines and newspapers, not all media. That anger inspired the October 17 memo, "The Rifle and the Shotgun," in which Magruder argued that it was time to focus the administration's heretofore scattered attacks on the media.[12]

Despite his disclaimers, Nixon's November 3, 1969, Silent Majority speech was a direct reaction to the apparent growing popularity of the movement.[13] His appeal to the "silent majority" was only an indirect attack on the media. The perceived network reaction to the speech led to the brutally direct approach taken by Spiro Agnew ten days later.

Nixon billed his Silent Majority speech, which he later considered the most important of his presidency, as offering a dramatic new policy in Vietnam. When it turned out that the speech offered very little that was new, some journalists reported that fact and expressed disappointment. For example, UPI's account in *The Daily Tribune* emphasized the president's less-than-revelatory discussion of the military situation and relegated the Silent Majority concept to the last paragraph of its lengthy account.[14] Obviously, the news service was looking for the Vietnam policy news, which the president's flacks had promised, not the powerful domestic thrust.

Yet Nixon actually had little to complain about in terms of the way the print media handled his address. The elite press treated it seriously, offering generous coverage, which in retrospect seems fair and perceptive. Of course, as Nixon should have expected, they had to offer space to doves as well for their reactions.

Though not one of the president's favorite papers, the *Washington Post* headed its lead story on November 4, "Nixon Asks Unity On Peace Plan/ Initiatives to Hanoi Rebuffed, He Says." And the next day, it placed on its front pages a picture of the president surrounded by favorable telegrams piled high upon his desk, along with the headline, "Nixon Claims Wide Support: Speech Disappoints Foes." When the Washington daily explained that Western Union was working overtime to send the deluge of mostly favorable telegrams to the White House, its correspondents did not know that some, if not many, of those cheering messages were not spontaneous.[15]

The *New York Times*, which offered four front-page stories about the speech, emphasized Nixon's "secret timetable" for a pullout and the fact that the president said for the first time that all American troops would eventually leave Southeast Asia. To be sure, the *Times* included a good deal of criticism from opponents of the president—"Congress Doves Unhappy; Protest Leaders Spurred"—and James Reston noted that the formerly moderate Nixon had "accepted the challenge of confrontation on the most emotional issue before the nation." Nevertheless, Nixon's arguments received a full hearing. If anything, the *Times* found more substance in the speech than others.[16]

Ten days later, *Time* published its interpretation of the speech. Like Reston, the newsweekly thought Nixon had "abandoned the politics of reconciliation, raising his voice to deliver a powerful, simplistic appeal." Even though the writer did not like the "hard-line" approach, he considered it effective. Moreover, one Nixon advisor, buoyed by the response, told him that the speech would hold the silent majority for at least four to six months and keep his critics at bay.[17]

Nixon's first reaction to the media's coverage of his speech concerned television.[18] The analyses presented on the three networks immediately after the speech, the so-called instant analyses, especially irritated him and his family.[19] Although all three networks offered balanced pros and cons, Nixon and his supporters saw mostly the cons, characterized by a long critique offered on ABC by W. Averell Harriman. Nixon media expert and speechwriter James Keogh now admits that the instant analyses on November 3 were not that bad.[20] In fact, it was Nixon's instant analysis of the television instant analyses that was unbalanced. In comparison, reports in the print media the next day appeared to be more positive.[21] However, it was in the nature of television roundtables, as compared to a lead story in the *Times* merely summarizing the speech, to offer equal time to partisan analysts from each party. Surely the president could not have expected all the analysts to be Republican apparatchiks. Yet Nixon may not have been totally off-base in his critique. Even before the great brouhaha following the Silent Majority speech, veteran journalist Eric Sevareid had told CBS chief William S. Paley that he thought instant analyses were not always good journalism.[22]

In retrospect, it appears that Nixon officials may have exaggerated their claims of television bias in their memoirs to justify the controversial anti-media campaign that had already begun. Or they may merely have reflected an extreme sensitivity to any criticism. No doubt they had prepared for the worst when Nixon asked Haldeman a week before the Silent Majority speech to prepare special "strike forces" to retaliate against the networks and *Time*, *Newsweek*, the *Post*, and the *Times* for their predictable criticism of the upcoming address.[23]

Immediately after the speech was delivered, Herbert Klein called media people around the country for their reaction. The director of communications received mostly rave reviews and even obtained a promise from CBS's Frank

Stanton to lean on Eric Sevareid for being unfair in his commentary. The Gannett publishing company's Paul Miller told Klein that his people rated the speech "far better than the commentators."[24] But Klein had called journalists known to be friendly to the administration. It is hard to imagine that an objective professional journalist would have found much fault with the evenhanded instant analyses.

The next day, official White House evaluations of those television commentaries were not positive. Beginning from the premise that most commentators are "confirmed doves," the monitor found NBC the most objective, CBS's Eric Sevareid "waspish," and Bill Lawrence on ABC "downright nasty and angry."[25] Network hostility was a product of the "firmness" of the speech that "stunned the doves," suggested the White House analyst in a phrase certain to please the president.

On November 4, the networks devoted considerable time on their newscasts to the speech. According to the White House news summary, although ABC "didn't hurt our cause" that day by also airing an MIT demonstration filled with images of Viet Cong flags, Brinkley and Sevareid were unfriendly in their commentaries on the other two networks. On the other hand, aside from those commentaries, the administration considered the straight news coverage—and not the instant analyses—of the Silent Majority speech to be favorable.[26]

At a November 5 cabinet meeting, Nixon expressed pleasure with the nationwide media reaction to the speech—"White House Press Corps is dying because of the effect of that television speech. . . . You can get across your point without having what you say strained through the press. And that drives the press right up the wall." Nixon advised his aides to remember that print and television reporters in Washington did not represent the whole country.[27] One wonders then why he was so upset at the networks. If the negative commentaries as seen in the instant analyses were so powerful, how was it that the president could report that the popular reception to the speech was favorable?

Moreover, two days later, Alexander Butterfield told him that White House mail was running 10 to 1 in his favor with the volume immense at 50,200 wires and 80,263 letters.[28] After one month, the total for both forms of messages was 182,500 pro and only 16,882 con.[29] As we have seen, not all of those letters were spontaneous. Many had been generated by enthusiastic Republican officials who knew the importance of being able to report such totals. Sometimes Nixon and others in the White House forgot that one reason for such outpourings of support was their own well-orchestrated letter-writing campaigns.

As for the print media, Nixon's analysts found the vast majority of the press supportive, with favorable commentary even in the dovish *Washington Post* and *Detroit Free Press*.[30] The eleven-page report concluded that the main negative voices, the *St. Louis Post-Dispatch*, the *Times*, the *New York Post*, and the *Nashville Tennessean*, were isolated in their editorial criticism.

Nevertheless, Nixon speechwriter and media specialist Pat Buchanan helped to organize a reinvigorated campaign against the media, particularly the networks. His activities culminated in the ghostwriting of the memorable speech Spiro Agnew delivered on November 13 in Des Moines at a meeting of the Midwest Regional Republican Committee. The less combative Herbert Klein and Ron Ziegler were not consulted about the Agnew address, which, after all, concerned their business.[31] The president offered a few editorial changes in the direction of moderation, but overall, he liked the speech because, as he told William Safire, it "really flicks the scab off."[32]

Agnew's address was merely the public side of an assault that had begun the day after the November 3 speech. That day an angry Nixon explained that his objective was "to go over the heads of the columnists" to the people.[33] On November 5, Dean Burch, the Nixon-appointed head of the Federal Communications Commission, asked the networks for transcripts of their November 3 instant analyses.[34] Although the administration claimed that no intimidation was meant by the request, it was taken as such by William Paley, the head of CBS. Paley was correct.[35] Both the administration and the newspeople were aware that recent polls revealed a growing antimedia bias.[36] Americans did not need much priming to rally around an administration that was allegedly being treated unfairly by the press.

A week after the Burch request, Agnew attacked television's "instant analysis" and "querulous criticism," and called attention to the "concentration of power" exemplified by the monopoly enjoyed by the three networks.[37] Agnew's attack against instant analysis was unfair, as Herbert Klein acknowledged later, since newspeople usually received embargoed copies of presidential speeches several hours before they were delivered to help with their deadline problem.[38] William Paley, however, saw some merit in the critique of instant analysis, a practice he stopped experimentally for five months in 1973.[39]

Agnew was pleased by the enthusiastic response to his speech, even greater than that which greeted the Silent Majority speech.[40] From 100,000 to 150,000 communications poured into the networks, with support for Agnew running at a ratio of 2–1.[41] By December 1, the White House had tallied 83,179 messages favoring the speech and only 3,793 opposing it.[42]

Bullied into carrying the Des Moines speech, the networks also were not very aggressive in their reporting of the event on the evening newscasts of November 14. However, in a bit of passive aggression, all three placed the story toward the end of their newscasts. NBC, which ran it last that evening, was the most critical. Chet Huntley offered an accurate background report about what he labeled a "carefully planned attack" orchestrated by people at the highest levels in the White House. He pointed to the coverage of the Silent Majority speech as the spark that ignited the firestorm. Julian Goodman, the head of NBC, had the last word on the subject, claiming that all three networks agreed with his characterization of Agnew's speech as an "appeal to prejudice" and an attempt to deny to television freedom of the press.

CBS was more circumspect. After reporting the untrue disclaimer from the White House that Nixon had nothing to do with Agnew's speech, the network revealed that after Agnew asked viewers to call in, it had received eighty-five hundred calls, forty-seven hundred in support of the vice president. The other two networks, according to CBS, received a comparable number of messages. Dean Burch and Nicholas Johnson then appeared, with Burch saying that he and the FCC were threatening no one's license and Johnson, a liberal FCC member, supporting Agnew in principle by calling for more—not less—commentary on television. Chicago Mayor Daley agreed with Agnew about the New York slant of the news and the "hatchet job" done to his city by the networks the previous year. Senator Muskie finished the segment with an attack on Agnew's "campaign of abuse" that had the "approval of the president." But Muskie was in the minority in Congress; according to one Nixon aide, a poll revealed that fully three-quarters of senators and representatives agreed with Agnew.[43] Despite the final Muskie clip, CBS was nervous about offering its own response to the Agnew attack.

On ABC, Howard K. Smith talked of the calls coming in at a 3–1 ratio in favor of Agnew and that Nixon had proclaimed his support for his vice president as well. It all began with Chicago, according to ABC, which also featured Mayor Daley. The historian of presidential campaigns, Theodore H. White, disagreed with Agnew's assault against the East when he pointed out that most of the major network newspeople were not from that region. Two senators, one pro and the other con, were then quoted, as was Herbert Klein, who claimed to have nothing against instant analysis as long as it was balanced. Dean Burch thought that Agnew's ideas were "thoughtful and provocative." These tepid responses from the networks belie Agnew's supporters' claims that there was a "wild reaction" from the media to his speech.[44]

A week later, the *Washington Post* and the *New York Times* took their lumps in an Agnew speech delivered in Montgomery, Alabama. Again, Pat Buchanan was the ghost writer with support from Nixon and opposition from Klein, Ziegler, Price, and Haldeman.[45]

How well did the Nixon-Agnew attack on the networks and the New York journalists work? For one thing, as we shall see, the Mobilization of November 15 received "spotty coverage."[46] Of course, that judgment is affected by what one might have expected from the networks in the absence of the Agnew offensive. Todd Gitlin thought that the campaign was generally effective in the period after the Agnew speech.[47] CBS did restrain itself from instantly analyzing Nixon's next speech, on December 15.[48] In general, the networks subtly toned down their instant analyses, making them somewhat less "free-wheeling."[49] Moreover, in January, 1970, Nixon's people made it more diffi-cult for the networks to offer such analyses when they, as a rule, stopped sending advance copies of speeches to the media.[50]

After Charles Colson, the architect of the media containment program, paid a visit to the network presidents in the fall of 1970, he felt that the situation was under control, the administration had won its point.[51] On the other hand, two media analysts found no dramatic change in the networks' handling of the Nixon administration after Agnew's speech.[52]

The Agnew offensive fed into the public's lack of confidence in the media's honesty and fairness, a fact of which the media were well aware. Coming as it did on the eve of the Mobilization, Agnew's speech affected the coverage of the demonstration. And even if some of that coverage proved to be favorable to the protestors, readers and viewers looked at what they read and saw with even more suspicion than before. The Nixon administration campaign to neu-tralize the press in its war for public opinion was successful, at least in the short run.[53]

The Moratorium and the Mobilization, November 13–15, 1969

As the Nixon administration feared, the November 15 demonstrations in Washington and San Francisco were the largest single-site demonstrations to date. Crowd estimates for the Washington activities ranged from 250,000 to 750,000, for San Francisco from 100,000 to 250,000.[54] Two nationwide anti-war organizations, the Mobilization and the Moratorium, cooperated in both cities with the latter following through on its promise to continue its protests monthly, adding a day each time, until the war came to an end. The recon-stituted Mobilization committee, which had been organized in Cleveland in July, had planned its November action well before the October 15 Mor-atorium. That committee was dominated by left-wing organizations, more militant than their temporary allies in the Moratorium.

The Nixon administration had warned Americans that the November event was controlled by radicals, determined to employ violent tactics.[55] It is true that the Weathermen, fresh from their October Days of Rage, demanded a twenty thousand dollar bribe from the Moratorium to keep their cadre away from Washington. Moreover, among the multitudes who planned to protest, several thousand were indeed bent on violent confrontation.[56] The vast major-ity, however, was not. But the administration's talk of violence and radicals, as well as White House point person John Dean's purposeful foot-dragging on granting parade permits, no doubt succeeded in scaring off scores of moder-ates from traveling to Washington. Finally, although the White House was able to secure enough busses for executive mansion fortification, many would-be demonstrators were frustrated by their inability to find enough busses to take them to the capital.

These factors suggest that the huge assemblage that did show up on November 15 was even more impressive than its unprecedented numbers suggested. Equally impressive is the fact that although Mobe participants were more militant than their Moratorium counterparts, the official events that weekend were completely peaceful.

The three-day Washington activity—two for the Moratorium, one for the Mobilization—began on November 13 with the March against Death. Carrying over forty thousand placards with the names of American soldiers who died in Vietnam or villages destroyed in the war, solemn Moratorium marchers led by seven drummers walked four miles through wind and rain from Arlington across the Memorial Bridge into the District to the White House. As they passed by the gates at 1600 Pennsylvania Avenue, marchers called out the name of the person or village they represented. They then moved on to the west steps of the Capitol where they deposited their placards in coffins. The walk took more than thirty-six hours. The 700 marshals trained for the activity performed superbly—the Moratorium's main contribution to that protest weekend went off without a hitch.

During this same period, 186 other demonstrators, led by, among others, Jane Hart, the wife of Senator Phil Hart (D-MI), were arrested for trying to hold a Catholic mass on the steps of the Pentagon. Two other events also preceded Saturday's mass demonstration. On Friday, November 14, after a ceremony at the National Cathedral, over 5,000 young people staged a kazoo concert, the largest of its kind in history.[57] More serious, and a portent of things to come, on that same day, 8 to 10,000 militants who gathered at Dupont Circle and the South Vietnamese Embassy had to be turned away by the police. The leaders of the Mobilization disavowed the extracurricular event that was followed by a second demonstration at the Justice Department where about 100 people turned in their draft cards. Police dispersed another smaller but more violent group of demonstrators at the South Vietnamese Embassy with tear gas.

November 14 also witnessed a nationwide flurry of Moratorium vigils and marches similar to those that took place on October 15. The most important of these was a mediagenic event in New York's Central Park where several thousand demonstrators, on signal, fell to the ground, feigning death, while thousands of balloons were released to the playing of "Taps." The black and white balloons symbolized those who had died in Vietnam and those who would die if the war continued.

The next day, November 15, Eugene McCarthy spoke at the assembly point on the Mall west of the Capitol from where Mobilization marchers moved down Pennsylvania Avenue, south on 15th Street, to the Washington Monument. The mostly white and young activists were led by three drummers who beat out a funeral cadence while "pallbearers" carried twelve coffins containing the placards from the March Against Death. A large banner held by other front-line marchers read, "Silent Majority for Peace." When radicals tried to divert marchers away from the official parade route to their own targets, disciplined marshals foiled their attempts.

Senators McGovern and Goodell and comedian-activist Dick Gregory were among the speakers at the Monument where Benjamin Spock and William Sloane Coffin served as co-chairs. Abbie Hoffman and Jerry Rubin were not permitted to speak. From all accounts, the speeches were not memorable that day. The music, however, was special with casts from four productions of *Hair*, Peter, Paul, and Mary, John Denver, Pete Seeger, Arlo Guthrie, Leonard Bernstein, and Mitch Miller (who led a massive ten minute "singalong" of "Give Peace a Chance") all lending their talents to the peace gala.

At 4:30, in a repeat of the October 21, 1967, rally before the Pentagon siege, Dave Dellinger announced that those who wanted to participate in a march to the Justice Department could follow him. He made it clear that his march would not be as peaceful or law-abiding as the official Mobilization demonstration. About ten thousand mostly young people took up Dellinger's invitation. Carrying Viet Cong flags and pictures of Che Guevara, among other radical symbols, they made their way to the Justice Department for a rally that ended with the breaking of windows, scattered looting, chants of "off the pigs," and arrests and injuries.

Nothing of the kind occurred in San Francisco's Golden Gate Park where the music of Bay Area rock groups was interspersed with political addresses representing a variety of factions in the peace and New Left communities. Wayne Morse and Rennie Davis were among the more prominent speakers. When David Hilliard of the Black Panthers harangued the crowd with obscene language, he was shouted down and compelled to leave the stage.

The networks did not cover the Mobilization live. CBS reporters who recommended such coverage were overruled by management.[58] During the day, NBC did offer their affiliates a few brief remotes from the scene, but overall, the networks paid scant attention to what was by far the largest antiwar demonstration in American history while it was going on.[59]

Nevertheless, as they ended their formal activities at the monument in the late afternoon, movement leaders had to have been pleased. Despite Nixon's vigorous offensive against them, they had been able to mount successful demonstrations both in terms of numbers and their generally dignified demeanor. As they read the "reviews," however, they must have questioned the magnitude of their tactical victory.

THE NOVEMBER DEMONSTRATIONS OFFERED MANY DRAMATIC visuals for telecasters. Six minutes into its show on November 14, ABC presented only three minutes on the dramatic antiwar actions of the day. Nevertheless, the March Against Death looked suitably somber and dignified. Viewers also heard about two noisier, albeit non-violent, demonstrations at the Justice Department. At the first one, Dr. Spock and "yippies" gathered for a while and then left with the pediatrician saying that there would be no violence. Another group, including some of the original protestors, returned for a ceremonial draft-card turn-in. Despite the relatively peaceful nature of the activities, ABC then described the precautions taken by the administration, which included a troop call-up to protect the capital against an expected two hundred thousand demonstrators on Saturday. Given the expectation of a smaller, violent crowd, when many more did show up and behaved decorously, the Mobilization might have been perceived as even more successful by ABC's staff—and viewers—than it was.

In New York's Central Park, a crowd smaller than expected, according to the correspondent, completed its remembrance of those killed in Vietnam by lying down in silence on the ground, symbolizing dead Americans and Vietnamese. The images of this demonstration, particularly of balloons being released to the accompaniment of "Taps," were almost as moving as those of the March against Death. Both the march and the lie-in were unique events that lent themselves to dramatic visual coverage.

CBS presented the Moratorium story at roughly the same placement in its newscast on November 14, but devoted two more minutes to it. Viewers might have pitied the one thousand marchers per hour who shouted out the name of war dead at the White House while making the long trek through the rain. The pictures belied the narration, which suggested that as few as one in twenty were not young people. Further, the reporter noted that the demonstration had been non-violent thus far. Obviously, he had picked up on the government's and some radicals' forecast of violence for the weekend.

At the end of the march at the Capitol, CBS cameras captured a few strains of a gentle young woman's impromptu performance of "Where Have All the Flowers Gone?" The mood evoked by that vignette was jarred by the sequence that followed of marines and paratroopers moving in for Saturday's demonstration. In a twenty-second account, CBS reported trouble at the Justice Department. The uncivil protestors were labeled "yippies," not part of the Mobilization, who were protesting the Chicago Seven trial, not the war.

CBS completed its coverage with the Central Park affair, noting the large number of American flags in evidence (something organizers planned on purpose). The narrator explained the significance of the balloon release and once again, as with the ABC coverage, the balloons, the bodies on the ground, and

"Taps" on the soundtrack all contributed to a moving sound bite. Those who had planned the event knew what would make good television.

NBC placed its own six-minute story on the events of November 14 in the same time-slot as its two rivals. Unlike the other two, however, its correspondent talked about hundreds of demonstrations in hundreds of places, reminiscent of the first Moratorium. NBC balanced Senators Mansfield and Republican Hugh Scott (R-PA), who praised the doves for their decorum, with a comment about Nixon's "apprehensiveness" as reflected in the measures taken to protect the city.

The March against Death received prominent placement on NBC. The mostly young marchers were orderly, and as was shown, even stopped for traffic lights on their four-mile trek. At the Capitol, NBC picked up the young woman singing "Where Have All the Flowers Gone?" The newscast also covered a small anti-Moratorium rally in Washington. Since the event attracted fewer than one hundred participants, this constituted disproportionate coverage. As for the rest of the city, forty-three thousand police and uncounted troops were said to be prepared for whatever would happen, although there had been no trouble yet.

NBC gave the Central Park demonstration some play, though its correspondent did not quite understand the balloon symbolism. The network's coverage ended with a very small incident in Sacramento where, when the names of war dead were read, several onlookers became upset with their usage by people they considered unpatriotic. One anti-antiwar critic referred to his opposite numbers as "heroes to Hanoi." Obviously, NBC decided to air this event because it was unique and offered spirited exchanges between anti and proadministration supporters. But the obscure Sacramento clash was hardly characteristic of the activities on November 14.

CBS's Saturday evening news on November 15 led with the Mobilization, deemed the largest demonstration to date. In addition, a "comparatively small group" marched on the Justice Department, but it was an "altogether peaceful rally." If that was the case, one wonders why the small action at Justice appeared at the beginning of the story? CBS's focus shifted to the Washington chief of police who estimated the crowd at 250,000 with other estimates given at between 300 and 500,000. The correspondent saluted the marshals for keeping militants in check. Viewers heard little from the speakers with Pete Seeger and other musicians said to have drawn the "loudest cheers." In San Francisco's Golden Gate Park, where Ralph Abernathy was seen speaking, a huge crowd of as many as 250,000 had turned out, with few over the age of thirty-five.

On CBS's Sunday Evening News, the Mobilization was again the lead with an organizer claiming that 800,000, a figure double other estimates, had shown up in Washington. In addition, he contended that the violent activity at the Justice Department was "partly to blame on the police." Whatever caused it, CBS acknowledged that Mobe participants were overwhelmingly non-violent. On the other hand, Attorney General John Mitchell appeared to blame the Justice action not just on the militants but on the Mobilization itself. In a counterpoint obviously not well-orchestrated by the administration, Herbert Klein complimented the marshalls for keeping order. All in all, the Mobilization did well on CBS that evening.

The story did not go away, receiving two minutes on ABC on Monday evening. Richard Nixon had no comment, and according to ABC's correspondent, would not be affected by the protests. Mitchell again stressed their violent aspects while Ron Ziegler noted they were generally peaceful. Hubert Humphrey, the last in a line of talking heads, assailed Spiro Agnew for his attacks on the media and dissenters that were polarizing the country.

CBS's coverage that night began with Dan Rather in front of the White House, a "White Bunker." The area around the mansion had been cleared for two blocks giving it the appearance of a ghost town with the president carrying on "business as usual" inside. Nixon was shown meeting with diplomats to punctuate that point. Herbert Klein saluted the effectiveness of Washington's security forces in keeping the peace. Cameras focussed as well on soldiers leaving the capital, mounds of litter at the Washington Monument, and broken and boarded windows in the area around the Department of Justice. Middle-aged Mobilization spokesperson Sidney Peck appeared at a press conference to proclaim that this mass non-violent demonstration could not be ignored by the administration.

The Mobilization was NBC's lead story that Monday night. David Brinkley called it the largest demonstration in history, and almost totally peaceful, a characterization virtually agreed to by the White House, which used the words "generally peaceful." Nevertheless, it would not change its policy on the war, according to the president's advisors. On this occasion, Mitchell's stress on violence was answered by Senator Mike Mansfield. Sam Brown was shown speaking to the media, complaining about Mitchell's interpretation of the event. Indeed, Brown noted, Washington's police authorities, who found him and his people very cooperative, were pleased with the tenor of the demonstration. Mitchell, however, refused to separate the 5,000 militants from the 245,000 others (NBC's figure) who protested civilly. NBC's reporter thought Mitchell made such comments to justify the administration's prediction of widespread violence. Clearly the attorney general appeared in a weak position on the newscast. Nevertheless, Brinkley concluded that this was probably the last mass rally of the antiwar movement.

The emphasis in this and other reports on the level of violence tended to deflect attention from the huge turnout, as well as from the demonstrators' political demands. Because the networks paid so little attention to the speeches and political positions taken by Mobe and Moratorium leaders, viewers may have had difficulty understanding what the protests were all about. The president was withdrawing troops from Southeast Asia on the road to Vietnamization. What these people wanted and how that differed from Nixon's position were questions left unanswered in media coverage that focussed on the charges and countercharges about violence. Indeed, that issue dominated the political commentary with demonstration leaders themselves appearing exuberant because their comrades had been peaceful, as if that had been the main goal of their demonstration.

Print journalists adopted interpretative frames for the events of November 13–15 similar to those of their colleagues in the broadcast media. On the day of the Mobilization, an Apollo space shot took the lead position in the *New York Times*. The front-page demonstration story was headlined, "Tear Gas in Capital Halts March on Saigon Embassy."[60] Despite the headline, the copy centered around other Mobilization events and pointed out that the demonstration's leadership was not involved in the violence perpetrated by a relative handful of radicals. If that was the case, why the headline that might cause some readers to skip what appeared to be another case of tear gas and protestors?

The *Times* illustrated the story on the jump page with photographs of the National Guard at the ready for anything that might happen, tear gas hovering over a crowd, and a map of where incidents took place. On that same page, another headline—"Policeman Stays Calm in Eye of Storm"—led one to expect more such events would take place on the main event day.[61] New York doves undecided about driving down to Washington Saturday morning could have been dissuaded by these pieces. After all, who wanted to risk police billy clubs and arrest?

In Sunday's *Times*, however, unruly activities played only a small part in accounts of the massive Mobilization marches and rallies. With a five-column head on page one and a picture of a huge crowd at the Washington monument, the Mobilization dominated the news on November 16.[62] Yet aspects of the coverage had to please administration supporters. The headline read "250,000 War Protestors Stage Peaceful Rally in Washington: Militants Stir Clashes Later." And under the picture, a caption noted that "Some wave flag of National Liberation Front of South Vietnam."

Four stories dealt with the day's activities—one on how marshals kept the march "cool," another on the radicals' attacks after the main rally, a third headlined: "More than 100,000 on Coast Demonstrate in a Moderate Vein," and the lead story about the "record throng" that was "a great and peaceful army of dissent moving through the city." The jump page featured a picture of that army on Pennsylvania Avenue described as being made up of mostly young, mostly left-of-center people.[63] Receiving somewhat less—and entirely appropriate—attention was the story of the six thousand or so militants, many of whom were carrying Viet Cong flags, who were the clear aggressors as they rampaged in the area around the Justice Department. Similarly, given the huge numbers of people on both coasts, one wonders why *Times* editors devoted so much space to the one thousand who were counted rallying to the president's support in the Bronx, or why they ran a story on forty-six counterdemonstrators at the Lincoln Memorial.[64]

No doubt, the overall impression was of a massive outpouring of antiwar sentiment, albeit not as middle-class or nationwide as the Moratorium. Yet there was enough space devoted to violence and counterdemonstrators to please those who felt that doves were a dangerous minority.

As usual, given the location of the demonstration, the *Washington Post* devoted even more space to the event than the *Times*, which itself was quite generous with its news hole. For the *Post*, size was the key—its huge headline blared, "Largest Rally in Washington History"—a message reenforced by a picture of a "sea of humanity."[65] The official count was 250,000 but even the capital's police chief suggested that the figure could be higher. The "impressively tranquil" demonstrators, who came from all over the country, were described as mostly white, young, and middle-class. A second page-one story told of the gassing of the radicals at Justice, although the reporter made clear that the "several thousand" militants were not representative of the Mobilization marchers. A third page-one story, "Middle-Class Youth Has Its Day," stressed the music and not the politics of this "Washington Woodstock."

According to the *Post*, there was a "majestic tone to [the] march," with an "endless cascade" of people.[66] Indeed, the crowd was so large that some people went home because they had arrived after the ceremonies were over or could not hear the speakers from the rear of the throng. The gentle demonstrators were met by even gentler capital police, some of whom apparently shared their political sentiments.

Most of the pictures that filled all of page 16 offered favorable views of the demonstration, with caskets from the March against Death and many American flags in evidence. The *Post* also presented excerpts from the day's speeches, most of which were moderate and reasonable, so much so that in a story on Jerry Rubin ("Peace Is Respectable") the Yippie leader appeared disappointed.[67]

The Washington daily stressed moderation and gentility as well in the story on San Francisco, where the largest rally in that city's history had been held.[68] Furthermore, the *Post*'s correspondent reported that many people who showed up at Golden Gate Park that day were new to protests. This suggested that the movement was on the move again.

Looking over the nation's two most important newspapers on November 16, demonstration organizers had to be relatively pleased. Both called attention to the record-breaking turnouts, though they may have underestimated the crowds, and both noted how peaceful the main event was, an event not spoiled by the militants at the Justice Department who had nothing to do with the demonstration itself. What was missing was the realization that the event was successful despite the fact that the Nixon administration, through press releases, leaks, and intimidation, had tried to keep demonstrators from Washington and the media from covering the story in any detail.

Newspapers that employed the wire services had more to work with that would please the president. One advance story in *The Daily Tribune* suggested its readers "Tie Viet Attacks to U.S. Protests."[69] Further, the same paper devoted much less space on November 15 to the demonstration than it had to the previous month's Moratorium. The Mobilization was the lead story, however, accompanied by two pictures of violent activity.[70] Most of the narrative dealt with the defensive measures taken by the administration to protect the capital.

On the same day, the *Macomb Daily* featured a page-one story on the tear gas employed on the "mob" at the Saigon embassy, and contended that the Mobilization would be tarnished by the violence.[71] In an AP roundup of GI reaction to the demonstration, three out of the four soldiers quoted opposed the Mobe. The *Daily*'s front page also featured a picture of young people rioting at the embassy. On an interior page, the suburban newspaper lavished more attention on the confrontations, with the March against Death buried in the story.[72] For two newspapers without a Sunday edition, the Saturday stories on Friday's activities may have colored some Michiganders' views of the weekend.

This news frame was reenforced by the relatively light coverage in Monday's issue of the *Tribune* that did (on page 14), refer to "the largest antiwar rally in history," but again stressed the militants' activities.[73] A page-one story dealt with "Agnew Defended, Rapped for Criticizing News Media," with eleven of the thirteen paragraphs in the article reflecting his defense. This report may have been slanted in Agnew's direction to compensate for a November 14 story in which the *Tribune* did not carry much about Agnew's speech of the previous night, even though it covered network officials' criticism of the vice president.[74]

Surprisingly, like the wire services, the *Guardian* and the *Village Voice* offered considerable material on the violence at the Justice Department in their accounts of the weekend's events.[75] This may reflect that the growing militance of New Left factions was indeed the big news in that community. However, in a twist not picked up by the mainstream media, the *Voice*'s Ron Rosenbaum contended that the attorney general was in good measure responsible for the confrontation because of the way he dealt with the two earlier marches on his building.[76]

Both left-wing weeklies thought that the establishment media had undercounted the crowd. The *Guardian* claimed that 800,000 had shown up in

Washington, 250,000 in San Francisco. Accepting a figure of 500,000 for Washington, the *Voice*'s correspondent complained that the Sunday papers used the Washington police chief's much smaller official figure of 250,000 in their headlines.[77] We will never know how many demonstrators rallied in the District that weekend but certainly citizens might have looked at the event differently had their headlines that Sunday morning claimed 500,000 rather than 250,000 or less.

The *Voice* did offer some explanation for why the media undercovered the speechmaking on Saturday—it was hard to hear and rather dull. No doubt, this was an accurate judgment. The larger the event, the more difficult it was to project the voices and also the more noise produced by people from the middle to the rear of the crowd who had given up trying to listen to anything but the music. More importantly, in its extensive account, the Greenwich Village weekly emphasized the fissures in the antiwar movement in which "coalitions are strained and everyone [is] unsure of just what allies they have made."[78] Finally, both left-wing weeklies noted the presence of many active duty GIs in the crowd, an important development in the evolution of the movement that was missed by most of the other media. Despite their obvious antiwar biases, the *Voice* and the *Guardian* offered perceptive and critical accounts of complicated events.

The mainstream newsweeklies did not do as well. *Time* was able to get most of the Mobilization story into its November 21 edition. The cover revealed the frame, with pictures of Nixon, Agnew, network newscasters, and protestors at the Washington Monument, and the banner, "Counterattack on Dissent." Despite the unprecedented November 15 throng, *Time*'s story began with the "politics of polarization," suggesting through pictures that there were two sorts of protests, those for and those against the president, and then devoted the next four pages to an analysis of Agnew and the media.[79] Only after exhausting that issue did *Time* begin covering the Mobilization (and without offering a representative picture of the large Washington crowd at that).[80] Most of the demonstrators were young, according to *Time*, and many moderates like Muskie, Kennedy, and Church had dropped out because of the Mobe's radicalism. After covering the violence at Justice, some of which may have been sparked by the Department's ambiguous position on permits, the story moved on to the March against Death, and finally to crowd estimates of 250,000, which made the Mobilization the largest event of its kind. If that was the case, and if the entire story was framed within a Nixon versus the protestors line, would not the size mean that the protestors had won and therefore that factor should have been the lead? Moreover, *Time* devoted almost one full page to covering Nixon supporters.[81] As for why few of their demonstrations were large or well-organized, entertainer Bob Hope explained, "It's pretty hard for good, nice people to demonstrate."[82]

Time certainly looked different than the newspapers on this story. Of course, it was true that Nixon was fighting back with his Silent Majority speech and the Agnew offensive, two activities related to the Mobilization. Nevertheless, the newsweekly was far less analytical and devoted far less space to the unprecedented demonstrations than it did to the first Moratorium.

Newsweek's advance story in its November 17 number, "Betting on the Silent Majority," also promoted the theme of Nixon versus the antiwar movement.[83] The issue opened with a story on Nixon's strategy, accompanied by the photograph of him surrounded by supportive telegrams that had been run in the *Post*. Mobe leadership, which eagerly took up the battle against the president, predicted the largest crowd in history on November 15.[84] The newsweekly reported that up to the last moment, Nixon's aides, fearing another Weatherman outburst, were withholding permits as twenty thousand troops girded themselves for what might happen.

The next week, the Mobilization, and not Agnew, was the lead story. Owned by the *Washington Post*, a particular target of the vice president, the newsweekly may have had its own agenda in downplaying his assault. *Newsweek* illustrated the protest profusely with pictures of throngs in Washington and San Francisco, the March against Death by candlelight, pleasant-looking demonstrators, and the Central Park balloon launch, as well as several of the violence in Washington and some Nixon supporters.[85] In quality and quantity, the doves won this encounter on the photographic front.

On the other hand, the accompanying text was not as upbeat, as seen in the story, "The Big March: On a Treadmill?" Here, reporters suggested that the movement faced problems from the Nixon-agitated right and from the Weathermen-agitated left as well as in determining its next move. The account of the demonstration itself, which stressed its peaceful nature, denigrated the rally a bit by comparing the music and festivities to Woodstock and referring in passing to the "obligatory oratory" at the Monument.[86]

At San Francisco, *Newsweek* judged that 90 percent of the 125 to 250,000 people demonstrating were under 25. The magazine also looked at the "Men behind the Mobe," with pictures of clean-cut types who nevertheless were deemed more radical than the October cadre.[87] The article described Mobe's leadership as "subordinating ideology" in a broad-based, still relatively moderate coalition. Concluding, the magazine felt that there was a "lack of fervor" aside from the demonstrations in Washington and San Francisco, and a "lethargic showing on campuses," an unfair critique since Mobe and Moratorium leaders had specifically concentrated their energies on those two cities.[88]

It was true, as *Newsweek* pointed out, that the antiwar movement was apparently no closer to success than it had been before the November event and it may have peaked. Part of this outcome may have been related to new manifestations of support for the president. Reporters found crowds of 100,000 in

Pittsburgh and Birmingham, Alabama, 85,000 in Chicago, 75,000 in Long Beach, and 50,000 in Hayward, California demonstrating that the Silent Majority had a voice.[89] These generous estimates left the impression that Nixon's message had a growing appeal. No doubt it did and the mobilization of the Silent Majority was a legitimate object for media focus. Yet, as we have asked before, how much coverage would be appropriate?

Like *Time*, *Newsweek* underplayed the massive nature of the demonstrations and overplayed Nixon's growing support. Nevertheless, the polls demonstrated that the majority of Americans were still in the president's camp, no matter how many doves the movement turned out on the streets. And the Nixon people knew it.

THE ADMINISTRATION WAS MORE PLEASED WITH THE COVERage of the Mobilization than it had been with the Moratorium. The Silent Majority speech and the Agnew attacks on the media had apparently worked. For example, Nixon's media monitors were gratified that Herbert Klein and John Mitchell received prominent attention on the November 16 newscasts.[90] All was not perfect in NBC's coverage, however; Pat Buchanan complained to the network about too much attention to antiwar demonstrators and not enough to administration supporters.[91] That NBC was singled out on this occasion exemplified the administration's general impression that it was the most anti-Nixon network, at least according to its survey of the networks from August to December 1969.[92]

Mort Allin's television watchers coded stories on the evening newscasts according to their favorable, neutral, or unfavorable depictions of the administration. They found ABC to be the most favorable (especially Howard K. Smith) by a 29–41–29 count, CBS the most neutral with 24–51–25, and NBC at the bottom with 16–40–44. The pattern held for news on Vietnam. The report noted that although the administration did not do too well in the coverage of Moratorium demonstrations, the specific "M-Day Reports, the most crucial reports, were at least balanced or favorable to our position." The administration therefore did better than it "could have expected." As for the commentators, Smith was the most favorable, ABC's Frank Reynolds and CBS's Dan Rather fair, Chancellor on NBC improving, with Eric Sevareid bringing up the rear in terms of administration support. The worst period on the newscasts extended from before the Moratorium to the Mobilization. After that point, the Nixon and Agnew speeches had apparently done the trick—the number of proadministration reports increased dramatically in November and December.

Characteristic of that development was the November 19 "Digest of Recent News Reports," which quoted the *Los Angeles Times*'s opinion that the Silent Majority did exist but that it was more antidemonstrator than prowar, and the

Wall Street Journal's view that the mostly young, large crowd on November 15 had "no broad base of support."[93]

As for the newsweeklies, according to Nixon's media monitors, although *Newsweek* gave the Mobe seven pages including two with color pictures, its correspondent thought that the moratorium movement itself was on its way down. Moreover, *Newsweek* devoted a reasonable amount of space to pro-Nixon rallies. The pleased media monitors were perceptive here.

They reported as well that *Time* highlighted the generally peaceful and cheerful mood of the Mobilization but concluded that only a minority in the country was for immediate withdrawal. Attesting to the power of pictures, one analyst noted, "Photo-wise we came out okay with the lead *Time* picture of the pro-Nixon rally at the Monument, a shot of violence at Dupont Circle and another Veterans' Day shot. The protestors also had three shots . . . none as predominant."

This analysis was somewhat at variance with the nature of the news-magazines' coverage, which included more material favorable to the antiwar movement than recognized by the Nixon White House. As with the Moratorium, this could have been a case of his people accentuating the positive since even more "unfair" treatment had been expected. They were also looking for proof that the important Silent Majority-antimedia campaign was working.

It was. Although the movement had organized another massive activity with many new and exciting mediagenic aspects, the November Moratorium and the Mobilization did not receive as favorable and comprehensive treatment from the press as had the October Moratorium. Nixon's media monitors were correct. The Silent Majority speech and Agnew's slashing attack against the allegedly liberal media had apparently slowed the momentum of the antiwar movement that had looked so threatening the previous month. The enthusiastic public response to those attacks worried the fourth estate.

The media's response to the second M Day cannot be fully explained as journalists playing down old or routine news. The events of November 13–15 were new and special and deserved fuller coverage. In the face of Nixon's vigorous, multi-faceted offensive against them, antiwar leaders had successfully built upon the momentum created by the first Moratorium. Yet the press suggested that they were on a treadmill and that a "silent majority" was becoming more visible and vocal. Those self-fulfilling prophecies would color subsequent analyses of the movement.

8

THE MOVEMENT REBOUNDS, APRIL 1970–MAY 1971

the radio and tv stations are saying that the success of shutting down the city was small. i disagree so much:

1. traffic *was* held up. no, we didn't keep people from work but we sure delayed them.

2. even though people did get to work, they hardly could keep their minds on it with all the action going on outside.

3. it showed how so many young americans are willing to put so much on the line (busted heads, jail terms, and prison records) for their ideals.

4. it cost the government an infinite amount of money: cops working overtime; judges likewise; prisons being filled, forcing guards, typists, etc. to work overtime, plus food for the prisoners.

5. it showed we could create havoc to get our point across.

6. most important, the poor blacks were behind us all the way. they know that their enemy is the same as our enemy. they cheered from windows and from their steps and many times they blocked out pigs who were chasing freeks.

we knew that the news would belittle us.[1]

U nderground journalist Ken Wachsberger analyzed the Mayday Tribe's attempt to close down Washington in this entry from his "Diary of a Mad Anarchist" for May 3, 1971. In contrast to observers from the mainstream press—and even demonstration organizer Rennie Davis—he judged the unprecedented action, in which thirty thousand activists engaged in civil disobedience in the streets of the nation's capital, to be a success. Whether it was or not, this last major antiwar protest was not the sort of activity to appeal to many Americans.

Richard Halloran, the reporter who covered the event for the *New York Times*, saw the event somewhat differently. His front-page account began with:

About 7,000 antiwar protestors were arrested yesterday morning after fighting running skirmishes with metropolitan police and Federal troops throughout large areas of the nation's capital.

About 150 were also injured in the six hours of disturbances as the protestors, demanding an immediate halt to the war in Vietnam, were thwarted in their plan to stop Government operations.

The protestors, who called themselves the Mayday Tribe, did succeed in disrupting the city's normal functioning by impeding traffic, harassing Government employees on their way to work using as weapons trash, tree limbs, stones, bottles, bricks, lumber, tires, rubbish bins, and parked cars.[2]

Nixon's assault against the media and the movement and his related campaign to energize a silent majority continued through the winter of 1969–70.[3] With little progress in the peace talks and with American troops continuing to return home, Nixon hoped to strengthen his domestic base to support a new escalation that would bring the peace with honor that had eluded him during his first year in office.

By the spring of 1970, his strategy was working well. The Moratorium, which after October 15, 1969, had appeared rather threatening with its program of escalating demonstrations each month until the United States left Southeast Asia, had run out of steam. Between December and March, its protests attracted little media attention. The once-promising idea was failing in part because it had become impossible to top the success of the first two actions.[4] When fewer people turned out each month after November 15, the moratoriums became less interesting and newsworthy. It was not easy to bring out more and more demonstrators month after month. There were good reasons why movement leaders had previously held only two mass gatherings a year. The Moratorium was on its last legs by April, 1970.

The Moratorium and Mobilization, April 15, 1970

The Moratorium and Mobilization committees called for a week of protests from April 13 through April 18 with tax day or April 15 the key date.[5] By that point, Nixon had recovered much of the support he had lost temporarily during the previous fall. Moreover, as he gained in strength and his police and intelligence services cracked down harder on dissidents, the language and actions of protest became more violent. Such was the case with the scattered demonstrations on April 15, which drew sizeable crowds but produced unprecedented violence, much of it initiated by protestors. The Young Socialist Alliance (YSA)- and SWP-dominated leadership, which eschewed violent tactics, proved unable to control the frenzy of militants who showed up to vent their spleens against the Nixon administration. Since 1969, that minority precipitated almost all of the rowdy and sometimes destructive behavior at antiwar actions. Prior to that date, counterdemonstrators had been primarily responsible for the limited amount of violence that accompanied the movement's marches and rallies.

The April 15 activities drew sizeable crowds of seventy-five thousand in Boston, forty thousand in New York, twenty-five thousand in Chicago, and twenty thousand in San Francisco, among other venues. However, militants from the PL faction of SDS broke up the affair in New York's Bryant Park, rioters trashed stores in Harvard Square, and Berkeley's campus experienced a major disturbance. Those actions certainly did not resemble the dignified protests of the original Moratorium.

Yet the antiwar movement was evidently still alive, though the crowds did not compare to those of the previous fall. However, even though almost all of the protestors behaved with decorum, the nihilistic activities of a small minority of lawless radicals colored the tax-day protests.

As we have seen with the McNamara incident at Harvard on election day in 1966, (see chapter 5), the daily news budget affected the tone, content, and placement of coverage of antiwar activities. The mission of Apollo 13, one of the most dangerous and fateful of the moon shots, was the major story from April 11 to April 17, 1970. Americans held their collective breath as they worried about whether the astronauts would be able to return to earth after experiencing serious technical problems with their vehicle. They were therefore probably even less tolerant than they might have been when hearing of another round of antiwar protests during this time of national crisis, no matter how the press portrayed the events. And, of course, with the Apollo shot dominating the headlines, the press had less space to devote to the dovish crowds in the streets.

For example, the *New York Times*'s huge lead on April 16 concerned the astronauts; the protest story, headed "Radicals Disrupt Antiwar Rallies," appeared at the bottom of the page.[6] The story itself belied the headline as the second paragraph pointed out that most of the protests nationwide were peaceful. But in the absence of huge crowds, that was not news.

Because the capital was not a major protest city, the *Washington Post* relegated the Moratorium to page 6 in a story dominated by accounts of the violence in Berkeley and Boston. Similarly, *The Daily Tribune*'s UPI account contained fifteen paragraphs, thirteen of which chronicled "rage and violence."[7]

The three networks, which variously devoted three and one half, four, and five minutes to the demonstrations on their April 15 nightly newscasts, generally offered more balanced coverage than the print media with genteel protestors appearing as frequently as militants. The CBS analyst even noted that the "antiwar feeling was as intense as ever." Yet one wonders what viewers remembered most from those images, the 60 to 70 percent showing decorous protestors or the 30 percent of wild attacks against property and the police.

The Nixon administration's media monitors were pleased with the coverage on television, and in the magazines for that matter, because of the attention shown to violent actions and also because the news stories correctly pointed out that the White House was uninterested and unaffected by the events of April 15.[8]

The tax-day demonstrations, crippled by media inattention and demonstration-related disturbances, left the movement in more disarray than usual. In fact, the Moratorium Committee decided to close down its offices while other organizations squabbled about what to do next. It appeared that the era of the mass demonstration was nearing an end. But those who sounded the death knell for the antiwar movement had not taken Richard Nixon into account.

Cambodia-Kent State Protest, May 9, 1970

The relative failure of the April Moratorium and Mobilization events helped to convince the president that the time was ripe to escalate the war in Southeast Asia in much the same way that the success of the Moratorium the previous October propelled him in the opposite direction. Although an invasion of Cambodia had been considered during the Johnson administration, Nixon did not authorize the major escalation of his administration until a few days after the April 1970 Moratorium's last gasp.[9] He probably would have gone ahead with the initiative no matter what happened on April 15, but the way the demonstrations fizzled certainly encouraged him.

His speech of April 30 announcing the "incursion" (not "invasion") into Cambodia and the killings at Kent State University on May 4 sparked a spontaneous—and unprecedented—outburst of antiwar actions on almost all major university campuses and in most large cities. Hundreds of universities had experienced strikes, demonstrations, and violent protests before the incident at Kent State—hundreds more joined in after May 4.

Even before the Kent State killings, leaders of the New Mobilization began to organize a demonstration in Washington on the weekend of May 9–10 to oppose the invasion of Cambodia.[10] Normally, at least fifteen-days' notice was required to obtain the use of federal park land for rallies; on this occasion, the authorities waived the waiting period. Shocked by the outburst of anger around the country, a besieged administration decided that it was best to allow the demonstrators to let off steam in Washington legally, rather than risk a replay of Chicago in 1968.

No previous mass demonstration had been put together in such a short time. Moreover, recent events had made it even more difficult for leaders to agree on a program or a strategy for the people drawn to Washington. Some talked about civil disobedience, others about revolutionary acts, but in the end, the main feature was yet another rally with speakers and music. The often bitter predemonstration wrangling among organization leaders caused many prominent leaders not to attend or to refuse to endorse the action and left final plans for the weekend unclear literally until the last speech was delivered.

Nevertheless, despite the notable lack of leadership, more than one hundred thousand gathered during that very warm and humid weekend in Washington, an astounding number given the lack of advance planning. The turnout reflected the widespread anger and frustration felt by many Americans with what they perceived to be an escalation in the violence abroad—and at home. In the few short days prior to the rally, three thousand marshals had been trained to contain what could have turned out to be a militant mob. The venue made the situation more tense since the rally took place at the Ellipse, directly across from the White House.

The most bizarre event of the weekend occurred early in the morning of May 9 when a restless Nixon and his valet made a surprise visit to young people camping out at the Lincoln Memorial. He later claimed that he had a useful dialogue with the students about international relations and political issues.[11] Some astonished students contended that he was rambling and unfocussed, choosing to talk about football and surfing rather than the war and Kent State. The truth is somewhere in between with Nixon trying unsuccessfully to engage the students in political discussions and then falling back on pleasant generalities about their lives and campuses. Nixon's spur-of-the-moment nocturnal journey also shocked his unprepared advisors and the Secret Service. Undoubtedly, the president tried to show students that he did sympathize with them, even if he did not agree with their position on the war.

The next day, news of his visit did not stop one of the speakers, Chicago Seven defendant John Froines, from leading a "Fuck Nixon" chant. Dr. Spock chaired the rally, which included a number of angry speeches that many did not hear because of the poor quality of the sound system. (This technical problem continued to haunt movement organizers and, from a media perspective, diminished the significance of the speeches.) Nine congresspeople appeared on the platform as Senators Brooke, Javits, and Goodell, among other luminaries, looked on from the crowd. Most of the demonstrators were young white college students, many of whom were attending their first antiwar rally.

Rumors abounded that some were going to march somewhere in the capital to commit acts of civil disobedience but without direction from the speakers' platform, the Ellipse rally broke up without incident. Despite the size of the crowd that journeyed to Washington that day, the demonstration struck many as a failure because it lacked spirit, purpose, and direction. Once it ended, few in attendance felt completely satisfied about their participation and fewer still had any ideas about the next steps to take to compel the president to bring the troops home from Southeast Asia more quickly.

The weather may have contributed to the torpor of the crowd as several cases of heat prostration were recorded. The police did arrest about four hundred people for civil disobedience unrelated to the official demonstration. The main unlawful acts at the Ellipse were committed by a small group of Nazis who scuffled with protestors. In addition to the Washington actions, as many as fifty thousand rallied in Minneapolis that weekend, sixty thousand in Chicago, twenty thousand in Austin, and twelve thousand in San Diego.

THE *VILLAGE VOICE* CAPTURED THE MOOD OF THE DAY BEST IN its story, headed "Twilight of Demonstrations, Dawn of the General Strike."[12] Its correspondent was "bitter" about the speakers, who seemed to be spouting the same old stuff at "just another Mobe picnic." Moving beyond the disappointing event itself, he concluded that the antiwar movement should adopt more radical tactics such as work stoppages.

Other newspapers picked up the theme of the emptiness of the protest, aside from its symbolic importance. On the morning of the Washington rally, the *New York Times* ran front-page stories on construction workers breaking up a New York rally and on widespread protests on campuses, which produced two hundred college closures and strikes at nearly four hundred others.[13] The former story took a decidedly anti-hardhat posture. The demonstration story, which documented acts of vandalism and arrests on campuses, reported official fears that the Washington protest would also lead to violence. The National Guard was on alert for this not-very-well-organized event at which the *Times* accurately predicted as many as one hundred thousand participants.

The rally was Sunday's lead story in the *Times*, accompanied by a picture of a large crowd, estimated at seventy-five to one hundred thousand, at the Ellipse. Even though the day's events were mostly peaceful, according to the *Times*, much of the first part of its story described scattered acts of violence. The crowd, which the reporter thought resembled the one at Woodstock, was resentful and angry but not violent. The reporter paid more attention to the arrests that took place after the rally than to the content of the speeches, and on the jump page the editor included a picture of tear gas wafting over Lafayette Park to break up one small ad hoc demonstration.[14]

The *Times* displayed its relative lack of interest in peaceful events compared to violent ones in its roundup article on the other activities of the day, which noted that "while peace prevailed on most campuses," there were exceptions.[15] The bulk of the article dealt with the exceptions. Of course, as we have seen time and again, reporters find it difficult to portray peaceful demonstrations in an interesting way, unless they have unique features, as was the case with the first Moratorium.

A third front-page story that Sunday morning dealt with Nixon's astonishing visit to the Lincoln Memorial. Here the reporter depicted a president under strain conducting a monologue that rambled erratically from irrelevant topic to irrelevant topic. One critic later noted that the *Times* account, which he felt was frivolous, was accepted by much of the rest of the media, even though an allegedly more accurate report was available in the *Washington Star*.[16]

The *Washington Post*'s front-page story and its follow-ups, which filled most of four other pages on May 10, were more comprehensive than those in the *Times*.[17] Several photographs reenforced the notion of "throng" (the word used in the headline to describe the crowd), which was viewed as mostly peaceful except for a few hard-core radicals who were shown trying to tip over a bus. The *Post* also reported nude swimming in the fountain at the Ellipse and the inadequate public address system that meant few could hear the speeches. "It Was Just Too Hot for a Revolution" noted another headline, and the familiar rhetoric of the speeches ultimately bored their listeners. Many were said to have been first-time protestors, compelled by their consciences to come to the capital. Overall, the *Post* was sympathetic to the protestors themselves but not impressed with the activities of their leaders.

As for the impromptu Nixon visit, also a page-one item, the newspaper devoted the first part of its narrative to the president's view of it. On the jump page, students had their say, with some finding him "absurd" and others refuting the claim that a meaningful dialogue had taken place.

The Daily Tribune on May 9 led its demonstration story with a picture of the president at the Memorial. The wire-service account that followed talked of thousands, some bearded, some clean-shaven, in "solemn witness" in a peaceful demonstration.[18] On Monday, May 11, the *Tribune*'s editors moved the story back to the front page of the second section along with a picture of a black man enacting the Crucifixion at the Ellipse. The caption quoted a police estimate of fifty thousand while the wire-service story itself noted that as many one hundred thousand may have turned up. Although the account covered the violence and strikes elsewhere, it also presented an image of responsible movement leaders working on peaceful protests in the future.[19]

Down the road, the *Macomb Daily*'s coverage on May 9 included a large front-page AP story, which at press time that Saturday estimated a crowd of from thirty-five to two hundred thousand. Observers had heard obscene chants, but no violence had taken place nor was any planned. For his part, the president appeared calm and helpful throughout the story.[20]

Time's May 19 cover featured a drawing of a huge feminine face with her mouth opened wide and the White House in the background. The banner headline read "Protest." *Time* devoted ten pages to the turbulent events on campuses with most of the attention going to Kent State.[21] Early in the story, the reporter noted that only on the eve of the demonstration did Nixon begin to understand the significance of Kent State. This new sensitivity was evidenced in his trip to the Memorial, which the newsweekly treated more generously than most—though he rambled, his comments related to the war, not to football.

Time was not far from the mark when it judged the Ellipse rally, attended by 100,000, a "letdown," perhaps because protestors had expended their passions the previous week. For whatever reason, it was a "canned rally" made up mostly of the "instant army of the young." The magazine blamed stale rhetoric and intense heat for the less-than-successful event. The only new element introduced by *Time* was the first display of the alleged Yippie flag, marijuana leaves against a red star. *Time* also noted that the demonstration had been taken seriously by the administration; the peace movement was still a significant force.

Newsweek also made the demonstration part of its May 18 cover story that featured the famous picture of an anguished young woman on her knees after the Kent State shootings. "Mr. Nixon's Home Front" offered several pleasant photos of the Ellipse gathering and individual demonstrators.[22] The president, "insensitive" and "isolated," had finally decided to begin the process of reconciliation as symbolized by his visit to the Memorial. His trip was judged "not successful" with an eyewitness noting, "I hope it was because he was tired, but most of what he was saying was absurd."

Newsweek counted seventy-five thousand at the Ellipse for a "peaceful anticlimax" to the weekend activities. Police-demonstrator relations were "amiable" at this "instant Woodstock." The magazine stressed the decorous nature of the event though it also briefly noted the actions of hard-core radicals in the District and elsewhere. In general, *Newsweek* thought that the antiwar movement was again on the move, this time in the control of moderates who planned non-violent "legitimate and creative activity."

Of all the single-event demonstrations to date, the Cambodian-Kent State protest in Washington received the most accurate print media coverage. Crowd estimates were on the mark as were analyses of the nature of the events, if perhaps exaggerating the rare moments of disorder. Moreover, in general reporters and editors seemed to sympathize with the protestors. Perhaps this reflects a subconscious antagonism toward the administration for its unrelenting war against the allegedly biased media. Some journalists may have felt that Nixon, hunkering down in the White House, was finally getting his comeuppance. To be sure, they were professionals who should not have been affected by such subjective factors but they were also human and had been taking quite a beating figuratively—and literally, at Chicago.

The relative accuracy and objectivity of the mainstream media's coverage of the Washington protest also reflected the fact that by 1970, journalists had learned how to report mass demonstrations better. And this one was relatively easy to cover since it took place in one venue in one city and lasted for a brief period. Whatever the reasons, the press's relatively dispassionate and accurate treatment of the movement in the wake of the Cambodian invasion and Kent State was less important than it might have been earlier. By 1970, most Americans had adopted dovish opinions—the war was a mistake and the United States had to withdraw. The only issue remaining was the speed of that withdrawal.

Television journalists, whom the administration pilloried even more than their print counterparts for biases, also appeared to sympathize with the protestors. Near the top of its May 8 evening telecast, ABC devoted a hefty six and one-half minutes to stories related to the weekend demonstrations. Most important that night was the Wall Street demonstration broken up by construction workers. ABC made it clear that the hardhats brutally stopped a lawful antiwar protest. Moreover, while workers roughed up young demonstrators, the "police did little to stop them." The tough hardhats "won the day," but it was a hollow victory according to the correspondent, and reflected sadly on the polarization in American society. Despite the ABC line, many viewers undoubtedly sympathized with the hardhats as they had sympathized with the Chicago police at the 1968 Democratic Convention.

As for the rally, ABC expected one hundred thousand to turn up as Washington "braced" for the event. Marshals were shown rehearsing crowd control techniques and National Guard troops were ready as well. ABC credited the White House with easing tensions by permitting the use of the Ellipse, even though both the Ellipse and Lafayette Park had been rejected previously as demonstration sites by the Park Service. In a scene from the halls of Congress, well-mannered young people lobbied their representatives. They were told by Senator McGovern, among others, to avoid violence, the underlying frame to the story. The report closed with harsh words from J. Edgar Hoover for the demonstrators, reminding his audience that communists had been involved in the November Mobilization.

CBS's four-minute story that evening dealt almost entirely with defense preparations for the next day's demonstration. The Justice Department expected one hundred thousand to show up at the Ellipse, a compromise venue. The key for the demonstrators was to obtain a place where the president could see them if he chose to look out a window of the White House. The threat of violence lingered over the advance story. To punctuate that threat, like ABC, CBS aired Hoover's warning.

NBC's three-minute report on the night of the 8th began by noting that Nixon was feeling "pressure" that would increase when the expected one hundred thousand demonstrators turned up the next day. The correspondent, however, gave him credit for the compromise decision to permit the use of the Ellipse for the rally. Underlying the significance of the event, he opined that it constituted Nixon's "seventh crisis." The president had decided to try to reach out to the young people, to be more sensitive to their concerns. The story concluded ominously with shots of young protestors in gas masks training for the event.

Despite the advance buildup, the television networks did not cover the demonstration live in its entirety, although a network of college radio stations did broadcast it to their limited audience. On the other hand, unlike previous demonstrations, the networks offered live remotes during the day, with NBC presenting specials before and after its Saturday afternoon baseball game. Moreover, all three networks offered prime-time wrap-ups.[23] It is interesting to note that CBS presented a similar prime-time wrap-up of the July 4 Honor America Day celebrations. CBS did not cover the May 9 event live in part because it feared that the fairness doctrine would mandate coverage of proadministration demonstrations live as well.[24] Nevertheless, the modest increase in live coverage of the May 9 event underscored the fact that the nation was in a major war-related crisis. No other antiwar demonstration either before or after took place during a period of national crisis.

On Sunday night, May 10, CBS wrapped up the weekend with a five-minute story that began with the singing of "Give Peace a Chance" by a handful of the remaining demonstrators the previous night. There had been some arrests and a bit of tear gas used against young people sitting in. As some of the 346 arrested were driven away, they began singing "America." The arrestees were clearly good-natured and non-threatening. Despite several bombings as well that night, the expected mass violence never materialized. Moreover, as seen from post-demonstration shots, the young people did a good job of picking up their own litter.

CBS's account of Nixon's early morning visit to the Memorial was decidedly uncomplimentary, with young people quoted as saying he "rambled," sounded manic, concentrated on travelogues, ignored their questions, and ended by saying "Have a nice day." "It seemed as if he thought we were on a picnic," commented one protestor. Nevertheless, the administration was quoted as being pleased with its handling of the demonstration and expressed "relief" that it was peaceful. This time, CBS depicted Nixon and his aides as trying to communicate with the young people.

On Monday night, CBS ran still more material on the Washington protest, summing it up as generally peaceful and thoughtful. The newscast featured Senator Edward Kennedy (D-MA) leading a church service in prayers for the war to end. Responding enthusiastically, the audience sang the "Battle Hymn of the Republic" while some of its members held up their fingers in the peace sign. Among the celebrities in the mature audience were Coretta Scott King who quoted Patrick Henry and encouraged everyone to reject "an inheritance of evil" from the "reactionary men" who ruled over them. In a final moving scene in this sequence, solemn young candlelight marchers flashed the peace sign as they passed a floodlit White House.

The movement looked even better in a feature story in which a CBS correspondent rode the bus to Washington on May 9 with students from Moravian College, a college without SDS or Weathermen. Asked why they were coming to Washington, earnest young people responded that the long war, fear of another Kent State, and the need to do something to express their concerns brought them there. They sang the plaintive refrains of "Where Have All the Flowers Gone?" to the accompaniment of an harmonica as they rode down the interstate. This was one of the most effective depictions of the movement ever seen on television considering the obvious sincerity and religious orientation of the students from a school not known for activism.

Assailed by the president and his aides since the previous fall for their allegedly skewed coverage of national and international affairs, the networks may have been looking for opportunities to place the White House in a poor light. This may have been one of the reasons why they broadcast feature stories such as the touching Moravian College pilgrimage. After all, with only a small percentage of a twenty-two and one-half minute news hole devoted to the protest, why linger so long on the obscure Moravian College story? To be fair to the newscasters, given the uproar over Cambodia and the Kent State killings, it was easy—and correct—to place the White House in a poor light.

CHARACTERISTIC OF AN ADMINISTRATION UNDER SEVERE pressure, its media analyses of this latest demonstration vacillated wildly. In the first place, they began from the premise that it was going to be a difficult weekend. Several months later, looking back at the invasion of Cambodia itself, Larry Higby noted that *Time*, *Newsweek*, the *Times*, *Post*, and the three networks all opposed the invasion "violently." This was the first time the White House aide could recall that all opposed a presidential action so strongly, an alleged reflection of their biases.[25]

Nevertheless, as the networks themselves reported, the administration appeared to be relatively pleased as the protest played out. On May 10, Nixon claimed he was "turning a corner this weekend"; the "students have overplayed their hands."[26] Of course, this was before the media analyses had come in. The next day, Nixon ordered Haldeman to embargo the *Times* and the *Post*, a reaction to his reading of the Sunday papers, and to call for a "shakeup" in his public-relations operation. Two days later, Nixon complained to Haldeman about the "lack of credibility" of the big seven news sources and called for a renewed offensive against them.[27]

One can see why Nixon was less than pleased with the media coverage, even though by May 10 he thought he had finally weathered the Kent State storm. For example, preparing for the weekend, John Ehrlichman reminded White House aides on May 9 to "be sure to go low on crowd count—give official number."[28] As we have seen, most of the press predicted a crowd of one hundred thousand on May 8 and stuck to that number on May 9 despite underestimates from official sources.

The White House was even more irritated with the media's treatment of Nixon's early morning visit to the Memorial. Egil Krogh, who caught up with Nixon and his valet and thus witnessed some of the conversations, complained about student accounts that said the president "kept rambling on from subject to subject." According to Krogh, this was not so; the president tried very hard to communicate but the students were "too stunned to respond at all." Ehrlichman himself admitted that he first believed news reports that depicted a tired president discussing surfing and other nonsense. Nixon was frustrated with reports that made what should have been a good story for the administration a public-relations fiasco.[29]

In their treatment of the antiwar movement, Nixon's media monitors, like the press, were becoming more perceptive.[30] Considering the seriousness of the domestic crisis that confronted the White House, it was difficult to find a silver lining in the television reports of the weekend. Analysts saw the May 9 news specials on the three networks as stressing the peaceful nature of the protest without giving enough credit to the White House for its role in helping to keep things cool. On the other hand, they quoted a CBS report, which despite referring to earlier angry words from Nixon, found that he was now listening to the students.

Harvard professors, billed as friends of Henry Kissinger, appeared on CBS to attack the Cambodian policy. Moreover, although cabinet members Robert Finch, Walter Hickel, and James Allen spoke with Dan Rather to defend the administration, analysts noted reporters' conclusions that Nixon was clearly affected by this demonstration more than the Mobilization of November 15 and even seemed a bit "out of control." For his part, Eric Sevareid did not think much of the antiwar speeches on the Ellipse and pointed out that the public was sick of both the war and the demonstrations. Finally, the media monitors noted that among those senators who opposed the invasion appearing on network specials on May 9 were Mathias, Hatfield, Brooke, and Goodell, who received unwelcome special attention as dovish Republicans.

Examining the May 10 newscasts, Nixon's media people noted that CBS and NBC offered generous coverage to the rally, which they estimated as ranging from sixty to one hundred thousand participants, impressive figures given the lack of planning time. The young people shown were generally clean-cut and the students interviewed who saw the president the previous morning were critical of the meeting. On the other hand, Dan Rather called Norman Thomas's Ellipse speech "rambling" and some in attendance complained that it was "difficult to hear." Although CBS quoted Nixon as saying "I really love those kids," the monitor scored the network for devoting too much time to radical Dave Dellinger. Worse still from the administration perspective, the sequence of students from Moravian College was "very favorable to the demonstrators."

In a summary of the themes of the "Major stories of the Week of May 4th," Mort Allin concluded that the "rambling talk in Memorial might hurt."[31] Moreover, he was disturbed that the frames of an administration out of control, national polarization, and an isolated Nixon dominated the media that week. The flip side was that by the end of the week, particularly over the weekend, things looked a little better with the media reporting that the White House now appeared more open. But it had been a rough week.

The situation did improve somewhat over the following weeks. Nevertheless, Nixon and his aides were leery of making any direct assault against antiwar protesters. In a poll privately commissioned by Haldeman during the week of June 17–23, respondents divided on dissent with 41 percent saying it was a healthy activity and 45 percent considering it a serious problem.[32] However, 57 percent of young people, 56 percent of wealthy people, and 53 percent of the college-educated were favorably inclined toward student protests. These figures may have been affected by the relatively positive media coverage of the doves.

The poll also revealed that there were limits to the general tolerance for antiwar activities. For example, 60 percent of those polled found student strikes unjustified. Haldeman advised Nixon that it would be difficult to exploit this issue because the majority of young people supported dissent. It would be even more difficult to exploit when eighteen-year-olds received the vote.

The administration had lost support in part because of what it perceived as unfavorable media treatment. This was especially true of the television networks, according to chief media analyst, Mort Allin. In July, he completed a survey of the previous months' news on the networks.[33] This was an astoundingly amateurish job, constructed in barely legible handwriting, full of crossouts, with obviously much room for error both in judgment and simple arithmetic. Prepared for Charles Colson and other aides, this report would not have passed muster as a term paper in a freshman journalism class.

Looking at the nightly newscasts' treatment of the war from March through the end of June, Allin judged ABC to be "almost beyond reproach" and CBS and Dan Rather not too bad, but NBC's Chancellor and Brinkley were "ready at the drop of a hat, to slip in a sarcastic comment." Considering the analyses presented here, which reflect very little difference between the networks in their coverage of demonstrations, it is difficult to see how Allin arrived at his conclusions. He was, of course, more interested in editorial comment and narration than the accompanying visuals. Whichever network was most hostile, the Nixon administration saw itself in deep trouble. The movement, despite its toothless demonstration, had temporarily gained the upper hand. Its advantage would not last for long.

IN MUCH THE SAME WAY THAT HE SLOWLY REGAINED POPULAR support after the success of the Moratorium in October, 1969, the president made selected public appearances in the spring and summer of 1970 where he delivered strong but somewhat conciliatory speeches to rally the public behind his plans for peace with honor in Vietnam. Even though the polls revealed that more and more Americans desired complete withdrawal from Southeast Asia sooner rather than later (55 percent in September), the Vietnam War was becoming less salient as American forces suffered fewer and fewer casualties and talks continued in Paris.

Leaders of the movement knew that the war had retreated from the head-lines—and from national consciousness. After the tactical confusion that marked the Cambodia-Kent State demonstrations, they retreated from direct confrontation with Washington. Part of the problem was lack of interest. For one thing, the president continued to bring the troops home and eschewed further escalation. For another, many students were distressed to discover that their campus antiwar activities during the previous May, which included the closure of many universities until the fall, interfered with graduation and other educational and vocational plans.

The invasion of Laos in early February, 1971, did not produce any signifi-cant mass demonstrations. That unsuccessful invasion took place during the dead of winter, not the best time for outdoor rallies, and most important, American troops were not directly involved. In addition, the disruption caused by the student strikes and university closures the previous spring caused some young people to think twice about taking up the cudgels against the Nixon administration again. Finally, the American battle-death count had fallen (while the Asian count had risen), as had the number of troops in Viet-nam, and the draft was winding down. On the other hand, there was little progress in the Paris peace talks, thousands of Asians were still dying each month in combat, and GIs were coming home at too slow a pace for some Americans.

Washington Demonstrations, April 19–May 6, 1971

Antiwarriors still dissatisfied with administration policies in Southeast Asia began preparing for yet another demonstration in Washington. Their leaders were split between those who wanted to continue lawful mass actions and those who advocated militant civil disobedience. The latter contended that another mass demonstration, no matter how large, would not influence Nixon or many of his supporters. They felt that unless the movement adopted new and more effective tactics, American bombs would continue to fall in South-east Asia.

The factions settled their tactical dispute in the late winter of 1971 with the call for two separate demonstrations in Washington.[34] The first would be a traditional one-day rally on April 24. The second, to take place one week later, would feature civil disobedience. The National Peace Action Coalition

(NPAC), a coalition dominated by the SWP, organized the rally. The People's Coalition for Peace and Justice (PCPJ), a group influenced by radical pacifists who had seceded from the moribund Mobilization, planned to disrupt Washington with several days of civil disobedience. In addition, the PCPJ had been circulating the People's Peace Treaty, declaring an immediate end to the war in Vietnam, which would play a role in its activities.

A third and independent element in the capital protests, and the most noteworthy, involved a contingent of antiwar soldiers, the Vietnam Veterans against the War (VVAW). In January, VVAW's war-crimes hearings in Detroit captured some headlines and sound bites. Following that event, the small but growing organization began planning a unique Washington protest for the week preceding the scheduled April 24 NPAC demonstration.

VVAW launched Operation Dewey Canyon III (the first Dewey Canyons were American offensives in the war) on April 19. Many of the two thousand vets who joined the protest encamped without permission on the Mall, an action that provided the administration with a means to disrupt what promised to be a highly mediagenic protest. Thus, government lawyers went to court to obtain authority to throw the "trespassers" off U.S. property. However, the Justice Department ultimately chose not to execute the court's eviction order fearing the negative publicity that would come with having to eject uniformed veterans forcibly, some of whom were in wheelchairs or on crutches. The administration feared the success of the unprecedented VVAW demonstration but feared even more the prospect of having to throw Vietnam veterans off the Mall, in full view of television cameras. The issue became moot when a District Court judge threw out the injunction and excoriated the Justice Department for its inconsistent actions.

The veterans became a highly visible presence in Washington from April 19 through April 23. Groups carrying toy weapons staged impromptu acts of guerilla theatre, such as search and destroy missions on the streets around the White House and the Capitol. Scores tried unsuccessfully to turn themselves in as war criminals, while others were initially barred from Arlington National Cemetery before gaining permission to visit the graves of their comrades. Still others lobbied and testified in Congress. On Capitol Hill, John Kerry, a decorated, former naval officer (later a Democratic senator from Massachusetts) made a long and impassioned statement on behalf of the veterans to the Senate Foreign Relations Committee.

Throughout the week, the VVAW kept their makeshift campgrounds tidy and protested non-violently. In their largest act of civil disobedience, 110 were arrested in front of the Supreme Court Building where they had been denied admission to pursue their cause. They surrendered to the police POW-style, hands held over their heads. On April 23, the week's protest came to an end with a dramatic ceremony in which from 600 to 1,000 of the veterans threw combat medals and ribbons over the fence of the Capitol. As they "returned" their decorations to Congress, many made brief statements citing fallen comrades as the people they memorialized through their act.

The weeklong VVAW protest was "unprecedented"[35] in American history and the most difficult for the Nixon administration to dismiss or ignore. Not massive, it was, however, new and imaginative. Providing the press with colorful and sometimes poignant stories and photographs, the veterans demonstrated that the size of a protest was not always the most important criterion for success. Washington had experienced larger demonstrations in the past; the city had not experienced anything like the VVAW "invasion."

On Saturday, April 24, the day after the moving medal-returning ceremony, as many as five hundred thousand people turned up for NPAC's demonstration, the single largest crowd in the history of the capital.[36] Busses entering Washington that morning were backed up for twenty miles on some routes. Demonstrators first gathered at the Ellipse and then marched down Pennsylvania Avenue to the Capitol steps for a noon rally. This was the first time Congress had permitted its steps to be used for a such a purpose. The president of the Senate, Vice President Agnew, had arranged for the permit.

April 24 was a pleasant spring day, perfect for a parade and rally. The march was led by a veteran in a wheelchair along with other veterans and notables, some of whom carried American flags. Among those who marched under the NPAC banner were contingents of Asian-Americans, Iranian students, left-wing Zionists, union members, gays, and blacks. Such diversity was admirable but the presence in newsclips of these groups which carried their own militant signs, alienated mainstream America. The crowd also included unaffiliated moderates and liberals, a large number of whom claimed to be at their first demonstration. Most of the doves were subdued, neither militant nor ebullient. Although their numbers alone had made the demonstration a fabulous success, the protestors were pessimistic, even despairing, as they held out little hope that their action would move the administration—or even the majority of the population, which seemed to be satisfied with the pace of withdrawal from Southeast Asia. If they felt that way, then perhaps journalists covering their activities had reason to play down the event, which, after all, though superficially spectacular, may not have been politically important.

Among those who spoke at the five-hour rally were Coretta Scott King, Senators Gruening and Hartke, the Reverend Ralph David Abernathy, Representatives Bella Abzug (D-NY) and Herman Badillo (D-NY), and John Kerry. Despite the presence of radical provocateurs, the affair was peaceful with the District police reporting only ten arrests. Moreover, like the encamped soldiers of the VVAW, the demonstrators cleaned up after themselves and did not trample flower beds. Later that weekend, 150 pacifists, including many Quakers, were arrested during sit-ins, and demonstrators on the way back to the New York area tied up traffic on the New Jersey Turnpike with slow-moving vehicles.

Thousands of protestors remained in Washington after April 24, many camped out at West Potomac Park, preparing for the civil disobedience that they hoped would paralyze the city. Sponsored by the PCPJ and what came to be called the Mayday Tribe, and with Rennie Davis as its most prominent leader, they began their protests on May 3. About thirty thousand mostly young people participated on that first day, mainly trying to tie up the bridges and other key arteries to make it impossible for workers to get to their jobs. Armed with precise intelligence it had gathered through legal and illegal means, the administration was well-prepared. Workers arrived at their offices earlier than expected while the police, in mass sweeps, indiscriminately arrested record numbers of demonstrators—and others—in the vicinity of the action. The civil disobedience continued in Washington through May 6 with the number of protestors dwindling each day.

Two stories emerged from the Mayday demonstrations. One involved the attempts by the young people to stop the government, which failed, though they did inconvenience many in the District on May 3 and 4. The other involved the illegality of the procedures employed for many of the mass arrests and the dreadful conditions in makeshift detention centers where the young people were detained. By the end of the week, despite disclaimers by administration spokespersons that the "ugly mobs of thugs" were arrested and detained legally,[37] the victory over the demonstrators began to be colored by a growing recognition that it had been obtained through illegal means.

From April 19 through April 25, and again from May 3 through May 6, Washington experienced the most sustained period of antiwar activities of any city in the history of the movement. This period was not easy to cover in the media given the large cast of characters and the diversity of the demonstrations. The VVAW was the biggest story though the mass outpouring of antiwar citizens on April 24 should have vied for media attention. Television journalists, especially, could find scores of interesting vignettes to fill their newscasts, from the colorful activities of the vets to the often bizarre attempts to stop the government. That medium might have found less of interest in the April 24 rally because it was so peaceful and uneventful—an important development in itself considering how violent sects within the New Left had become over the previous two years.

THE VVAW ACTIONS, WHICH OCCURRED AT PLACES LIKE THE Supreme Court steps and Congress and involved discrete colorful activities, were made to order for television. On the evening of April 22, ABC began its six-minute treatment near the top of the newscast with the Supreme Court story where viewers saw the veterans sitting down and then being arrested for trespass. The arrests were peaceful, some vets carried American flags, and, as ABC noted, the protestors were soon set free. The correspondent also reported that despite a court order, the District police did not remove the vets from the encampment on the Mall. The scene then switched to the Foreign Relations Committee hearings where Lieutenant John Kerry presented an "eloquent indictment" of American policy in Indochina. The handsome and soft-spoken Kerry looked intelligent and sincere, the senators looked pensive. ABC also aired a critique from the head of the Veterans of Foreign Wars (VFW) who said the media were overplaying the story of a handful of unrepresentative antiwar veterans. In fact, he claimed some of those protesting in Washington were not even veterans of the war. The VVAW admitted that some in their van were not veterans but added that twenty-three hundred veterans had come to the capital of whom 93 percent had been in the combat theatre. Moreover, one member of the VVAW claimed that he represented the political views of 75 percent of Vietnam veterans. The last word, however, went to the communist delegations at the Paris Peace Talks who offered words of encouragement to the demonstrators. Surprisingly, by this late date, they still had not learned the rudiments of good public relations in the United States.

CBS's four-minute report, also near the beginning of its April 22 broadcast, began with the defiance of the unenforced court order to vacate the Mall and shifted to the Supreme Court where the arrests took place POW-style. An extended excerpt from Kerry's testimony followed but again the VFW commander alleged that the VVAW was a small and unrepresentative group.

NBC's five-minute account that night also began at the Supreme Court, showing two veterans in wheelchairs who were not arrested even though they tried to join the others. The network offered little explanation for why the arrests for "disorderly conduct" took place. However, the dignified Kerry received considerable attention from NBC as the "war hero" suggested that the United States was still in Vietnam to protect Nixon from being the first president to lose a war.

ABC began its April 23 broadcast with the VVAW, noting that Washington "has been filled with veterans" protesting the war non-violently. That constituted the segue into the main part of the story about the violence expected at Saturday's demonstration where two hundred thousand protestors might show up. Attorney General John Mitchell was shown talking to student editors about the radicals and spies involved in the demonstration and the likelihood of "substantial harm" done to property and people. When Mitchell asked the students how many expected violence, about half raised their hands. When opponents of the administration made such predictions, viewers must have been worried. Stories such as these reenforced the White House's efforts to keep the crowds small on Saturday.

The last part of ABC's antiwar coverage, which should have been the first, showed the veterans throwing their medals over the fence in a "remarkable ceremony." Representative Ron Dellums (D-CA) who was in attendance referred to it as "symbolic expression." Most viewers certainly would have been moved by the ceremony. The one jarring note was the fact that many of the vets appeared scruffy, dressed in rumpled fatigues, and sporting long hair and mustaches or beards. All the same, according to ABC, they had a great impact on the city, more than the likely impact of the mass demonstration the next day.

CBS began its newscast that night with a Soviet space flight and then switched to the veterans for six minutes. The medal ceremony received top billing where the mood was described as one of "anger and mourning." Several vets offered comments for the camera with their "contempt showing" for the government. The scene made for compelling drama as viewers saw and heard the vets dedicating their medal-return to friends who "died needlessly" in the war. Shots of vets in wheelchairs or otherwise handicapped were especially poignant as was the point when the narrative fell silent for more than twenty-five seconds for the playing of "Taps." A final scene showed the father of a boy killed in Vietnam dissolving into tears as he tried to discuss his reasons for being in Washington.

Attorney General Mitchell then appeared to warn of violence at the next day's demonstration perpetrated by some who were inspired by "outside interests." The bulk of this account dealt with preparations being made by the authorities and shopkeepers for dangerous eventualities. Despite Mitchell, the sponsors of the demonstration said it would be peaceful. Mitchell, it now appears from hindsight, was directing his attention primarily to those who would stay on for civil disobedience after the Saturday demonstration. He was correct, of course, about the upcoming Mayday actions. But viewers could easily have thought he was talking exclusively about the Saturday demonstration or at least might link the two activities.

NBC's lead story on April 23 was the medal ceremony, medals that were considered by the VVAW to be "symbols of shame." A man without a leg was seen throwing his medals over the fence, while other longhaired vets stood by. Although some seemed very angry, tears and hugs dominated the scene. After the climactic event, the VVAW was shown cleaning up their encampment with Senator Mansfield attesting to their impact.

On the day of the mass demonstration, only the tiny National Education Network carried the rally live. (This means that the Cambodia-Kent State protest had received somewhat more live coverage from the networks than did the largest demonstration in the capital's history.) CBS did lead with the protest on its Saturday evening newscast, devoting almost nine minutes to it. Beginning with an assertion that the demonstration drew the largest crowd in Washington's history, with more than two hundred thousand, and maybe as many as the five hundred thousand claimed by the organizers, the network offered almost uniformally positive coverage. Above all, the demonstration was "peaceful as promised." According to Roger Mudd and the visuals, the crowd was older than previous ones with a sprinkling of union hats and members of black organizations, along with the expected young white people and Viet Cong flags. Veterans of the war were among the marchers. The assemblage was much larger than had been predicted and organizers literally ran out of standing space. Those tuned to CBS that evening saw the charismatic Kerry addressing the crowd, gently but firmly promising that he and his colleagues would be back again and again to pressure legislators and if need be, to work in the upcoming elections. Vance Hartke then offered Nixon a plan to end the war: merely "announce a date for withdrawal" and "get them out now." Pop artist John Denver sang "Last Night I had the Strangest Dream" as the camera panned to the masses of people in the crowd who linked arms and sang along.

After a commercial break, San Francisco received attention with its march led by vets, including one in a wheelchair. Nevertheless, most of the nearly 250,000 were young people, "college kids and radicals" who always turned out for such things. There were, however, others from the middle-class and union ranks on this occasion, as could be seen in the visuals. Golden Gate Park's rally produced "hardly any trouble" as rock musicians played and comedian Dick Gregory promised to fast until the war was over. Both the Washington and San Francisco demonstrations appeared to be impressive events, different in terms of composition and gentility from many previous demonstrations. Only the Moratorium had received such generous treatment from the cameras.

Despite the networks' coverage of Mitchell and the VFW Commander, as well as hints that the movement's tactics were about to change for the worse from a middle-class perspective, antiwar leaders had to be encouraged by their "reviews" on the nightly newscasts. No doubt, the predictions of a smaller crowd than eventually turned up and the rally's well-documented peaceful nature contributed to viewers' positive impressions of the protests. Those impressions commingled with the often touching impressions of the VVAW protests of the previous days.

The print media approached the two demonstrations in a manner comparable to that of the broadcast media. For example, the *New York Times* was sympathetic to the VVAW. Its front page on April 23 featured a photograph of the arrests at the Supreme Court and an accompanying story in which a judge "rebuked US aides" for trying to evict the veterans from the Mall.[38] On page 4, *Times* readers found a flattering portrayal of VVAW spokesperson John Kerry, a Yale man who had been wounded three times in Vietnam. As for the main Saturday rally, the newspaper expected a crowd that might range from fifty to two hundred thousand. Readers might have concluded that when more than two hundred thousand showed up, the rally was a success.

Although it was not the lead story, the medal-discarding ceremony made the front page of the *Times* the next day, along with a photograph of one vet throwing his over the fence in the "last and most emotional demonstration" of VVAW week. Other stories relating to the event appeared inside the paper with the VVAW described as having "an impact far greater than its numbers."[39] The left, or second, lead on Sunday, April 25, dealt with the Saturday demonstration, along with an impressive crowd photograph. The headline used the "official" crowd estimate of 200,000 that came from the District police even though the story itself noted that organizers claimed 500,000. The *Times* also tacitly accepted San Francisco's official estimate of 150,000. Given the size of the crowd in the capital, it was surprising that the *Times* devoted only one interior page to an account of the events of the day.[40] Further, that account described the demonstration inaccurately as smaller than the Mobilization of November, 1969. However, the reporter did note the large number of adults who participated.

The follow-up the next day continued the emphasis on the gentle and genteel nature of the event.[41] An accompanying picture of the small Quaker sit-in, however, belied the copy that stressed the peaceful and law-abiding. Despite this mixed message and the usual absence of interest in the political goals of the demonstrators, the antiwar movement's activities in Washington received generally favorable coverage from the *Times*, if slightly less prominent than deserved.

The *Post* devoted considerable attention as well to the demonstrations in the District. On April 23, its page-one story—"Judge Lifts Ban on Vets, Scolds US"—concerned the administration's convoluted legal maneuverings.[42] The main picture on the page centered around a tall fence that had been erected in front of the Capitol in anticipation of Saturday's demonstration. At the bottom of the page, John Kerry was shown testifying before the Senate Foreign Relations Committee. The story of his testimony, which was a "highly emotional plea" delivered "to a receptive and sympathetic committee," appeared, along with excerpts, on an interior page.

Another long story dealt with the plight of one protestor who had to be taken to a hospital for treatment of old war wounds, while a picture showed soldiers engaged in mock guerilla warfare on a Washington street. Overall, the photographs and pictures were sympathetic to the vets who appeared sincere, committed, and non-radical.

The next day, the medal ceremony captured the lead position in the *Post*.[43]

The story also served as an advance for the demonstration that day where organizers expected two hundred thousand, the police one hundred thousand. After describing several of the veterans at the Capitol and explaining their actions, mentioning a protesting Gold Star mother and the playing of "Taps" by a man whose son had been killed in Vietnam, the story moved on to John Mitchell's warnings and the preparations being made to contain the expected violence. In addition, the *Post* ran a moving photograph of six vets leaving the capitol, walking with arms around each others' backs, as one limped along on a crutch.[44]

The front page also offered a retrospective on demonstrations that had become a "Washington staple." The names may change but the themes remained the same according to the feature writers. All had three things in common— predemonstration wrangling over permits, disagreement about the number of people who showed up, and especially recently, proclamations that this would be the last such mass demonstration. The article was perceptive but emphasized that we had seen this all before. Like the *Times*, the *Post* preferred the VVAW's invasion of Washington with its unique and heartfelt brand of protest to the presumably less interesting mass demonstration to come.

Nevertheless, on Sunday the Washington daily lavished more space on the Saturday demonstration than did the *Times*, with five front-page stories, including the lead, topped by a banner headline.[45] That headline, however, used a figure of one hundred seventy-five thousand even though larger estimates of 500,000 were reported. Whatever the numbers, the newspaper found it a "Vast and Peaceful Throng" of "unprecedented numbers" of people, many of them first-timer protestors. *Post* reporters based that conclusion on unscientific polls that revealed as well that the crowds represented a cross section of the population. They did not write much about the speeches at the Capitol because, according to one reporter, they were not important and had been heard before.[46] What was considered important was the size and the nature of the crowd.

Like the *Times*, the *Post* found the crowd more pessimistic than angry. In addition, the *Post* reported that on this occasion the many tourists on the street supported the demonstrators' activities.

Only the Moratorium had received such positive treatment in the two elite dailies. Both papers, by this time highly critical of the Nixon administration in many areas, were attracted to the peaceful, surprisingly mainstream nature of the event. On the other hand, both underplayed the size of the crowd and as usual, paid scant attention to the political positions taken by the organizers and speakers.

Perhaps the two elite dailies should not be faulted for their somewhat limited and unenthusiastic coverage of what was the largest protest in history. The *Village Voice* emphasized the activities of the VVAW and the upcoming

Mayday actions in its own reportage on the demonstrations.[47] For example, all of its front-page pictures in the edition covering the protests dealt with the VVAW. Downplaying the "mass spring rite of exorcism of guilt," its correspondent concluded that large crowds and stale speeches are ineffective—the peace movement was changing its approach. As had been the case in the past, however, the *Guardian*, while impressed with the "profound" impact of the VVAW on the public and Congress, was impressed as well with the five hundred thousand in Washington and the three hundred thousand in San Francisco who demonstrated that the antiwar movement was alive and well. Further, the *Guardian* also took seriously the speeches delivered at the two rallies.[48] Throughout this era, the *Guardian* was one of the few papers consistently to print long excerpts or even the entire remarks of demonstration speakers. Many of these were thoughtful and programmatic, not just vehicles for invective and sloganeering. But few Americans ever found that out.

Relying on the wire services on April 23, *The Daily Tribune* offered a brief front-page news note on the veterans throwing their medals over the fence. It also ran a UPI story that stressed the unique nature of the VVAW demonstration, and claimed that the Senate and others were listening to the often dignified protest from the veterans—"Antiwar Veterans Make Impression on Nation's Leaders."[49] Moreover, the UPI account favored the VVAW in the argument over the Mall permit.

According to Saturday's UPI story in the *Tribune*, the demonstration of two hundred thousand mostly white and young people was close to breaking the November 1969, participation record. Viet Cong flags were noted in the crowd, as were veterans, and members of Congress. Two other stories that day presented quotes from veterans about atrocities committed in Vietnam and a claim that the White House had shut down because of the rally.[50]

By Monday, the *Tribune*'s focus had switched to the change in tactics expected by protestors who remained in Washington.[51] In addition, a picture showed Quakers being arrested at the White House with one trying to get his baby arrested as well.[52] The caption on a photo of marchers on Pennsylvania Avenue suggested that more than 200,000 had protested while the copy in the AP accompanying story—"Massive Antiwar Rally Peaceful: Hard Core Militants Remain"—reported that the numbers may have exceeded the record-breaking 320,000 of the November 15, 1969 Mobilization. The 320,000 figure was a stunner since 250,000 had been the widely accepted figure at the time. However large the April 24 gathering may have been, the AP hailed the demonstrations as the "most peaceful of their kind to date." The San Francisco march of 156,000 was dealt with in one sentence.

The *Macomb Daily*'s advance Newspaper Enterprise Association (NEA) story on April 24, buried on page 7, was straightforward but ended on a flippant note, with one marcher quoted as saying, "I'm going to march but I'm

having difficulty deciding the group I want to join. . . . So it goes. Another
year, another demonstration."[53] Its April 26 follow-up AP story, very similar
to the one in the *Tribune*, was headed "War Protestors Besiege Congress" and
quoted the police as saying it may have been the biggest protest in history.[54]
(Besiege" is not a particularly accurate verb to describe the peaceful demonstration in front of the Capitol.) The front-page story noted that many journalists thought the organizers' estimates of crowd size may have been more
accurate than the police's. The rally's sponsoring group was said to have had
a leftist tinge, but nevertheless, the last paragraph of the *Daily* story repeated
the line about the most peaceful demonstration to date, with only twenty-five
arrests tallied.

Despite their editorial support for the Nixon administration, both Michigan
dailies offered their readers positive glimpses of the demonstrations. And in
this case, it was not just because of relatively favorable wire-service copy.
The local editors' choice of headlines and photographs also contributed to that
outcome.

The newsweeklies offered a somewhat different view of the April events.
Time's somewhat snide advance story "Demo Time Again" referred to this
"regular feature of spring in the capital."[55] Of course, that comment is entirely
accurate. The small story did report that relations between demonstrators and
the government were better, with even Spiro Agnew cooling his rhetoric. Yet
the notion of a regular feature suggested that some in the media were no
longer interested in antiwar demonstrations.

Those events were major stories the next week, with pictures of a vet
marching on crutches and huge crowd scenes.[56] The line, "part festival, part
political mass meeting," captured *Time*'s ambivalence. The crowds, undercounted as 200,000 in Washington and 125,000 in San Francisco, were said
to contain fewer college students and more "teeny-boppers," with some union
members as well. A "layer of despair" hung over the event, a characterization
made by other observers as well.

And like other media, *Time* took the part of the vets on the issue of demonstration permits over the Justice Department, which ended up with "egg on its
face." One veteran offered his glass eye as proof that he was the real thing in
order to counter administration claims that many had not seen combat. The
medal-tossing scene was one of "simple eloquence" as was a picture of a vet
throwing his cane over the fence. A large insert included excerpts from
Kerry's testimony.[57] Overall, *Time* devoted far more space to the veterans
than to the Saturday demonstration.

Newsweek's advance story, like *Time*'s, viewed the demonstration in a
slightly jaded way.[58] We've seen them before, the weekly seemed to say, so
what else is new? The organizers were described as radical, except for the

VVAW which was running its own show. Interestingly, *Newsweek* noted that crowd estimates had been scaled down from 250,000 to 50,000.

Its readers were in for a surprise in the next issue when at least 200,000 participants were counted with as many as that number in San Francisco.[59] A photograph attested to the mass turnout in the capital. Nevertheless, the protestors apparently had no one to convince; everyone, especially Congress, was working rapidly to wind down the war. In San Francisco's largest rally ever, the magazine's correspondents noted the usual number of gays and "inevitable VC flags," but it was also described as "benignly spring like." Again the vets were taken more seriously with Kerry ("totally nonviolent") quoted, the government looking somewhat silly, and the VVAW effective with its "theatrical style of protest."

Newsweek, more favorable to the protests in general than *Time*, was nevertheless more explicit in its view that the success of this latest round of demonstrations really did not matter much after all. The light at the end of the tunnel was in sight; some wanted to race towards it while the majority seemed satisfied with the administration's more leisurely pace. Both newsmagazines' emphasis on the VVAW and somewhat casual approach to the mass demonstration reflected the media's interest in novelty. That interest made a relatively small demonstration, which may not have reflected mainstream veteran attitudes, into something more important than it really was. The VVAW had succeeded in capturing the media's attention with new and imaginative approaches to protest.

NOT SURPRISINGLY, THE ADMINISTRATION THOUGHT THAT THE media had treated it unfairly once again. ABC newscasts topped the enemies list at this juncture. Surveys conducted by the White House revealed that the once friendly network had replaced NBC and CBS as offering the most unfair coverage of the Vietnam War. The network also carried the Dick Cavett talk show, which was allegedly full of guests critical of the administration.[60] The White House was well aware of the public-relations problems posed by the VVAW. Consequently, a few days before its arrival, Colson discussed with Haldeman the need to get out the word that not only were its ranks tiny compared to the vast majority of patriotic veterans but that those ranks were swelled by camp followers.[61] Colson predicted correctly that the VVAW would receive considerable attention and thus the administration needed to discredit the organization. A few days later, he reported limited success in a memo entitled "Non-Veterans Demonstration," which summarized his program to smear the VVAW.[62] Colson exulted that we "made ABC news tonight, along with a good shot of Rainwater"(the VFW Commander).

The news summaries compiled by the administration captured the popularity of the VVAW with the networks. All three covered the veterans on their shows on April 20 with CBS offering a "very sympathetic portrayal" of the men at Arlington National Cemetery and NBC spotlighted for its favorable coverage of the Foreign Relations Committee hearings.[63]

The next day's summaries noted that both ABC and CBS led off their broadcasts with the march to the Court, where veterans tried to turn themselves in as war criminals.[64] Eric Sevareid seemed sympathetic, as was Senator Kennedy who was shown commenting on VVAW activities. But ABC and NBC also aired a critique from an African-American hero, General Chappie James, who produced a sound bite that pleased administration media monitors.

Reacting to the generally positive treatment of the VVAW, Pat Buchanan advised Haldeman on April 21 not to throw the veterans off the Mall; "They are getting tremendous publicity," he wrote, from journalists much more sympathetic to them than other demonstrators.[65] This assessment of the media's treatment of the VVAW played a central role in the Justice Department's decision to permit the vets to remain on the Mall.

The April 22 newscasts again reflected a defeat for the administration with analysts noting the coverage for Kerry who was called "eloquent" by ABC, in his "brilliant performance" that was "highly effective."[66] VFW Commander Rainwater appeared to oppose him on ABC and CBS and Howard K. Smith and CBS both noted that the antiwar vets' activities encouraged the enemy, but the analyst was impressed by the Kerry footage on all three channels, as well he or she should have been.

By April 23, a frustrated Haldeman had to admit that the attempts to blunt the impact of the VVAW had failed. The media "by their own obsession created a major thing out of what should have been almost totally ignored." (His assistants gave information about this allegedly scandalous situation to former White House aide James Keogh who was writing a book about the media and Nixon.)[67] At meetings that day, others expressed similar concern. Colson wanted to go on the offensive against the press and its obvious bias in favor of the VVAW and its almost total disregard of proadministration veterans and active soldiers and officers. The small number of antiwar vets were getting far too much publicity. Another aide noted, the "media are killing us—what can we do? . . . [the networks] run the Vets every nite." Another complained, "How can we fight back?" They worried about the "impact of 5 days of Vets as lead story."[68]

The Nixon people's readings of the VVAW coverage were correct. To some degree, one can sympathize with their anger, considering the small number of veterans in Washington. On the other hand, any number of veterans protesting a current war was news in much the same way as the first demonstration in Washington in April of 1965, which drew "only" twenty thousand people, was a major news story because of its novelty and historic dimensions. Moreover, the administration was fortunate that, by and large, journalists did not link the VVAW story with a major problem it confronted, declining morale in the U.S. military in general.

On the eve of Saturday's rally, White House analysts took some comfort in Mitchell's appearance on all three telecasts.[69] They commented on ABC's contention that the veterans were more important than the rally, an observation that was true but, as the compiler commented sardonically, only because the media had built them up. NBC and CBS were viewed as sympathetic to the medal tossers, with Harry Reasoner on CBS heaping praise upon John Kerry. That morning, the aide responsible for looking at the CBS morning news expressed consternation that Fred Halstead had been interviewed without the network identifying him as a leader of the SWP.

Scanning the news reports on the main demonstration the day after it took place, Nixon aides commented that the media were "totally positive for demos"; they were not, however, "anti-Nixon," and the demonstration was written off as "big but w/o balls." They also called attention to the perception that more blacks, suburbanites, and middle-aged types had turned out and that the "movement is a movement again."[70] Looking over the news summaries himself, Nixon was struck by the *Washington Post*'s evaluation of the new mood on the part of the tourists towards the demonstrators.[71]

There was not much good news for the administration in the news analyses of the Sunday papers and the Saturday telecasts. The demonstration "dominated" all the major media that weekend with NBC and CBS offering special coverage. The *Washington Star* talked of a "mighty tide of humanity," as many as five hundred thousand, and the tide was "gentle but giant." One analyst noted that both NBC and CBS focussed on the untrampled tulip beds and that the networks had reported that the attorney general had been wrong in his prediction of violence. Worrisome also was the *Post*'s informal survey of demonstrators, which revealed many first-timers and many who had journeyed more than 200 miles to Washington. Overall, the media monitors saw the networks and the newspapers as presenting a most favorable impression of the events. The administration's evaluations were accurate.

Several days later, its magazine survey for the week of April 26 scored *Time* and *Newsweek* also as complimentary to the demonstration and the veterans with *Newsweek*'s lead story calling attention to the "poignance" of the vets highlighted, as well as its comments concerning the size of the Saturday crowd.[72] However, a monitor was pleased with *Time*'s more flippant view of the festive atmosphere as well as its less than complete support for Kerry. On the other hand, he or she characterized *Time* as generally impressed with the VVAW overall and critical of the administration for its aborted attempt to evict the vets from the Mall. This analysis missed both newsweeklies' general line about the lack of political import of the Saturday demonstration.

Administration complaints about the media were frequent from April 24 to the end of the month. Mort Allin reported angrily to Colson that on the morning of April 24, CBS News showed definite hostility to those who were supportive of the administration while two days earlier demonstration leader Sidney Peck was treated with "deferential respect if not sympathy."[73] Three days later, Colson complained to Haldeman about the "moods created by TV. Two weeks ago, 'Meet the Press' had the VVAW on, [and] Allan [*sic*] Lowenstein was on this week," which meant that for three weeks in row, guests were "beating the antiwar drums. . . . I'm not paranoid, just mad."[74]

Colson was not alone in his consternation. Immediately after the demonstration he asked political observers and officials around the country what they thought of the coverage. These analysts, all friendly to the administration, thought the press was unfair and "overplayed" the story of the vets in particular—the "Washington Post blew the whole thing way out of proportion."[75]

One wonders about those complaints. The veterans' encampment though small was unique and authentic. The Saturday demonstration itself was the largest in history and it was peaceful and non-radical to boot. What did the administration expect the press to do with the two stories?

THE MAYDAY ACTIONS THAT BEGAN ON MONDAY MAY 3 DID not receive as favorable a press. Most journalists, and certainly most Americans, did not sympathize with lawbreakers who tied up traffic and blockaded buildings in order to close down the government, even if they were generally non-violent about their civil disobedience. The *Village Voice* complained that the media treated non-violence as if it were violence in an attempt to convince their readers and viewers that they were not pro-left. The *Voice* concluded sadly that reporters' hostile responses to Mayday demonstrated that principled civil disobedience could not work. The *Guardian*, equally critical of the media, especially their inattention to police violence, was nonetheless more optimistic about the utility of the tactic in the future.[76] Both left-wing weeklies' critiques did not apply to the *New York Times* and the *Washington Post*, whose relatively balanced coverage of Mayday activities was an exception to the rule.

On May 4, the first foray of the Mayday Tribe made the *Times*'s front page with a report that the cadre of thirty thousand was "routed" by the authorities and surprised by the mass arrests. The newspaper was fair in its description of the odd coalition that tried to bring "creativeness, joy and life against bureaucracy and grim death."[77] Its analysis of how Rennie Davis planned to create chaos through militant non-violence was accurate and dispassionate as well.

The next day, the protests vied for front-page space with other major stories including one on the Supreme Court and the death penalty and another on the resignation of East German President Walter Ulbricht. A large front-page picture showed soldiers guarding a detention center filled with some of the estimated 7,000 arrestees. Some disruption did take place in the streets of Washington on May 4, according to the *Times*, with the police and protestors "fighting running skirmishes," but in general it was still business as usual in most government offices.[78]

The protests stayed on the *Times*'s front page for the third straight day on May 6. The main frame again was lawbreaking with another 2,680 arrests noted and an increase in violent tactics used by both sides. The civil disobedience had become less civil. The *Times* was not ready to compare Washington in 1971 to Chicago in 1968, but things were beginning to move in that direction as the police arrested anyone with long hair or a "raffish appearance."[79]

The *Washington Post* was quicker than its New York rival to identify illegal measures used by the police. In its May 4 number, three-quarters of the front page dealt with Mayday, along with a picture of a policeman macing protestors who were sitting in. A banner headline proclaimed the largest one-day arrest in history. Rennie Davis, who was arrested after speaking to the press, was quoted as saying that his group underestimated the government's response and consequently failed in its primary goal.[80] Other pictures showed the authorities using force against the demonstrators, including one of a police dog biting a young person on the leg. A separate story suggested that the police had indiscriminately gassed and rounded up all sorts of people on streets where there was trouble.[81]

On May 5, the *Post* again made the Mayday actions its lead with pictures of demonstrators at the Justice Department accompanying four separate front-page stories. Reporters delineated the legal problems encountered with such mass arrests and how, apparently only inadvertently, errors had been made by harried judges and police personnel. In a human-interest story favorable to the Mayday Tribe, the protestors appeared to be gentle and reasonable young people, including one who brought flowers to the Justice Department "to emphasize nonviolence," a photo caption noted.[82]

The protestors in most of the *Post*'s accounts appeared less hippie-ish and radical than in comparable stories in the *Times*. Both newspapers, however, were rather friendly to them, considering the fact that they were purposefully breaking the law. The two elite dailies' apparent acceptance of uncivil protests on this occasion, compared to earlier ones, may again have subconsciously reflected some reporters' own general exasperation with the Nixon administration.

The wire services were more balanced in their approach. Readers of *The Daily Tribune* received early reports of the May 3 actions that afternoon in a lead wire-service story that announced that the protest had failed and that six thousand activists had already been arrested.[83] The next day, the AP account was again on the front page with a description of tactical changes on both sides. Some troops were being pulled back because the threat had receded, while protestors held an altogether peaceful rally at the Justice Department.[84] By May 5, the story left the front page of the *Tribune* but the procedures employed to arrest and detain the protestors emerged as a major issue according to the AP. Even though the seven thousand arrested on May 3 represented the largest number ever arrested in a single day, two days later, *Tribune* editors buried the story deep in the interior of the paper.[85] Their readers thus received the message that the illegal arrests were unimportant.

Also relying on the Associated Press, the *Macomb Daily* noted the failure of the Mayday protest in its page-one story on May 4. The last line of the account quoted one protestor as saying, "What a bummer." The next day, the AP's tally of ten thousand arrests reenforced the failed-protest theme, with the police using heavy-handed but non-violent means to meet the civil disobedience, which did include a bit of vandalism as well.[86] The tone of the story was generally sad but not far from the mark—the police had won, the demonstrations had been futile, and few citizens approved of such actions. In the polarized United States of the spring of 1971, the great silent majority dismissed complaints of civil libertarians about the violations of the rights of antiwar protestors who were, after all, breaking the law.

Time led off its news section in the May 10 issue with a picture of a young person being arrested at the Justice Department.[87] Other photos showed a mock battle outside Secretary of Defense Melvin Laird's home and a peaceful sit-in at the IRS. *Time* found the latest in the long series of spring demonstrations different, with some of the thirty thousand demonstrators, especially those camped out at West Potomac Park, openly using drugs and engaging in petty theft. These demonstrators, according to *Time*, destroyed the favorable image left by the VVAW and were denounced by other doves. Rennie Davis, however, received some credit for his organizational skill.[88]

By *Time*'s deadline for its next edition, the Mayday story had come to an inglorious end. Near the beginning of its May 17 number, the newsweekly devoted almost three pages to the events of the first week in May, including pictures of arrested demonstrators and nude campers.[89] "Self Defeat for the 'Army of Peace'" blared the headline for the story about that "preposterously ill-organized" bunch of radicals who were absurd to think they could really stop the government. On the other hand, the police did make "thousands of illegal arrests."[90] Yet *Time* found this preemptive tactic superior to merely gassing and clubbing. If anything, the constitutional slights saved more blood than might have been shed. Inside the stockade where protestors were detained, a *Time* reporter described "Ho-Ho-Ho Chi Minh, Ho Chi Minh is gonna win," and "One two three four, we don't want your fuckin' war" chants intoned by young people more petulant than angry, some of whom played frisbee or smoked marijuana in a carnival-like atmosphere. The reporter found the scene sad, with forlorn hippie types and the occasional adult engaging in endless "colloquies."[91] For *Time*, this was the end of the antiwar movement.

Newsweek's lead story for May 10 asked "What Price Protest?"[92] Several pages of pictures showed scenes of violence and marchers with North Vietnamese flags and Mao posters. The newsweekly's reporters noted correctly that the change in antiwar tactics pleased hardliners in the Nixon administration, which had taken a beating the previous week.

The next week, the magazine's cover featured young people under arrest behind a fence and the lead story devoted six pages to "The Biggest Bust" of "peace freaks," but not necessarily violent or angry types.[93] Despite the arrests and the tear gas, like the other media, *Newsweek* did not consider the authorities' responses to be as severe as those that had taken place in Chicago during the nihilistic Days of Rage. The only way to stop the Mayday protestors was to arrest them, the magazine concluded, even though the effective defense of the capital involved violating civil liberties and producing "unequal justice under the law."[94] Among those amendments violated were the fourth, fifth, sixth, and eighth.[95] In addition, reporters found the centers used to confine the protesters unsanitary and unsafe. *Newsweek*'s coverage was balanced, accepting administration tactics but worrying about the cost.

The Mayday protest was quite telegenic. In its lead story on May 3, ABC's evening newscast judged the protest a failure. Although the lively examples of confrontations aired were competitive for a while, the police triumphed in most of them. Moreover, few viewers appreciated the shots of demonstrators harassing unsympathetic suburban motorists and even pulling distributor caps from vehicles in attempts to block traffic. ABC paid little attention in its twelve-minute report to the motivations of the Mayday Tribe. Thus, most viewers had to sympathize with the police and the military compared to the often unkempt-looking young people breaking the law. They certainly must have been disgusted by the several protestors who dropped sacks of manure on the Pentagon doorstep in front of the ABC news team.

CBS also made Mayday its lead story that evening with Walter Cronkite comparing it inaccurately to Chicago in August of 1968. Washington, he said, "faltered" but did not shut down. Most people got to work, a tribute in part to the better training and organization of the authorities over the demonstrators. Viewers saw protestors throwing trash cans in the street, setting up barricades, and slashing tires as the police responded with tear gas. The trash-can throwing and the tire-slashing in particular, which certainly angered many viewers, was not a tactic used by the vast majority of civil disobedients. As usual, the cameras tried to capture the most sensational activities, even if they were not representative. After looking at such sequences, how many viewers sympathized with a lawyer for the militants who complained to CBS about the mass arrests and the conditions in the detention centers including, he said, tear gas used on those already inside the wire enclosures?

On NBC, John Chancellor thought that though the demonstration had failed, May 3 had been a "memorable day." The police, who were congratulated by Nixon, had been effective. NBC used its no-narration technique for several minutes of film showing cars abandoned by demonstrators in streets, trash can and rope barricades, sirens blaring, police chasing, and tear gas wafting over the scenes. Few of those arrested resisted; most were young people and some had been arrested for no reason. During scenes of conflict, one could hear the protestors curse the police as bastards and pigs. The pictures, more than the narration that followed, made one root for the forces of law and order, who here did not appear to be too unlawful in their procedures.

The next day, May 4, ABC again made the demonstration its lead story and, interestingly, its second story was on a Kent State memorial. The protestors were said to have given up, traffic was not impeded on May 4. The newscast covered a sizeable demonstration at Justice as well as the release of many who had been arrested the day before without being charged. There was a suggestion here of indiscriminate arrests. The two-hour rally at Justice was orderly and without incident until the police ordered the protestors to leave. Then arrests were made with only one documented case of a "vigorous nightstick." Eight hundred in all went peacefully into the waiting buses as John Mitchell looked on.

Like ABC, CBS felt that the "heart had gone out" of the demonstrations that day. The police easily scattered the few who tried to impede traffic, as was seen in a shot of rough police tactics. The main part of the lead story that night dealt with the Justice action, for which a permit had not been granted. The demonstrations and arrests that followed were orderly and almost a "youth culture carnival" as those waiting to be arrested danced about to the music of flutes.

David Brinkley on NBC that same evening described the failure of the demonstrators lightheartedly when he quipped that even presidents could not stop the government bureaucracy. The by-then-leaderless Mayday group was disbanding, bereft of new strategies. To viewers, the march on Justice seemed unusually civil with demonstrators stopping for traffic lights. One scene did show an older woman shaking her head as the young people walked by chanting, "One two three four . . ." Mitchell was then seen watching from his office, while the illegal demonstrators sang "Give Peace a Chance." Like CBS, NBC included footage of the almost joyful dance to the waiting paddy wagons after the police ordered the crowd to disperse.

By the evening of May 5, both ABC and CBS had dropped the story from the lead position. ABC examined antiwar demonstrations in other parts of the nation, reporting mostly violent activities. As for Washington, the marchers found "unexpected allies" that day when a large group of federal employees rallied in Lafayette Park. A crowd of three thousand was then shown on Capitol Hill being addressed by four congressmen. ABC recorded their attempt to effect a People's Peace Treaty, one of the first times the reason for Mayday received some play. A score were arrested as Congressman Ron Dellums scuffled with a policeman.

CBS noted that the doves had been invited to the Capitol by four members of Congress. All were gathered to support the People's Peace Treaty. The police began arresting people who were only standing around listening to speeches. During the week, the number of arrests overwhelmed the justice system and created a "legal headache" for the government. Amid charges of illegal arrests, CBS ran footage of hippie-looking internees.

Congressman Robert Drinan (D-MA) was among those CBS showed complaining about police violation of rights that included sheer "lawlessness." The main problem was said to have occurred on Monday, May 3, when even press secretary Ron Ziegler was said to have admitted that illegal arrests did occur, although not many.

NBC led with the Capitol story on its May 5 telecast, showing one demonstrator with a Viet Cong flag and another who was nude, though the vast majority who listened to the congresspeople were peaceful and clean-cut. NBC then moved on to the arrests that had caused the machinery of the justice system to break down. Accepting the protestors' criticism about overcrowding in the detention centers and sloppy paper work, NBC reported that the government had admitted that 80 percent of the arrests were illegal and most of the first seven thousand arrestees improperly charged.

Despite the media's increasing attention to illegal arrests as Mayday week wound down, there is no doubt that most Americans felt little sympathy for the rowdies who tried to close down the government using illegal means. Coming so soon after the VVAW and April 24 demonstrations, the civil disobedience in Washington, no matter how fairly the media portrayed it, was bound to tarnish some of the more pleasant images of antiwar protestors created during the previous month. Of course, by this point, those participating in Mayday were little concerned about demonstrating in order to win over the American public to their cause. They really thought that they could slow or even close down government operations with their tactics. And some even thought they came close to their goal. At the least, one underground journalist participant-observer claimed "that the straight press did a shitty job of reporting" because it underplayed the fact that "it took 6,000 armed cops, soliders, and mp's representing the strongest government in the world" to make 12,000 illegal arrests.[96]

IN GENERAL, THE ADMINISTRATION WAS PLEASED WITH THE media coverage of the Mayday demonstrations. To be sure, Richard Nixon was disturbed when John Chancellor referred to May 3 as "a memorable day" (as evidenced in his marginalia, "Colson note!") and also when on the same newscast NBC noted that some people were arrested just because they were in the vicinity. On the other hand, Eric Sevareid's commentary on CBS, which hailed the police for acting with restraint, earned Nixon's approval.[97] This comment seemed to convince Charles Colson, who on May 5 told Haldeman that the administration had earned widespread support for its demonstration control. "I think this has really turned out to be a great plus for us."[98]

However, four days later, the president was not entirely satisfied. He felt that the administration had been "gun-shy on this issue [disruptive demonstrations] because of our seeing it so closely through the eyes of the Washington press corps." He wanted his people to talk and act even tougher because they appeared too indecisive and weak.[99] Nixon's response is surprising considering the media's view that the administration acted anything but weakly with the Mayday protestors. Of course, the president may have been reacting to the fact that government spokespersons had conceded that there might have been some illegal arrests in the confusion.

AS THE ERA OF MASS ANTI-VIETNAM WAR DEMONSTRATIONS came to a close in the spring of 1971, the media had improved their coverage to a point where it became more difficult to fault them for being routinely unbalanced or unfair as had been the case in the sixties. For its part, the Nixon administration had become more accurate in its analyses of how the media covered the movement. To be sure, the president remained painfully sensitive to any coverage favorable to the movement, even if it appeared in an even-handed account. Nevertheless, by the time the media, the administration, and the doves reached this point in the summer of 1971, the war had wound down to such a degree that whatever the antiwar movement was up to made little difference to most Americans.

9

CONCLUSION

One of the chief myths to emerge from the era of the Vietnam War is that the dovish American media lost the war by failing to report military progress in Southeast Asia while devoting disproportionate and favorable attention to the antiwar movement. Other scholars have successfully challenged the myth of antiadministration biases in reporting from the primary combat theater. In this study, I have concentrated on the secondary—although by no means unimportant—combat theater, the streets of the United States. There the contest was not for turf or body count; it was for the hearts and minds of the American public.

Through marches, rallies, vigils, teach-ins and scores of other activities, antiwar leaders tried to convince Americans, from Main Street to Pennsylvania Avenue, that involvement in the Vietnam War was a mistake. The messages from the doves to their audiences, as conveyed through media filters, were often counterproductive to the development of a broad-based antiwar movement. To be sure, a handful of movement-friendly publications like the *Guardian* and the *Village Voice* offered different filters. But their limited readerships did not need much convincing to oppose American policy in Southeast Asia. This was not the case for most of those who read the *New York Times* or watched the "CBS Evening News," especially during the Johnson administration.

From the first major demonstration in April, 1965, to the wild Mayday activities of May, 1971, the media framed their stories in terms of the size and composition of the crowds attending antiwar events, and especially the absence or presence of violent, bizarre, or countercultural behavior. Aside from reporting that the protestors wanted out of Vietnam, the media virtually ignored the political discourse that served as the centerpiece for most antiwar activities. They rarely exposed casual readers and viewers, who constituted the bulk of their audiences, to the rationales behind protest activities.

Throughout the period, the movement, the media, and the administrations argued over crowd size. Observers on both sides of the parade barricades judged the relative success of each event partly in terms of numbers. Moreover, each succeeding event had to be larger than the previous one in order to demonstrate that momentum was moving in the doves' direction, as well as to maintain media interest. But there was no way to arrive at a consensus about crowd size because the problems posed by determining an accurate count empirically ranged from difficult to virtually impossible.

Most of the time the media accepted police or government crowd estimates as the "official" estimates, and usually used those figures in their headlines or first paragraphs. To be sure, demonstration organizers exaggerated their own crowd estimates, in part to combat underestimates from government officials. Those estimates often appeared further down in the stories.

But this was not the major problem posed by the way the media covered the antiwar movement. After all, aside from activists who kept asking themselves, "How are we doing?" many readers or viewers did not really care whether an event attracted one hundred thousand or two hundred thousand participants. No doubt, they were affected when a reporter undercounted a crowd and then referred to its size as disappointing, something that happened with disconcerting frequency during the period. Nevertheless, the more important frame for those who covered the movement was not crowd size but the sorts of people who were protesting against the war and the types of activities in which they engaged. This frame was related to the size frame in the sense that in order to bring out more and more people to impress the media, leaders lost control of their ability to influence or dictate the behavior of those on their fringes. To attract ever-increasing crowds, antiwar coalitions had to accept everyone under their broad banners, even groups that could—and did—embarrass them.

Print and broadcast journalists concentrated on violent aspects of demonstrations and marches that often did not reflect their true nature. From 1965 through the fall of 1967, when almost all of the disorder at demonstrations involved unprovoked attacks by handfuls of counterdemonstrators against the doves, headline writers and their editors and camera operators and their directors emphasized arrests and physical clashes to a point where readers and viewers had to conclude that violent behavior and demonstrations went hand in hand. Even when events were virtually violence-free, journalists pointed that out at the beginning of their stories or in the headlines, thus reenforcing the notion that demonstrations meant violence. By 1969, especially when sects within the New Left did begin to strike the first blow against property and police, organizers themselves considered the absence of violence as a major criterion of success.

When the media associated instability and disruption with mass oppositional activities, they influenced many Americans who had doubts about the war to remain on the sidelines, out of harm's way. After all, those demonstrations did look dangerous when the television cameras "shot bloody." The decision to stay home was affected as well by administration warnings that upcoming antiwar activities would become violent or that the leadership was dominated by revolutionary subversives.

Even more important, others who would not join a mass protest for any reason but who thought of deserting Johnson or Nixon stayed on board when they reasoned that if the unattractive ruffians the media portrayed were the sorts of people in the antiwar movement, they wanted nothing to do with them or their arguments. If antiwar meant radical and hippie, they supported the presidents.

Journalists usually did point out somewhere in their stories that most uncivil activities took place at the fringes of the action and that the vast majority of protestors were law-abiding. Moreover, they did not accept uncritically the red-baiting tactics employed by the presidents. This is an important matter since many in the leadership of the antiwar movement came from political positions beyond the left of the Democratic party. Indeed, at no other time since the late thirties had Marxists, socialists, and Trotskyists enjoyed such influence. All the same, while not engaging in crude red-baiting, journalists paid disproportionate attention to Viet Cong flags, pictures of Che Guevera, revolutionary and foul-mouthed sloganizing, and beatnik- or hippie-looking young people.

The physical appearance of the protestors was a very important issue as those youthful activists who went "clean for Gene" McCarthy during the 1968 presidential campaign understood. By 1967, most college students from elite and urban campuses, the largest group of foot soldiers in the movement, began to adopt sloppy, long-haired, countercultural fashions that offended many adults.[1] Whether they were politicos in the Mobe or dope-crazed, free-loving hippies of Haight-Ashbury, they all began to look the same from their unruly unisex hair to their tie-dyed T-shirts, torn jeans, and sandals.

Magazines, television newscasts, and newspapers, including the august *New York Times*, are businesses seeking to attract the largest possible audience in order to increase advertising revenues. After a while, large demonstrations featuring speeches from the same talking heads mouthing the same clichés lose their newsworthiness, or if they are newsworthy in the abstract, they presumably no longer interest readers or viewers after the second or third iteration. Photos of people dressed in colorful garb engaging in antisocial activities are interesting and sell papers, even if they have little to do with the main event. Reportage of confrontations between doves and hawks or protestors and the police make for more lively copy than excerpts from speeches by senators or authors.[2] This was especially true for television with its twenty-two-and-one-half precious minutes to cover the entire world's news each evening.

Movement leaders recognized this problem and sought to produce ever bigger crowds engaged in more and more unusual activities highlighted by ever more lustrous speakers and artists. This was the only way to continue to attract media attention, and thus, the attention of public officials and the American masses. The relatively poor coverage of the seemingly impressive Second

International Days of Protest and the April 1969 rallies demonstrate how difficult it was to obtain press interest in the absence of something new or especially big. Ultimately, the demands of the print and broadcast journalists determined the agenda of many movement activities from the sorts of placards that were carried to the time and place of marches and rallies.

To be fair, no one can say for certain what adequate or fair coverage for antiwar activities would have been. Editors' decisions to emphasize certain aspects of those activities, where to place the stories, and how much space to allocate are complicated ones. For the years from 1965 through 1968, even though media coverage was often negative, the fact that such stories appeared on the front pages energized those who participated in mass demonstrations and, at the least, indicated to the rest of the population that the antiwar movement was an important matter. When another generation of editors decided to under-cover the Gulf War peace movement, they led most Americans to believe that it was an unimportant matter.

The media's emphasis on "unpatriotic" slogans and flags, revolutionary rhetoric, and countercultural garb and lifestyles did contribute to the general notion that the country was falling apart in the late sixties and early seventies. Many Americans associated the assault against their value system with the war—maybe their children would "come home," would return to the "happy days" of the 1950s if the war ended. Some movement leaders recognized the possibility that their activities, which sometimes were disorderly and destabilizing, could contribute to an end to the war. As moratorium organizers contended, there would be no "business as usual" until the United States withdrew from Vietnam. But there was also the danger that such an approach could lead to the increased polarization of society and government repression against critics.

There was another audience to which the movement directed its many messages, the Washington leadership. Both the Johnson and Nixon administrations worried about the impact of images of the besieged Pentagon or young people burning their draftcards on other countries. When the media overemphasized the violent aspects of protests, they presented a picture to the outside world of a weak United States, riven by domestic conflict. Such images were not pleasing to movement leaders who were trying to influence Americans to join them, but they allegedly did please the nation's Cold War enemies. Indeed, both Johnson and Nixon expressed concern that those images encouraged Hanoi to fight on until increasingly popular dovish forces compelled Washington to end its intervention in Southeast Asia.[3]

There were differences, over time, in the way that the media covered the movement. By 1968, a majority of the public had decided that America's involvement in the war in Vietnam was a mistake. Prominent national leaders and moderate newspapers and magazines reached a similar conclusion about the same time. Antiwar perspectives, if not all antiwar activities, became more acceptable to Americans. The derided "Vietniks" and "beatniks" of 1965 became the more legitimate "doves."

During the Nixon years, the Moratorium, the Washington demonstration after Kent State, and the VVAW and NPAC Washington protests in late April 1971, all received full and relatively fair coverage from most of the media examined in this study. At the least, the coverage was more positive than that accorded comparable movement activities before the Tet Offensive. In part, journalists may have been responding to the Nixon administration's direct attacks against them, especially the three networks and the *Times* and the *Post*.

However, those events were indeed special. The massive October 15, 1969, Moratorium was an altogether unique event involving as many as three million middle-class Americans, the solemn and civil Washington demonstration after Cambodia reflected the nation's shock over the events of the first week in May, the VVAW's unprecedented guerilla theater provided many moving vignettes, and the April 24, 1971, Washington rally was not only the largest in the nation's history but it was also amazingly peaceful given the violence and vitriol of the period.

This is not to say that the media's coverage of those and other events pleased doves and displeased hawks. As we have seen, newspapers, magazines, and the networks bent over backwards to offer time and space to counterdemonstrators and administration spokespersons. This was especially true for the television stations, which were federally licensed and operated under a fairness doctrine that implied that virtually every Democrat who appeared on the air had to be balanced with a Republican, every dove with a hawk. Thus, for example, although distressed by the media's treatment of the Moratorium, the Nixon administration took comfort in the fact that many of its people appeared on television to offer the White House perspective.

Both administrations also took comfort in the way thousands of regional papers depicted the movement in their wire-service reports. In general, the Associated Press and the United Press International were more consistently proadministration than the seven media focussed upon in this study. They offered enough antidovish photographs and copy to permit local, often conservative, editors to place a spin on stories different from that in the *Times* and the *Post*.

Yet try as they did to ignore the elite media, both Johnson and Nixon understood that the *Times* and the *Post*, *Newsweek* and *Time*, and the three television networks exercised a powerful influence over other media as well as over important opinion leaders in Washington and throughout the nation. Locally edited wire-service copy favorable to the White House in one thousand *Daily Tribune*s meant little when the *Times* and *Post* lined up against the president.

At the same time, the elite media's influence was not unlimited. The Nixon administration's offensive against them convinced millions of Americans that they were unpatriotic and liberal. Even before that offensive, as seen in the public's response to the Chicago Convention riots, a majority of viewers did not always believe what they saw on television or read in newspapers and magazines. It was difficult in the late sixties and early seventies for revolutionary-*looking* young people to come out ahead in any confrontation with the authorities, no matter how the press depicted it.

The two thin-skinned presidents who occupied the White House from 1963 through 1974 were not as sanguine about their many built-in advantages against oppositional mass movements. As we have seen, especially with the media-obsessed Nixon administration, they tended to see more support for the movement in the press than was actually the case. To some degree, this had to do with their need to have universal approval in all the major media outlets. Overly sensitive to the smallest amount of generous treatment afforded their adversaries, they lashed out when reporters did not depict the movement as subversive and unpatriotic. Much of the time, the White House had a lot to be pleased about, even when the *Times* and the *Post* finally adopted antiwar editorial positions.

Most interesting of all in this respect, neither Johnson nor Nixon employed professional journalism experts to analyze the media for them. Political operatives with little understanding of how the media influences the public produced methodologically suspect surveys for their bosses. Frequently, they told the presidents what they wanted to hear by searching for ostensibly negative comments. Furthermore, the television monitors in Nixon's elaborate system often paid little attention to the visual content of the nightly newscasts, thus misunderstanding the likely impact of a story. Both Johnson's and Nixon's often inacurate analyses of media opinion influenced their policies toward the fourth estate, the public, and even the enemy. One wonders what difference, if any, it would have made had professional media analysts been included in the White House entourages. Of course, Johnson and Nixon, untutored in academic media theory, were nonetheless very successful politicians who must have understood something about the interaction between the press and the public in order to get elected time and again.

Much has changed in the media and in American political culture since the Vietnam War era. The influence of the cable networks' CNN worldwide and the existence of C-Span has altered the significance and even role of the nightly network newscasts. In addition, the impressive showing in 1992 of Ross Perot, whom the media generally derided, suggests that the rules of the game for oppositional mass movements may be changing. In that election campaign, Perot and Bill Clinton advocated the institution of electronic town halls where citizens could bring their concerns directly to officials without a media filter. In fact, one in the series of presidential debates, which up to 1992 had employed only journalists as interrogators, followed a town-hall format.

Despite these dramatic changes, oppositional movements can still draw lessons from the experiences of the anti-Vietnam War activists and their attempts to win American hearts and minds. In the first place, mainstream media like those studied here still reflect middle-class, moderate values and still are influential in shaping the public debate. During the Vietnam War era, these media reacted negatively to the prospect of disorder and to political rhetoric that took the debate beyond the wings of either political party. One could see this in their responses to the radical International Days of Protest in 1965 and 1966, Harrison Salisbury's controversial dispatches from an enemy capital in wartime, and the Reverend Martin Luther King, Jr.'s strident condemnation of American imperialism in April 1967.

Such allegedly extreme activities did not offend or worry just the capitalist publishers of the print media or the presidents of the networks. They offended working journalists as well, even though the majority of them were either moderates or liberals. Of all the antiwar activities of the period, their favorites were the televised teach-in of May 1965 and the Fulbright hearings of the following winter. In both cases, reasonable and well-behaved people argued with one another in meeting rooms. No one carried a Viet Cong flag in those locales and no one threatened to leave the rooms to march on the Pentagon or the Justice Department. They were also very easy to cover.

One wonders what would have happened if leaders of the antiwar movement had scheduled more teach-ins and fewer mass demonstrations or if the networks had chosen to air more Foreign Relations Committee hearings rather than "I Love Lucy" reruns. Most likely, the media—and their audiences—would have tired of those bland and scholarly exercises for talking heads once they lost their unique quality.

One could see this reaction in the media's treatment of the dignified November 1965 SANE demonstration, which they liked, compared to the more rowdy and radical First International Days of Protest the previous month, which they did not. Although reporters approved of the way the moderate adult leadership of SANE ran its event, they did not find the event itself especially interesting or spirited.

Any attempt to learn about how to run an oppositional movement from the Vietnam War experience is confounded by the historic image of that experience itself. Even though much of the material in this study refutes the idea that the media favored the antiwar movement, most of those who control the media—as well as most Americans—believe that myth. Thus, one of the lessons journalists have learned is to avoid the appearance of being too favorable, in terms of space and approach, to comparable antiwar protests. This was certainly the case during the 1991 Gulf War crisis.[4] How those who oppose their nation's foreign policy can maneuver around this legacy of the Vietnam War is a difficult issue.

At bottom then, even if contemporary protestors study the Vietnam era for clues about how to get their messages across to the public through the media in the most effective manner, that era has so colored the way the society looks at dovish demonstrators that the first order of business is to show that the media did not present an especially flattering picture of the antiwar movement from 1965 through 1971. And, that, of course, is what this book has been all about.

Beyond correcting this legacy, we also encounter what may be an insurmountable problem in a nation where much of the political debate takes place near the center. Most Americans, including journalists, are leery about marches and rallies sponsored by organizations not associated with the major parties, no matter the cause they advocate. During the Vietnam era, many left-wing politicos contended that mass demonstrations, for all their psychic rewards for participants, were not the most effective tactic. There were too many things that could go wrong that were out of the control of the organizers, not the least of which was unflattering coverage that could produce support for the administration. Perhaps a better approach, as recommended by some strategists, was to devote more energy to the often unglamorous and anonymous activities of grassroots organizing, lobbying, and electoral politics, activities the media could not very easily distort. After all, did not the work in the McCarthy and Kennedy primary campaigns help to produce Lyndon Johnson's March 31, 1968, decisions? Of course, it is unclear whether those campaigns would have been viable without the national mass organizing and demonstrating efforts that preceded them.

The development of oppositional mass movements outside the political mainstream remains a complicated business. A study of the anti-Vietnam War movement's relationship with the media offers interesting but certainly not definitive suggestions for those who agitate for dramatic political change in the contemporary United States.

APPENDIX A

WASHINGTON PRO-CHOICE DEMONSTRATION, APRIL 9, 1989

On Sunday, April 9, 1989, groups opposed to the alteration or overturning of the Supreme Court's *Roe v Wade* decision held one of the largest demonstrations in American history. The gathering of from three hundred to six hundred thousand abortion-rights activists to march and listen to speeches naturally was a major news story for print and electronic media. Like many in the antiwar movement before them, supporters of this demonstration would not be entirely pleased with media coverage. Some of their complaints revolved around the familiar issues of crowd estimates and attention to counterdemonstrators.

On April 10, the *New York Times* made the demonstration its lead story, although its editors did not feel that the huge turnout merited banner headlines.[1] Four photographs accompanied the story. The main shot on page 1 showed a throng carrying banners. The jump page offered three more pictures, one of another large crowd, another of several placard-bearing demonstrators on the steps of the Capitol, and a third of a pro-choice demonstrator engaging in spirited conversation with three pro-lifers. The last of the four pictures is the one that might have irritated demonstration leaders. The *Times* referred to only a few hundred counterdemonstrators out of a total of at least three hundred thousand demonstrators. Why devote any attention to them?

Further, by emphasizing the lowest crowd estimate (three hundred thousand over six hundred thousand), the *Times* may have contributed to the downplaying of the event nationwide. One participant complained to the *Detroit Free Press* about its use of the three hundred thousand figure—"The difference may not be significant except to those, like myself, who stood ready for four hours, marched for another two hours, and stood another hour listening to speakers at the rally. I realize it is routine to take the conservative figure when reporting gatherings of this nature. However, leaving out half the marchers who attended leaves me wondering if political influence was a factor in deciding the tally reported by the media."[2]

Aside from choosing the lowest crowd estimate and devoting space to the handful of counterdemonstrators, the *Times* offered flattering coverage of abortion-rights activists, who were mostly middle-class and who were joined by celebrities, political leaders, and many mother-daughter tandems. The reporter wrote sensitively of the intensity of emotions felt by those in attendance, including scores of people who offered testimony of their own abortion experiences before 1973, when the procedure became legal in the Untied States. Moreover, the main article and an accompanying feature presented many direct quotations from movement organizers and participants concerning their motivations and political agendas.

Television did not treat the march as its lead story that same Monday morning.

There was no comparable event or crisis of similar magnitude that morning, if one is to use the size of the march as a measure of its importance. Nonetheless, the pro-choice march did not lead the 8 A.M. news on any of the four networks (ABC, CBS, NBC, and CNN). It was slightly old news by then, having made the previous evening's editions, but few watch the Sunday evening news and CBS canceled its newscast to carry the completion of the Masters golf tournament.[3]

ABC and CNN led with a story about disturbances in Soviet Georgia, CBS with the ongoing trial of Oliver North, and NBC with continuing clean-up efforts at the Alaskan oil spill. All four treated the demonstration positively in terms of attractive spokespersons and shots of huge crowds.

CBS used the three hundred thousand figure in its voice-over. Even that low figure, according to the quoted organizers, constituted the "largest women's rights demonstration ever." The network also offered a clip of angry exchanges with pro-lifers that was balanced with a bite from actress Lee Grant claiming six hundred thousand participants.

Along with its crowd shots, ABC presented a picture of 4400 crosses and Stars of David that had been placed in the ground by abortion opponents to symbolize the number of fetuses that allegedly are killed each day by abortions. Perhaps that counter-demonstration belonged in the brief story on the march even though it was put together by only a relative handful of people. More important to the editors, it made for a striking visual.

In its story, NBC referred to hundreds of thousands of people who traveled from all over the country from all walks of life, including a ninety-four year old former suffragette.

CNN, which devoted three minutes to the march as part of its half-hour telecast (the other networks' news reports ran for about six minutes at the beginning of each half-hour segment of their morning shows), did not mention the size of the crowd although its pictures gave the impression of a huge number of people. The all-news network offered comments or glimpses of clean-cut college students, two members of the House of Representatives, Reverend Jesse Jackson, actress Whoopie Goldberg, and others. CNN devoted about twenty seconds to the pro-abortion demonstrators and mentioned, but did not show, the symbolic graveyard.

Overall, the media sampled here treated the event favorably although one might question whether it received enough recognition for its apparently unprecedented magnitude. After all, large demonstrations were uncommon in this period and abortion opponents were able to rally only sixty-seven thousand in Washington in January of the same year. Nevertheless, columnist Joseph Sobran, a pro-life supporter, argued that the media bent over backwards to promote the march. He was critical of the advance stories that included directions for travel to Washington, maps, and schedules of events. Further, he noted that few pictures of the pro-life symbol, a poster of an aborted fetus, were carried in newspapers or on television.[4]

Unlike some of the antiwar marches, there is no doubt that the media presented the demonstrators' message clearly. Of course, it was a fairly simple message—people had come to Washington to support the law of the land, the *Roe v Wade* decision, a decision supported by a majority of the population. In addition, all of the media noted one dominant symbol, the coat hanger, which was carried on many placards. That gruesome symbol might have disconcerted some viewers, but that was not the media's fault.

In many ways, little had changed since the antiwar demonstrations. The press emphasized national leaders or celebrities in attendance, paid considerable attention to the counterdemonstrators no matter how minuscule a part of the crowd they constituted, and were unclear about the magnitude of the event. Indeed, on the latter issue, only two of the five sources examined in detail here offered precise crowd figures.

Yet the pro-choice demonstrators, who received extensive if not overwhelming coverage, did manage to get their message out in stories generally flattering to their cause. Of course, that message was more popular than that of antiwar dissenters, as we shall see in Appendix B.

APPENDIX B

WASHINGTON ANTI–GULF WAR DEMONSTRATION, JANUARY 26, 1991

On January 26, 1991, opponents of the initial American military response to Saddam Hussein's August 1990 invasion of Kuwait gathered in Washington for a day of speeches and music. Thousands more than the official estimate of seventy-five thousand doves showed up to support a continuation of the U.N.'s economic boycott and to oppose the U.S.-led coalition's air war, which had begun on January 16. This was the centerpiece for nationwide protests that were highlighted on the West Coast by a crowd of twenty-five thousand in San Francisco. Members of that crowd engaged in conflict with the police that led to one thousand arrests. Despite the sizeable protests against an ongoing war and the fact that three weeks earlier the Senate approved of George Bush's policy by a slim 52–47 vote, there was no doubt that the president enjoyed the backing of a large majority of the American population.

The previous weekend, about twenty-five thousand mostly radical activists had also protested in Washington. The January 26 antiwar contingent was more moderate in its makeup. Having learned from the Vietnam War experience, its leaders made certain that participants carried American flags and also that speakers expressed support for the men and women in combat. Among those who addressed the crowd were Reverend Jesse Jackson, Molly Yard, the head of the National Organization for Women, and Representative Charles Rangel (D-NY).

The media brimmed over with Gulf War news that day, including the fear that a major oil spill would soon lead to environmental disaster. The *New York Times* relegated the demonstration to page 17 and offered only one photograph, that of some doves arguing with a hawk.[1] The story was accurate with its description of seventy-five thousand demonstrators (the Park Service estimate) amid a "blizzard of American flags." Nevertheless, although the reporter noted that the organizers had learned from the Vietnam War, he still saw the event as a "throwback to the sixties." His story, which covered only one half of the top half of the page, was split between the Washington event and antiwar activities elsewhere. Overall, the *Times* piece was perceptive and fair-minded. But why did the editors place it on page 17?

The *Washington Post* put the demonstration on its front page with a photograph of an impressive crowd scene. More important, on three interior pages, along with more pictures, its reporters presented a detailed survey of the backgrounds and views of 827 demonstrators, the majority of whom came from outside the local area.[2] However, in the second paragraph of its lead story, the influential daily reported that its own *Post-ABC* poll revealed that 75 percent of the population backed the president. That gratuitous comment, which belonged on the editorial page, took some of the bloom off the rather generous treatment that the *Post* afforded the protest. It was as if to say, look, place this event in context—the doves are in the minority and do not represent most Americans. Further, the tiny bit of scuffling between a handful of counterdemonstrators and demonstrators in the capital received four paragraphs worth of attention from the *Post*'s reporter. And although the speakers were mentioned, what they had to say was not.[3] In many ways, this was the Vietnam War redux.

One could say the same for the *The Daily Tribune*'s AP account.[4] Of its nine paragraphs buried on an interior page, only one dealt with the Washington protest. Moreover, the editors included only one photograph of the nationwide activities. Like the *Post*, however, the AP did note that organizers disputed the seventy-five thousand official number and claimed that two hundred thousand joined in the march and rally in the capital.

For its part, *Time* magazine simply ignored the protests, even though its issues, which were dominated by the war, contained sections on the "Home Front."[5] *Newsweek* paid only slightly more attention. In its January 28 issue, writers briefly mentioned the antiwar movement, and offered a photograph of arrests in San Francisco. The following week, at the end of a story on the home front, *Newsweek* called attention to "150,000" [*sic*] who rallied on the Mall, but offered no photographs or discussion.[6] This is even more inexplicable than *Time*'s treatment. If 150,000 Americans turned out to protest, should not the magazine have said something about it?

As was the case during the Vietnam War, the *Village Voice* covered the protests in detail and what is more, complained editorially about how the mainstream media went about "silencing the protestors with sneers when not ignoring them altogether."[7] A picture of the demonstration took up all of the cover of the weekly's February 5 issue and the related reportage suggested that the 250,000 organizers' estimate was more accurate than the official 75,000 count. Moreover, the *Voice*'s correspondent noted that demonstration leaders worked hard not to alienate those with sons and loved ones in the Gulf and that in general, the crowd was a "lot more mainstream" than those that appeared at the early Vietnam War rallies.[8] Anyone looking for information about the speeches and political groups involved in this important protest would have been better served by reading the *Village Voice* than the mainstream press.

The Gulf War dominated the news budgets of all three major networks that night with extensive stories on oil spills, the air war, Scud missiles, and diplomacy. NBC alluded to the Washington protest in a half-minute story on protests around the world, ABC "lavished" ninety seconds on a comparable story, and CBS spent twenty seconds on prowar rallies in Albany and Miami as well as antiwar protests in Europe.

To be sure, the war was the news that day, not the protests. Nonetheless, the previous weekend's worldwide antiwar protests, including the radical, much smaller, but perhaps more photogenic demonstration in Washington, had received more attention.

The nation, including previously skeptical congresspeople, had rallied around the president, the air war was going well, and the unprecedented international coalition was holding fast. The antiwar movement was simply not important in the overall scheme of things, at least to journalists and editors who may have remembered the controversy over their coverage of the earlier movement. But by treating the movement as unimportant, by marginalizing it, they contributed to making it unimportant or invisible to the vast majority of Americans, some of whom were not entirely enthusiastic about the war in the Gulf.

ABBREVIATIONS

ANS	Annotated News Summaries, President's Office Files, Richard M. Nixon Presidential Materials Project
AP	Associated Press
CALCAV	Clergy and Laymen Concerned about Vietnam
CNV	Committee for Non-Violent Action
DT	*Daily Tribune* (Royal Oak, Mich.)
GRD	*National Guardian*
LBJL	Lyndon Baines Johnson Presidential Library
MD	*Macomb Daily* (Warren, Mich.)
Mobe	Spring (and National) Mobilization to End the War in Vietnam
NAG	National Action Group
NCCEWVN	National Coordinating Committee to End the War in Vietnam
NEA	Newspaper Enterprise Association
NET	National Education Television
NLF	National Liberation Front
NP	Richard M. Nixon Presidential Materials Project
NPAC	National Peace Action Coalition
NSC	National Security Council
NSCVN	National Security Council File on Vietnam, Lyndon Baines Johnson Presidential Library
NSF	National Security File
NW	*Newsweek*
NYT	*New York Times*
PCPJ	People's Coalition for Peace and Justice
PDS	Presidential Document Series
PL	Progressive Labor
POF	President's Office Files

PPF	President's Personal Files
SANE	National Committee for a Sane Nuclear Policy
SDS	Students for a Democratic Society
SNCC	Student Nonviolent Coordinating Committee
SWP	Socialist Workers Party
UPI	United Press International
VFW	Veterans of Foreign Wars
VV	*Village Voice*
VVAW	Vietnam Veterans against the War
WDT	Willie Day Taylor clipping file, Lyndon Baines Johnson Presidential Library
WHCF	White House Central Files
WILPF	Women's International League for Peace and Freedom
WP	*Washington Post*
WRL	War Resisters League
WSP	Women Strike for Peace
YSA	Young Socialist Alliance

NOTES

1. Introduction

1. For a discussion of its relative effectiveness see Melvin Small, *Johnson, Nixon, and the Doves* (New Brunswick, N.J.: Rutgers University Press, 1988), 20–23, 225–234; and Charles DeBenedetti with Charles Chatfield, *An American Ordeal: The Antiwar Movement of the Vietnam Era* (Syracuse, N.Y.: Syracuse University Press, 1990), 387–408.

2. John F. Mueller, *War, Presidents, and Public Opinion* (New York: John Wiley, 1973), 164–165. William Berkowitz correlated the dates of fifteen antiwar activities with polling data gathered in periods following those demonstrations. The weak correlations he discovered between demonstrations and presidents' Vietnam approval ratings went in a counterintuitive direction. That is, demonstrations were followed by periods in which presidential popularity rose. In his follow-up study, E. M. Schreiber reported similar findings, concluding that there was no evidence that demonstrations affected the development of public attitudes against the war. William Berkowitz, "The Impact of Anti-Vietnam Demonstrations upon National Public Opinion and Military Indicators," *Social Science* 2 (March 1973): 1–14; E. M. Schreiber, "Anti-War Demonstrations and American Public Opinion on the War in Vietnam," *British Journal of Sociology* 27 (June 1976): 225–236.

3. Jerome Skolnick, *The Politics of Protest* (New York: Simon & Schuster, 1969), 23.

4. Laimbeer on WJR radio, "Sportsrap," Detroit, May 28, 1993. In describing why Ron Rothstein had been fired, Laimbeer claimed that there had been no serious problems between the Pistons and their coach until the media began reporting about them.

5. For an informed view of the impact of television on one famous demonstration, see Reuven Frank, "On Tiananmen Square; Echoes of Chicago," *New York Times* (hereafter *NYT*), June 4, 1989, sec. 2, p. 27.

6. Typical is the view of former CIA Director William Colby, expressed in *Lost Victory: A Firsthand Account of America's Sixteen-Year Involvement in Vietnam* (Chicago: Contemporary Books, 1989), which ignores the research of Todd Gitlin, *The Whole World Is Watching: Mass Media in the Making and Unmaking of the New Left* (Berkeley: University of California Press, 1980); Daniel C. Hallin, *The "Uncensored War": The Media and Vietnam* (New York: Oxford University Press, 1986); and William M. Hammond, *Public Affairs: The Military and the Media, 1962–1968* (Washington, D.C.: Center for Military History, 1988). Clarence R. Wyatt, *Paper Soldiers: The American Press and the Vietnam War* (New York: Norton, 1993) and Nicholas O. Berry, *Foreign Policy and the Press: An Analysis of the New York Times's Coverage of U.S. Foreign Policy* (Westport, Conn.: Greenwood, 1990), two more myth-debunking studies, appeared too late for Colby's enlightenment.

7. See Appendix B. In one study of network news coverage of the Gulf War from August 8, 1990 to January 3, 1991, researchers found that only 29 of 2,855 minutes were devoted to antiwar activities. Martin Lee and Tiffany Devitt, "Gulf War Coverage: Censorship Begins at Home," *Newspaper Research Journal* 12 (winter 1991): 20.

8. Hallin devotes some attention to the peace movement in *The "Uncensored War,"* 191–201.

9. An early brief analysis of this issue that criticizes the media for their inaccurate and unfavorable portrayal of the antiwar movement is Nathan Blumberg, "Misreporting the Peace Movement," *Columbia Journalism Review* 9 (winter 1970–71): 28–32.

10. DeBenedetti, *An American Ordeal*, 404. Charles Chatfield, the assisting author, wrote the concluding chapter after DeBenedetti died.

11. Charles Chatfield with Robert Kleidman, *The American Peace Movement: Ideals and Activism* (New York: Twayne, 1992), 143–145.

12. Early in his administration, Bill Clinton also tried to weaken the influence of the elite media by working with other journalistic outlets. *Detroit News* (May 31, 1993): 6.

13. Small, *Johnson, Nixon, and the Doves*, 13. More recently, Bush administration staffers all claimed to read the *Times*, the *Post*, the *Wall Street Journal*, and the *Washington Times*. John Podhoretz, *Hell of a Ride: Backstage at the White House Follies, 1989–1993* (New York: Simon & Schuster, 1993), 55.

14. Because of that readership, the newsweeklies may be even more important in affecting elite opinion than television. Herbert Gans, *Deciding What's News: A Study of "CBS Evening News," "NBC Nightly News," "Newsweek," and "Time"* (New York: Random House, 1980), 221–224.

15. With the arrival of CNN and other cable stations in the 1980s, the nightly network newscasts declined in prominence.

16. The identification of the seven most influential sources of news and opinion, as seen by the White House, is comparatively easy when one examines the daily comments on the media in files at the Lyndon Baines Johnson Presidential Library (hereafter LBJL) in Austin, Texas and the Richard M. Nixon Presidential Materials Project (hereafter NP) in Alexandria, Virginia.

17. For other approaches to sampling and coding media, see Mark S. Rozell, *The Press and the Carter Presidency* (Boulder, Colo.: Westview, 1989), 5–6; and Hallin, *The "Uncensored War,"* 255–273.

18. I am influenced here by Elihu Katz and Paul F. Lazarsfeld, *Personal Influence: The Part Played by People in the Flow of Mass Communications* (Glencoe, Ill.: Free Press, 1955).

19. One interesting attempt to compare news content with editorial posture is Birgitte Lebens Nacos, *The Press, Presidents, and Crises* (New York: Columbia University Press, 1990).

20. At least, this seems to be the philosophy behind the "new journalism" seen in such publications as *USA Today*.

21. Letter to the editor from Sharon McPhail, *Detroit Free Press* (September 27, 1993): 10A.

22. I did use newspapers as well for these reconstructions. Examined with care,

they are still important sources. The best account of the Mayday 1971 actions, for example, was written by George W. Hopkins primarily from newspaper accounts. Hopkins, "'May Day' 1971: Civil Disobedience and the Vietnam Antiwar Movement," in Melvin Small and William D. Hoover, eds., *Give Peace a Chance: Exploring the Vietnam Antiwar Movement* (Syracuse, N.Y.: Syracuse University Press, 1992), 71–90.

23. Although these neighboring papers later combined operations, they were separate institutions during the period under examination.

24. For problems encountered working with original wire-service reports, see Harvey Molotoch and Marilyn Lester, "Accidental News: The Great Spill," *American Journal of Sociology* 81 (September 1975): 239–240.

25. I had forgotten that Todd Gitlin had demonstrated a similar point when he compared the *New York Times*'s coverage of the April 17, 1965, SDS demonstration with that of the *Guardian* in *The Whole World Is Watching*, 52–60. For interesting histories of the *Guardian*, see John Trinkl, "Something to Guard," *Crossroads* 29 (March 1993): 27–31; and Jack A. Smith, "The *Guardian* Goes to War," in Ken Wachsberger, ed., *Voices from the Underground: Insider Histories of the Vietnam Era Underground Press* (Tempe, Ariz.: Mica Press, 1993), 99–106. At its height during the period, the *Guardian* had twenty-four thousand paid subscribers.

26. For the frustrations one researcher encountered dealing with this problem, see Gitlin, *The Whole World is Watching*, 296–305.

27. During the war, the Department of Defense monitored the news programs. Unfortunately for this project, it took very seriously its mandate to cover only military-related news, not the antiwar movement. Thus clips from newscasts, not the entire newscasts, are available in the National Archives. See the comments on this issue by George Arthur Bailey in "The Vietnam War According to Chet, David, Walter, Harry, Bob, Howard, and Frank: A Content Analysis of Journalistic Performance by the Network Television Evening News Anchormen, 1965–1970" (Ph.D. dissertation, University of Wisconsin, 1973), 19–20.

28. The format I have adopted does lead to some repetition as I "call the roll" of the newspapers, magazines, and networks following each demonstration. I could have ignored distinctions among the media and organized my analyses around general themes that appeared in all of them. But had I done that, I would not have been able to demonstrate clearly how the *New York Times* differed from the wire services and *Time* from *Newsweek*, and even how the networks rarely differed from one another. I am as interested in differences among a variety of media sources over time as I am in how the media portrayed the movement.

29. The newspaper of record, the *New York Times*, did run a small story about the three-hundred-person protest on February 11.

30. David Dellinger, *More Power Than We Know: The People's Movement Toward Democracy* (Garden City, N.Y.: Doubleday, 1976), 60; Sidney Lens, *Unrepentant Radical: An American Activist's Account of Five Turbulent Decades* (Boston: Beacon Press, 1980), 367–368.

31. Todd Gitlin, *The Sixties: Years of Hope, Days of Rage* (New York: Bantam, 1987), 41.

32. Dellinger, *More Power*, 8–9, 21, 60.

33. A Vietnamese diplomat is convinced that the movement was more important

during the Nixon years than during the Johnson years. Author's interview with Bui Xuan Ninh, New York, N.Y., June 15, 1983.

34. Small, *Johnson, Nixon, and the Doves.*

35. All of the mass demonstrations that drew more than ten thousand participants are catalogued in Berkowitz, "The Impact of Anti-Vietnam Demonstrations." The key events that I summarize but not survey in detail, are, in 1965: the SANE rally in Washington on November 27; in 1966: the Senate Foreign Relations Committee hearings in February, the Second International Days of Protest on March 25–27, Robert S. McNamara's confrontation with Harvard radicals on November 7, and Harrison Salisbury's dispatches from North Vietnam, which began to appear in the press on December 25; in 1967: Martin Luther King, Jr.'s break with the Johnson administration on April 4, and the New York demonstration on April 15; in 1968: the New York demonstration on April 27, and the Chicago Democratic Convention riots of August; in 1969: the April 5–6 protests; and in 1970: the April 15 nationwide demonstrations.

36. The leading historian of the antiwar movement, Charles DeBenedetti, suggests that the media was an important factor in evaluating the success of the movement. Charles DeBenedetti, "Lyndon Johnson and the Antiwar Opposition," in Robert A. Divine, ed., *The Johnson Years*, Vol. 2 (Lawrence: University Press of Kansas, 1987), 480 n. On the other hand, Michael Mandelbaum concludes that neither the media nor the demonstrations had much influence on public opinion during the war. Mandelbaum, "Vietnam: The Television War," *Daedalus* 3 (fall 1982): 167.

. 37 Herbert G. Klein, *Making It Perfectly Clear* (Garden City, N.Y.: Doubleday, 1980), 418. Another keen observer of the media-opinion nexus feels that even though television obviously transforms events and the way people think about them, it is difficult to determine how. Michael J. Arlen, *The Living-Room War* (New York: Viking, 1969), xi. For a discussion of the complications inherent in an assessment of media impact, see George Donelson Moss, "News or Nemesis: Did Television Lose the Vietnam War?" in his *A Vietnam Reader: Sources and Essays* (Englewood Cliffs, N.J.: Prentice Hall, 1991), 250–252.

38. Small, *Johnson, Nixon, and the Doves*, 41.

39. George C. Reedy, *The Twilight of the Presidency*, rev. ed. (New York: New American Library, 1987), 109.

40. Maxwell McCombs and Sheldon Gilbert, "News Influence on Our Pictures of the World," in Jennings Bryant and Dolf Zillman, eds., *Perspectives on Media Effects* (Hillsdale, N.J.: Lawrence Erlbaum, 1986), 1–14; Christopher J. Bosso, "Setting the Agenda: Mass Media and the Famine in Ethiopia," in Michael Margolis and Gary A. Mauser, eds., *Manipulating Public Opinion: Essays on Public Opinion as a Dependent Variable* (Pacific Grove, Cal.: Brooks-Cole, 1989), 153–174.

41. Lutz Erbring, Edie N. Goldenberg, and Arthur H. Miller, "Front Page News and Real World Cues: A New Look at Agenda Setting by the Media," *American Journal of Political Science* 24 (February 1980): 16–49; Shanto Iynegar and Donald R. Kinder, *News That Matters: Television and American Opinion* (Chicago: University of Chicago Press, 1987), 60.

42. On the importance of lead stories see Iynegar and Kinder, *News That Matters*, 45. For a tribute to the role of the media in putting reform and ultimately revolution on all Eastern Europeans' agendas, see Johanna Neuman, "The Media: Partners in the Revolution of 1989," occasional paper (Washington, D.C.: Atlantic Council, 1991).

See also Robert Sheppard's column, "Lots of Ballyhoo: Not Much Audience," in *The Globe and Mail* (Toronto), (August 18, 1993): A21, for a discussion of how environmentalist protesters in Clayoquot, British Columbia had been unable to draw much media and thus public attention.

43. Edwin Diamond, *The Tin Kazoo: Television, Politics, and the News* (Cambridge: MIT Press, 1975), 165–168.

44. Michael Parenti, *Inventing Reality: The Politics of the Mass Media* (New York: St. Martin's Press, 1986), 89.

45. *Detroit News* (April 25, 1993): 15A; Walter Goodman, "When Gay Images and Reality Conflict," *New York Times* (July 20, 1993): B3.

46. Gitlin, *The Whole World Is Watching*, 146–179, 180–204; John R. Searle, *The Campus War: A Sympathetic Look at the University in Agony* (New York: World, 1971), 22–27.

47. William Small, *To Kill a Messenger: Television News and the Real World* (New York: Hastings House, 1970), xi.

48. Hallin, *The "Uncensored War,"* 197; Gans, *Deciding What's News*, 54.

2. The Media and Oppositional Movements

1. Among those who assail the media for their support for the antiwar movement are Edith Efron, *The News Twisters* (Los Angeles: Nash, 1971); and Russ Braley, *Bad News: The Foreign Policy of the "New York Times"* (Chicago: Regnery Gateway, 1984).

2. David L. Altheide, *Media Power* (Beverly Hills: Sage, 1985), 59; Gans, *Deciding What's News*, 58; Stuart Hall, "A World at One with Itself," in Stanley Cohen and Jock Young, eds., *The Manufacture of News: Social Problems, Deviance, and the Mass Media* (Beverly Hills: Sage, 1981), 147–156; Iynegar and Kinder, *News That Matters*, 128–133; Graham Murdock, "Political Deviance: The Press Presentation of a Militant Mass Demonstration," in Cohen and Young, eds., *The Manufacture of News*, 206–225; Harry J. Skornia, *Television and the News: A Critical Appraisal* (Palo Alto, Cal.: Pacifica Books, 1968); J. Mallory Wober and Barrie Gunter, *Television and Social Control* (Aldershot, U.K.: Brookfield, 1988), 86.

3. Edward S. Herman and Noam Chomsky, *Manufacturing Consent: The Political Economy of the Mass Media* (New York: Pantheon, 1988), 35.

4. Gans, *Deciding What's News*, 42. See also Allan Rachlin, *News as Hegemonic Reality: American Political Culture and the Framing of News Accounts* (Westport, Conn.: Praeger, 1988), 5–33.

5. Lewis H. Lapham, *The Wish for Kings: Democracy at Bay* (New York: Grove Press, 1993), 120–152.

6. Hallin, *The "Uncensored War,"* 197; Gans, *Deciding What's News*, 269. In covering the student movement in general, the networks supported official symbols of authority. Richard A. Pride and Barbara Richards, "Denigration of Authority: Television News Coverage of the Student Movement," *Journal of Politics* 36 (August 1974): 637–660.

7. Gans, *Deciding What's News*, 61. See also Johan Galtung and Mari Ruge, "Structuring and Selecting News," in Cohen and Young, eds., *The Manufacture of News*, 56.

8. Michael Margolis and Robert E. Burtt, "Revolutionaries of the Status Quo: The Denominational Ministry Strategy, the Unemployed and the Powers That Be," in Margolis and Mauser, eds., *Manipulating Public Opinion*, 199.

9. Dellinger, *More Power Than We Know*, 192.

10. Harvey Molotoch and Marilyn Lester, "News as Purposive Behavior: On the Strategic Use of Routine Events, Accidents and Scandals," in Cohen and Young, eds., *The Manufacture of News*, 129. See also Gans, *Deciding What's News*, 150.

11. Maxwell McCombs and Sheldon Gilbert, "News Influence on Our Pictures of the World," in Bryant and Zillman, eds., *Perspective on Media Effects*, 4.

12. Doris A. Graber, *Mass Media and American Politics* (Washington: Congressional Quarterly Press, 1980), 63–65; Mark Fishman, "Crime Waves as Ideology," in Cohen and Young, eds., *The Manufacture of News*, 103; Altheide, *Media Power*, 95, 242.

13. James D. Halloran, Philip Elliott, and Graham Murdock,, *Demonstrations and Communication: A Case Study*, (Harmondsworth, U.K.: Penguin, 1970), 70.

14. Gans, *Deciding What's News*, 92.

15. Ibid., 88; Edward Jay Epstein, *News from Nowhere: Television and the News* (New York: Random House, 1973), 108–109.

16. David L. Paletz and Robert M. Entman, *Media Power Politics* (New York: Free Press, 1981), 130.

17. Gans, *Deciding What's News*, 91.

18. During the Vietnam War era, the costs of covering antiwar *and* civil rights protests "strained the resources of the news organizations." Reuven Frank, *Out of Thin Air: The Brief Wonderful World of Network News* (New York: Simon & Schuster, 1991), 332.

19. See, for example, the many attacks on the media in Colby, *Lost Victory*, as well as Robert Elegant, "How to Lose a War: Reflections of a Foreign Correspondent," *Encounter* 57 (August 1981): 73–90; and Winant Sidle, "The Role of Journalists in Vietnam: An Army General's Perspective," in Harrison E. Salisbury, ed., *Vietnam Reconsidered* (New York: Harper and Row, 1984), 110–112.

20. David Broder talks of the "nearly unanimous" opposition to the war among his colleagues in his *Behind the Front Page: A Candid Look at How the News Is Made* (New York: Simon & Schuster, 1987), 140.

21. Gay Talese, *The Kingdom and the Power* (New York: World Publishing, 1969), 444–445; Joseph C. Goulden, *Fit to Print: A. M. Rosenthal and His Times* (New York: Lyle Stuart, 1988), 156–157; and Robert Sam Anson, *War News: A Young Reporter in Indochina* (New York: Simon & Schuster, 1989), 71. See also Hammond, *Public Affairs*, 49.

22. Gans, *Deciding What's News*, 187; Hallin, *"The Uncensored War,"* 201. The media were hostile to "peaceniks" in the nineteenth century as well. See Sandi E. Cooper, *Patriotic Pacifism: Waging War on War in Europe, 1815–1914* (New York: Oxford University Press, 1991), 77–78. See also James C. Schneiders, *Should America Go to War? The Debate Over Foreign Policy in Chicago, 1939–1941* (Chapel Hill: University of North Carolina Press, 1989), 107.

23. Gitlin, *The Whole World Is Watching*; David Halberstam, *The Powers That Be* (New York: Knopf, 1979), 507.

24. Gitlin, *The Whole World Is Watching*, 80; Gans, *Deciding What's News*, 29.

25. James Miller, *"Democracy Is in the Streets"* : *From Port Huron to the Siege of Chicago* (New York: Simon & Schuster, 1987), 236–237, 402 n. 45.

26. Halloran, Eliott, and Murdock, *Demonstrations and Communication*, 305; Mark Fishman, "Crime Waves as Ideology," 106; Marilyn A. Lashner, *The Chilling Effect in TV News: Intimidation by the Nixon White House* (New York: Praeger, 1984), 46; Robert MacNeil, *The People Machine: The Influence of Television on American Politics* (New York: Harper & Row, 1968), 30; Gans, *Deciding What's News*, 15. Much to their mutual chagrin, *Time* and *Newsweek* often run the same cover stories.

27. Gans, *Deciding What's News*, 180.

28. Even as late as 1989, ABC conceded the impossibility of fulfilling its promise to create a completely live, big-budget, prime-time documentary feature, "Prime Time Live."

29. Small, *Johnson, Nixon, and the Doves*, 12; Lashner, *Chilling Effect*, 7.

30. Bailey, "The Vietnam War," 375 and passim; Paul H. Weaver, "Newspaper News and Television News," in Douglass Cater and Richard Adler, eds., *Television as a Social Force: New Approaches to TV Criticism* (New York: Praeger, 1975), 90.

31. Av Westin, *Newswatch: How TV Decides the News* (New York: Simon & Schuster, 1982), 11. For a recent tribute to the influence of television in affecting decision-makers' agendas, see Patrick O'Heffernan, *Mass Media and American Foreign Policy: Insider Perceptions on Global Journalism and the Foreign Policy Process* (Norwood, N.J.: Ablex, 1991).

32. Richard M. Nixon, *In the Arena* (New York: Simon & Schuster, 1990), 138.

33. Lawrence W. Lichty, "Video Versus Print," *Wilson Quarterly* 6 (1982): 54–55. Another supporter of the importance of print over electronic media is Moss, "News or Nemesis," 254–255.

34. Bailey, "Vietnam War," 61; Lashner, *Chilling Effect*, 151. Not all local affiliates carried national news shows offered by their networks. William Small, *To Kill a Messenger*, 6.

35. Benjamin I. Page and Robert Y. Shapiro, "What Moves Public Opinion," *American Political Science Review* 81 (March 1987): 23–43.

36. Oscar Patterson III, "Television's Living Room War in Print: Vietnam in the Newsmagazines," *Journalism Quarterly* 61 (spring 1984): 35–40. See also Patterson, "An Analysis of Television Coverage of the Vietnam War," *Journal of Broadcasting* 28 (fall 1984): 397–404.

37. Bailey, "Vietnam War," 365–367; Joseph F. Fowler and Stuart W. Showalter, "Evening News Selection: A Confirmation of Judgement," *Journalism Quarterly* 51 (winter 1974): 712–715; James B. Lemert, "Content Duplication by the Networks in Competing Evening Newscasts," *Journalism Quarterly* 51 (summer 1974): 238–244.

38. American diplomats attested to the importance of the ABC coverage. Over an eleven-month period, the network devoted 301 minutes to Bosnia, while NBC and CBS devoted 179 and 177 minutes respectively. *Detroit Free Press* (April 29, 1993): 22A.

39. Halloran, Eliott, and Murdock, *Demonstrations and Communication*, 133.

40. Lashner, *Chilling Effect*. See also chapter 7.

41. Halloran et al., *Demonstrations and Communication*, 306–307. David Altheide drew a similar conclusion in *Media Power* when he compared Associated Press

stories with television news stories. Because of the emphasis upon the visual, television news tends to be more limited than radio news. Sally Bedell Smith, *In All His Glory: The Life of William S. Paley* (New York: Simon & Schuster, 1990), 362.

42. Weaver, "Newspaper News and Television News," 91, 87.

43. Todd Gitlin even suggests that the narrative is more important than the picture. Gitlin, *The Whole World Is Watching*, 265.

44. Thomas Powers, *The War at Home: Vietnam and the American People, 1964–1968* (New York: Grossman, 1973), 73.

45. Chatfield, *The American Peace Movement*, 129.

46. Michael Lipsky uses a slightly different formulation when he suggests that demonstrations are held to nurture the organization, and maximize exposure, impact on third parties, and chances for success with those in government. Michael Lipsky, "Protest as a Political Resource," *American Political Science Review* 62 (December 1968): 1144–1159. Among other things, these "periodic self-satisfying rituals" serve as "psychological breakthroughs" for participants who had up to that point remained on the sidelines. David Dellinger, *From Yale to Jail: The Life Story of a Moral Dissenter* (New York: Pantheon, 1993), 297.

47. Lipsky, 1153–1154; Dellinger, *More Power*, 117; Kim McQuaid, *The Anxious Years: America in the Vietnam-Watergate Era* (New York: Basic Books, 1989), 139–144.

48. Kirkpatrick Sale, *SDS: Ten Years toward a Revolution* (New York: Random House, 1973), 185; Searle, *The Campus War*, 24–25. West Coast Communist party leader Dorothy Healey remembers being carried away by the excitement at several Progressive party rallies in 1948. Dorothy Healey and Maurice Isserman, *Dorothy Healey Remembers: A Life in the American Communist Party* (New York: Oxford University Press, 1990), 110. See also Wini Breines, *Community and Organization in the New Left, 1962–1968: The Great Refusal* (New York: Praeger, 1982), 32–34.

49. Jerry Rubin, *Do It! Scenarios of the Revolution* (New York: Ballantine, 1970), 106.

50. Miller, *"Democracy Is in the Streets,"* 243–244.

51. For the SDS's opposition to more demonstrations even after their successful April, 1965 Washington rally see Dellinger, *More Power Than We Know*, 12.

52. George Reedy, oral history, tape 3, 37–38, LBJL.

53. Gitlin, *The Whole World Is Watching*; Gans, *Deciding What's News*, 171.

54. Public opinion polls after the Kent State killings in 1970 revealed increased support for the president, in part because of the turbulence on college campuses. Dwight Chapin to H. R. Haldeman, June 3, 1970, Polls, 1969–1972 folder, box 22, Chapin files, White House Staff Files (hereafter cited only by name of staff member), NP.

55. Small, *Johnson, Nixon, and the Doves*, 184–185.

56. Halloran, Elliott, and Murdock, *Demonstrations and Communication*, 237; Hallin, *The "Uncensored War,"* 199–200; Robert M. Entman and David L. Paletz, "The War in Southeast Asia: Tunnel Vision on Television," in William C. Adams, ed., *Television Coverage of International Affairs* (Norwood, N.J.: Ablex, 1982), 192–193.

57. Galtung and Ruge, "Structuring and Selecting News," 54.

58. One organizer suggests that a gathering of one hundred in 1958 was a "mass"

peace demonstration. Bradford Lyttle, *The Chicago Anti-Vietnam War Movement* (Chicago: Midwest Pacifist Center, 1988), 8.

59. *Detroit Free Press* (May 21, 1989): 3B.

60. Throughout his book on Berkeley during the sixties, W. J. Rorabaugh expresses frustration at his inability to report with precision the size of the crowds at various events. W. J. Rorabaugh, *Berkeley at War: The 1960's* (New York: Oxford University Press, 1989).

61. It is even difficult to count a stadium crowd. In a stadium that officially seats fifty thousand, ten to fifteen thousand more people might be able to squeeze in bleacher-style.

62. Taylor Branch, *Parting the Waters: America in the King Years, 1954–1963* (New York: Simon & Schuster, 1988), 730.

63. Stanley Cohen, "Mods and Rockers: The Inventory as Manufactured News," in Cohen and Young, eds., *The Manufacture of News*, 276.

64. The same sort of thing happened during the period prior to U.S. entry into World War II. Schneiders, *Should America Go To War?*, 107.

65. Sale, *SDS*, 186 n; Tom Wicker, oral history, 48, LBJL. Wicker describes how during the 1964 presidential campaign he deflated the police estimate of a Johnson rally in San Francisco (a Democratic city), from 500,000 to 350,000, a judgment that irritated the president. See also Lyttle, *The Chicago Anti-Vietnam War Movement*, 48, who tends to split the difference between the police and movement leaders.

66. Small, *Johnson, Nixon, and the Doves*, 244 n. 66.

67. Limbaugh also complained about the brief sound bite chosen by telecasters, which he felt reflected unfairly upon the nature of his fifteen-minute address. Dan's Bake Sale is the name given to a rally of Limbaugh supporters who traveled to Ft. Collins to raise money for "Dan," a listener who could not afford Limbaugh's newsletter.

68. Margolis and Burtt, "Revolutionaries of the Status Quo," 200.

69. During the Nixon administration, White House aide Charles Colson was aware of this issue and tried to organize counterdemonstrators to obtain media time. Paletz and Entman, *Media Power Politics*, 128.

70. See the discussion of this issue in David J. Garrow, *Bearing the Cross: Martin Luther King, Jr., and the Southern Christian Leadership Conference* (New York: Morrow, 1986).

71. Gitlin, *The Whole World Is Watching*, 42, 182; Gans, *Deciding What's News*, 53–54, 150.

72. Molotoch and Lester, "Accidental News," 128–129.

73. Epstein, *News from Nowhere*, 254–256, 176.

74. Wyatt, *Paper Soldiers* 146–148. As Wyatt demonstrates, "shooting bloody" did not mean showing terrible war scenes and mangled bodies, but was merely a colorful term for showing grunts in the field.

75. Daniel Berrigan, *To Dwell in Peace: An Autobiography* (New York: Harper & Row, 1987), 243.

76. David Farber, *Chicago '68* (Chicago: University of Chicago Press, 1988), 38.

77. Vincent Nobile, Jr., "Political Opposition in the Age of Mass Media: GI's and Veterans against the War in Vietnam" (Ph.D thesis, University of California, Irvine, 1987), 20.

.78. Melvin Small, "The *New York Times* and the *Toronto Globe and Mail* View Anti-Vietnam War Demonstrations," in *Peace and Change* 14 (July 1989): 324–349. It is true, however, that Canadian media were somewhat less interested in violence than their American counterparts. Benjamin D. Singer, "Violence, Protest, and War in Television News: The U.S. and Canada Compared," *Public Opinion Quarterly* 34 (winter 1970–71): 612–616.

79. Graham Murdock, "Political Deviance: The Press Presentation of a Militant Mass Demonstration," in Cohen and Young, eds., *The Manufacture of News*, 206–225.

80. Throughout his memoirs, Dave Dellinger notes that most of the demonstrations that he organized and attended were peaceful but that they all attracted provocateurs, crazies, and wild people of the left in their van. Dellinger, *More Power Than We Know*. See also Sanford Gottlieb, "Discussion," in Leon Friedman and William F. Levantrosser, eds., *Watergate and Afterward: The Legacy of Richard M. Nixon* (Westport, Conn.: Greenwood, 1992), 147.

3. The White House and the Media

1. See Klein, *Making It Perfectly Clear*, 197, on how the Nixon administration misinterpreted television coverage of the ABM issue. In a more celebrated case, Franklin D. Roosevelt misinterpreted newspaper reactions to his Quarantine speech in 1937. Dorothy Borg, *The United States and the Far Eastern Crisis of 1933–1939* (Cambridge: Harvard University Press, 1964), 397–398; Travis Beal Jacobs, "Roosevelt's Quarantine Speech," *Historian* 24 (August 1962): 483–502.

2. Broder, *Behind the Front Page*, 163. John F. Kennedy was another who was overly concerned about the influence of columnists. Richard Reeves, *President Kennedy: Profile of Power* (New York: Simon & Schuster), 113–114.

3. On the chaotic nature of media surveying in the Johnson White House, see Peter Benchley, oral history, 35, LBJL.

4. Johnson meeting with three *Washington Star* columnists, November 15, 1967, box 1, Tom Johnson's Notes of Meetings, LBJL.

5. George Christian, *The President Steps Down: A Personal Memoir of the Transfer of Power* (New York: Macmillan, 1970), 6. Johnson considered columnists especially important. McGeorge Bundy to Johnson, February 13, 1965, box 2, vol. 8, McGeorge Bundy's Memos to the President, National Security File (hereafter NSF), LBJL; Meeting with correspondents, October 5, 1967, box 3, Meeting Notes File, LBJL. See also Joseph A. Califano, Jr., *The Triumph and the Tragedy of Lyndon Johnson: The White House Years* (New York: Simon & Schuster, 1991), 159–160.

6. Christian, *The President Steps Down*, 6. According to one story, Johnson did not know very much about the relatively new process of taping television programs until the night in 1966 that he lamented that he had to miss "Gunsmoke" and was informed that it could be recorded for him. From the summer of 1966 on, he used recordings frequently, especially for the Sunday afternoon news shows. David Culbert oral history interview with George Christian, 2, LBJL.

7. Dan Rather, oral history, 23–26, LBJL. John F. Kennedy was also known to call or have his aides call television stations during broadcasts. Reeves, *President Kennedy*, 300.

8. Doris Kearns, *Lyndon Johnson and the American Dream* (New York: Signet, 1977), 7.

9. George Christian, oral history, tape 2, 14–15; Culbert interview with Christian, 5, LBJL. For Johnson's likes and dislikes among columnists see George Reedy, oral history, tape 3, 39–40, LBJL.

10. Robert Kintner to Johnson, November 2, 1966, box 72, ND19CO312 confidential, LBJL. See also a leak of a Lou Harris poll in a memo from Hayes Redmon, June 17, 1965, box 80, PR 15–4 E, confidential, LBJL.

11. George E. Reedy, *Lyndon Johnson: A Memoir* (New York: Andrews and McMeel, 1982), 5. Similarly, during the presidential campaign of 1992, Ross Perot suggested that reporters tried to write the most sensational stories possible in order to earn bonuses and promotions.

12. George Reedy titles a chapter on Johnson's press relations, "A Gap of Understanding," in his *Lyndon B. Johnson*, 59–69.

13. Harry McPherson, *A Political Education* (Boston: Little, Brown, 1972), 265.

14. Interview by author with George Christian, February 20, 1989, Austin, Texas; Christian, *The President Steps Down*, 6.

15. On August 25, 1965, for example, she clipped and pasted on paper the following: a column by Philip Geyelin from the *Wall Street Journal*, columns from the *Herald Tribune* and the *Baltimore Sun*, excerpts from a white paper that the *New York Times* published, Max Frankel's column in the same paper along with the front page, and stories from the *Daily News*, the *Washington Post*, and the *Washington News*. Box 174, Taylor clipping file (hereafter WDT), LBJL.

16. Office Files of Fred Panzer, LBJL.

17. Christian, oral history, tape 2, 20, LBJL. See also significant events reports in box 83, 1967, 1968, PR 18, confidential, White House Central Files (hereafter WHCF), LBJL.

18. Kearns, *Lyndon Johnson*, 335; Roche to Johnson, January 10, 1967, box 223, ND19 CO312, LBJL. See also, for example, McGeorge Bundy to Johnson, February 14, 1965, box 2, vol. 8, McGeorge Bundy Memos to the President, NSF, LBJL.

19. See Eugene Pulliam to Jack Valenti, February 1, 1966, box 219, ND19CO 312, LBJL.

20. Mentioning these sources as well as two wire services and two pollsters, Johnson told Spiro T. Agnew, "They're all so damned big they think they own the country." Quoted in Halberstam, *The Powers That Be*, 596. See also for Johnson's concern about several columnists, Christian, *The President Steps Down*, 186; and Turner, *Lyndon Johnson's Dual War*, 56–58. For a notion of which other newspapers might have been important, see Dixon Donnelly's survey of editorials in thirty-three "outstanding" newspapers, in Donnelly to Christian, May 19, 1967, reel 7, "Vietnam, the Media, and Public Support for the War," Presidential Document Series (hereafter PDS) (Frederick, Md.: University Publications of America, 1986). On the other hand, Christian remembers that he rarely devoted much attention to newspapers beyond those from the East Coast. Author interview with Christian.

21. Christian, *The President Steps Down*, 192, 207.

22. Stewart Alsop, oral history, 7–8, LBJL.

23. Culbert interview with George Christian, 7, LBJL.

24. George Christian to Colonel Albright, July 7, 1967, UT 1–1. WHCF, LBJL;

Peter Benchley, oral history, 42–43, LBJL; Box 128, Office Files of Fred Panzer, LBJL. See also R. C. Bowman to Walt Rostow, November 17, 1967, box 98, National Security Council (hereafter NSC) country file, Vietnam (hereafter NSCVN), LBJL, for a survey of 26 newspaper editorials on bombing in Vietnam, and Rostow to Johnson, November 28, 1967, box 99, ibid., for another survey of editorial opinion.

25. Bundy to Johnson, March 29, 1965, vol. 9, McGeorge Bundy Memos to the President, NSF, LBJL. See also July 1, 1965, ibid., for an incomplete but extensive list of Bundy's press contacts during the month of June.

26. See the entire file in PR 3, WHCF, LBJL for criticism of the media and their responses; Rostow to Johnson, October 20, 1967, box 99, NSCVN, LBJL.

27. Turner, *Lyndon Johnson's Dual War*, 209; Kearns, *Lyndon Johnson and the American Dream*, 331.

28. Johnson's meeting with Max Frankel, September 20, 1967, box 3, Meeting Notes File, LBJL; Johnson's meeting with Australian Broadcast group, September 20, 1967, ibid. See also, Benchley, oral history, 45, LBJL.

29. Bundy to Johnson, February 14, 1965, vol. 8, box 2, McGeorge Bundy Memos to the President, NSF, LBJL; Benchley, oral history, 3; Katherine Graham, oral history, 25–26, 35, LBJL. See also, Carol Felsenthal, *Power, Privilege, and the Post: The Katherine Graham Story* (New York: G. P. Putnam's Sons, 1993), 239–244, 255–260.

30. Halberstam, *The Powers That Be*, 429–430; Turner, *Lyndon Johnson's Dual War*, 223.

31. Barry Zorthian quoted in Kim Willenson, *The Bad War: An Oral History of the Vietnam War* (New York: New American Library, 1987), 183.

32. Benchley, oral history, 42–43, LBJL. At NBC, Chet Huntley was personally pro-Johnson and David Brinkley was more skeptical about the president. Gans, *Deciding What's News*, 198.

33. For difficulties in evaluating mail, see Larry Levinson to Joseph Califano, February 12, 1966, box 219, ND19CO312, LBJL, and Califano to Johnson, February 24, 1966, box 9, WH 5–1, LBJL.

34. William E. Porter, *Assault on the Media: The Nixon Years* (Ann Arbor: University of Michigan Press, 1976), 27–28, 35; Joseph Spear, *Presidents and the Press: The Nixon Legacy* (Cambridge: MIT Press, 1984), 68.

35. H. R. Haldeman to Pat Buchanan, October 23, 1969, memos to Pat Buchanan, box 53, Haldeman files, NP; John Ehrlichman, *Witness to Power* (New York: Simon & Schuster, 1982), 332.

36. Ehrlichman, *Witness to Power*, 266.

37. See the discussion of this issue in Haldeman to Buchanan, July 10, 1969, in Bruce Oudes, ed., *From: The President: Richard Nixon's Secret Files* (New York: Harper & Row, 1989), xii.

38. Pat Buchanan to Haldeman, May 6, 1971, box 1, Buchanan files, NP.

39. Richard Tanner Johnson, *Managing the White House: An Intimate Study of the Presidency* (New York: Harper & Row, 1974), 219–220; Spear, *Presidents and the Press*, 67; Porter, *Assault on the Media*, 57–59; Daniel Schorr, *Clearing the Air* (Boston: Houghton Mifflin, 1977), 33.

40. Haldeman to Klein, July 8, 1969, Haldeman folder 1, box 1, Klein files, NP.

41. Spear, *Presidents and the Press*, 67.

42. Colson to Anderson, April 12, 1971, box 1, Buchanan files, NP.

43. Stephen E. Ambrose, *Nixon: The Triumph of a Politician, 1962–1972* (New York: Simon & Schuster, 1989), 248–251.

44. Magruder to Haldeman, early 1971, box 4, Buchanan files, NP.

45. Haldeman to Ehrlichman, Ronald Ziegler, Klein, Kissinger, and Bryce Harlow, July 21, 1969, in Oudes, ed., *From: The President*, 36–37.

46. Even professionals make this error. Frank, *Out of Thin Air*, 41.

47. Alexander Butterfield to Nixon, October 7, 1969, November 1969 folder, box 138, Memoranda for the President, Haldeman files, NP.

48. Haldeman to Buchanan, October 23, 1969, box 53, H. R. Haldeman Memos to Buchanan, Haldeman files, NP; Nixon to Haldeman, November 24, 1969, box 1, President's Personal Files (hereafter PPF), NP; Nixon to Haldeman, May 11, 1970, 1970 folder, box 138, Memos from the President, Haldeman files, NP.

49. Haldeman to Magruder, February 4, 1970, in Spear, *Presidents and the Press*, 101; Raymond Price, *With Nixon* (New York: Viking, 1977), 181–182; Nixon to Ehrlichman, February 5, 1969 and Colson to Haldeman, August 16, 1971, in Oudes, ed., *From: The President*, 310. For an example of a successful campaign of unspontaneous letters from College Republicans in *Newsweek*, see Klein to Nixon, October 30, 1969, Memos to the President, box 3, Klein files, NP.

50. Porter, *Assault on the Media*, 60; Spear, *Presidents and the Press*, 144–146; Haldeman to Buchanan, September 9, 1969, in Oudes, ed., *From: The President*, 41. Interestingly, in an earlier period, George Christian also thought that ABC was the fairest network. Christian, *The President Steps Down*, 196. By 1970, even ABC adopted an antiwar perspective. Gitlin, *The Whole World Is Watching*, 218.

51. Seymour M. Hersh, "Nixon's Last Cover-up: The Tapes He Wants the Archives to Suppress," *New Yorker* (December 14, 1992): 92.

52. Colson to Haldeman, September 25, 1970, press and media folder 1, box 141, Haldeman files, NP. See also Julius Duscha, "The White House Watch Over TV and the Press," *New York Times Magazine* (August 20, 1972): 9, for Buchanan's comments. CBS head William Paley reported that Colson was polite, not threatening. Paley, *As It Happened*, 241.

53. Charles Colson, oral history, 39, 40, NP.

54. Ziegler to Haldeman, November 25, 1969, box 141, Press and Media File 2, part 2, Haldeman files, NP; Klein to Nixon, December 5, 1969, ibid. For an exhaustive list of the slants of national columnists compiled for Nixon, see Klein to Haldeman, June 11, 1969, Haldeman folder 1, box 1, Klein files, NP.

55. Price, *With Nixon*, 150, 183; Klein, *Making It Perfectly Clear*, 285.

56. Colson to Haldeman, April 5, 1972, box 95, Haldeman files, NP.

57. Price to Higby, February 5, 1971, box 129, ibid.

4. The Launching of a Movement

1. Quoted in Powers, *The War at Home*, 93.

2. *Washington Post* (hereafter *WP*), (November 28, 1965): 1.

3. DeBenedetti, *An American Ordeal*, 111–112; Nancy Zaroulis and Gerald Sullivan, *Who Spoke Up? American Protest against the War in Vietnam, 1963–1975* (Garden City, N.Y.: Doubleday, 1984), 38–43, 73–76; Gitlin, *The Whole World Is*

Watching, 46–60; Gitlin, *The Sixties*, 81–86; Sale, *SDS*, 185–194; Miller, *"Democracy Is in the Streets,"* 231–234; Fred Halstead, *Out Now: A Participant's Account of the American Movement against the Vietnam War* (New York: Monad Press, 1978), 36–44; Dellinger, *From Yale to Jail*, 194–199; Gregory Nevala Calvert, *Democracy from the Heart: Spiritual Values, Decentralism, and Democratic Idealism in the Movement of the 1960s* (Eugene, Ore.: Communitas Press, 1991), 151–156.

    4. *NYT* (April 17, 1965): 3.

    5. *NYT* (April 18, 1965): 3.

    6. Lapham, *The Wish for Kings*, 159. For a critique of the way the media misreported the massive July 12, 1982 anti-nuclear demonstrations and how they ignored "its causes and political ramifications [and] the substance of its speeches," see Robert Spiegelman, "Media Manipulation of the Movement," *Social Policy* 13 (summer 1982), 9–16.

    7. Hallin, *"The Uncensored War,"* 88.

    8. Gitlin, *The Whole World Is Watching*, 46–59, 75.

    9. *WP* (April 18, 1965): 1, 18. The figure of sixteen thousand came from the Park police; none was reported from the leaders of the march in this instance.

    10. *The Daily Tribune* (hereafter *DT*), (April 17, 1965): 1.

    11. At a peace demonstration in Boston that same year, NBC reporter Sander Vanocur told Lewis Bateman, a well-dressed young man, that he was not a candidate for an interview because the network was not interested in people who looked like him. Author interview with Bateman, Washington, D.C., June 21, 1991.

    12. *National Guardian* (hereafter *GRD*), (April 24, 1965): 1, 4.

    13. Bundy to Johnson, April 14, 1965, box 9, McGeorge Bundy's Memos to the President, NSF, LBJL.

    14. Valenti to Johnson, April 19, 1965, box 357, PR 18, LBJL.

    15. Mail Summaries, box 1, WHCF, LBJL.

    16. DeBenedetti, *An American Ordeal*, 107–108; Powers, *The War at Home*, 61; Halstead, *Out Now*, 50–54; Louis Menashe and Ronald Radosh, eds., *Teach-Ins U.S.A.: Reports, Opinions, Documents* (New York: Praeger, 1967).

    17. Small, *To Kill a Messenger*, 111.

    18. The figure of seven hundred probably came from the membership of the group that put together the teach-in. Bundy later agreed to appear at another teach-in, a one-hour televised debate at Georgetown University on June 21, where his opposite number was University of Chicago political scientist, Hans Morgenthau. For discussion of this event, see Small, *To Kill a Messenger*, 111–112.

    19. *NYT* (May 16, 1965): 1, 62.

    20. *NYT* (May 17, 1965): 30–31.

    21. *WP* (May 16, 1965): 1, 21.

    22. Ibid., 23.

    23. *DT* (May 15, 1965): 1.

    24. *DT* (May 17, 1965): 12.

    25. *Newsweek* (hereafter *NW*) (May 24, 1965): 28.

    26. *Time* (May 21, 1965): 25.

    27. Cooper to Valenti, May 17, 1965, reel 6, PDS, NP.

    28. Rostow to Rusk, May 17, 1965, box 18, files of McGeorge Bundy, NSF, LBJL.

29. Box 174, WDT.

30. Small, *Johnson, Nixon, and the Doves*, 50–51.

31. Box 1, Mail Summaries, LBJL; poll figures found throughout Small, *Johnson, Nixon, and the Doves*.

32. DeBenedetti, *An American Ordeal*, 125–127; Gitlin, *The Whole World Is Watching*, 85–87; Zaroulis and Sullivan, *Who Spoke Up?* 56; Halstead, *Out Now*, 68–91; Powers, *The War at Home*, 85–88; Sale, *SDS*, 288–331; Rorabaugh, *Berkeley at War*, 95–98.

33. Women in general rarely received leadership designations from the media despite their often central roles in the movement. See the articles by Amy Swerdlow, Alice Echols, and Nina Adams on the subject in Small and Hoover, eds., *Give Peace a Chance*, 159–198.

34. *NYT* (October 16, 1965): 1, 2.

35. Sale, *SDS*, 228.

36. *NYT* (October 17, 1965): 1, 43.

37. *WP* (October 16, 1965): 1, 12.

38. *WP* (October 17, 1965): 1.

39. For a discussion of the attempt by Walter Lippmann, who was antiwar, to get rid of Wiggins earlier than 1968, see Ronald Steel, *Walter Lippmann and the American Century* (New York: Vintage, 1981), 571.

40. *DT* (October 16, 1965): 1.

41. *DT* (October 18, 1965): 12, 15.

42. Ibid., 15.

43. *Macomb Daily* (hereafter *MD*), (October 16, 1965): 1.

44. *MD* (October 18, 1965): 6

45. *Village Voice* (hereafter *VV*), (October 21, 1965): 3. The *Voice* began publication in 1956 devoted primarily to its New York neighborhood. In 1965, it was still a very slender, mostly cultural newsweekly with little space devoted to political news. With the rise of the New Left, the antiwar movement, and the counterculture, it became much thicker and much less parochial with a readership, by subscription, extending throughout the United States.

46. *GRD* (October 23, 1965): 1, 6.

47. *NW* (October 25, 1965): 98.

48. See also, ibid., 30.

49. *NW* (November 1, 1965): 25, 31.

50. Ibid., 25–26, 31–34.

51. Ibid., 26.

52. Ibid., 31.

53. Ibid., 32.

54. *Time* (October 22, 1965): 25.

55. This advance report also included mention of demonstrations in Madison and New York, as well as a statement from Senator Dodd that the leadership of the demonstration had passed from "moderates to Communists and other extremist elements."

56. Gitlin, *The Whole World Is Watching*, 94.

57. September 16, 1965 memo, box 196, NSCVN, LBJL.

58. Box 174, WDT, LBJL.

59. Box 1, Mail Summaries, LBJL.

60. DeBenedetti, *An American Ordeal*, 131–132; Gitlin, *The Whole World Is Watching*, 116–123; Powers, *The War at Home*, 89–93; Halstead, *Out Now*, 93–94, 112–115; Zaroulis and Sullivan, *Who Spoke Up?* 63–66; Sale, *SDS*, 242–244; Dellinger, *From Yale to Jail*, 204–208.

61. Dellinger, *From Yale to Jail*, 206.

62. *NYT* (October 28, 1965): 1; *WP* (October 28, 1965): 1. See also *NW* (December 6, 1965): 28–29; and *Time* (December 3, 1965): 27.

63. *GRD* (December 4, 1965): 1,4,6.

64. Lee White to Bill Moyers, December 2, 1965, box 357, PR 18; poll, December 14, 1965, box 346, PR 18; boxes 174 and 175, WDT; box 180, Office Files of Fred Panzer, LBJL.

65. Cooper to Bundy, November 27, 1965, box 57, Hu-4 Freedoms, confidential, LBJL.

5. From Fulbright to the Pentagon

1. Norman Mailer, *The Armies of the Night: History as Novel, The Novel as History* (New York: New American Library, 1968), 297–298.

2. *NYT* (October 23, 1967): 1.

3. Box 180, Panzer files, LBJL.

4. Small, *Johnson, Nixon, and the Doves*, 78–81; Hammond, *Public Affairs*, 247–250, Zaroulis and Sullivan, *Who Spoke Up?* 71–77; Halberstam, *The Powers That Be*, 503–507; Powers, *The War at Home*, 109–116; Friendly, *Due to Circumstances Beyond Our Control*, 212–265.

5. Zaroulis and Sullivan, *Who Spoke Up?* 75; Hallin, *"The Uncensored War,"* 192.

6. Hayes Redmon to Bill Moyers, February 27, 1966, box 71, ND19CO312 confidential, LBJL.

7. *NYT* (February 9, 1966): 1; *WP* (February 9, 1966): 1.

8. *NW* (February 21, 1966): 27. See also *Time*, which took the administration's side, quoting Truman on Fulbright as an "overeducated Oxford s.o.b." (February 18, 1966): 22.

9. Richard Berlin (the president of the Hearst corporation) to Johnson, February 21, 1966, and Ernest K. Lindley to Jack Valenti, March 4, 1966, box 432, FG 431 F, LBJL; Mail Summaries, box 1, LBJL. The administration was so proud of Rusk's and Taylor's performances that it used them in newsreels made for distribution in Europe. Hammond, *Public Affairs*, 248–249.

10. Reedy to Johnson, February 17, 1966, box 80, ND19CO312, LBJL.

11. Zaroulis and Sullivan, *Who Spoke Up?* 79–80; Powers, *The War at Home*, 169; Halstead, *Out Now*, 139–144; DeBenedetti, *An American Ordeal*, 149–150.

12. Powers, *The War at Home*, 121.

13. *NYT* (March 25, 1966): 3, (March 26, 1966): 1; *WP* (March 26, 1966): 8, (March 27, 1966): 1. See also *DT* (March 26, 1966): 1; and *MD* (March 26, 1966, March 28, 1966): 1, 6.

14. *NW* (April 4, 1966): 32, (April 11, 1966): 34.

15. In its April 8 number (p.28), *Time* did run a brief story about how patriots in South Boston beat up several draft-card burners but did not mention the International Days of Protest.

16. *VV* (March 31, 1966): 1, 18–19.

17. *GRD* (April 2, 1966): 1–6.

18. Box 347, PR 16, LBJL. See also clippings for March 28 and 29, 1966, box 202, WDT, LBJL. The International Days of Protest was one of those rare demonstrations that produced more dovish than hawkish mail in the White House mail bags, however. Mail Summaries, box 1, LBJL. The Defense Department did not register comparable tallies. Califano to Johnson, April 7, 1966, box 9, WH 5–1, LBJL.

19. Zaroulis and Sullivan, *Who Spoke Up?* 94–96; Steve Kelman, *Push Comes to Shove* (Boston: Houghton Mifflin, 1970), 54–61; Powers, *The War at Home*, 135–137.

20. *NYT* (November 8, 1966): 1, (November 9, 1966): 3; *WP* (November 8, 1966): 1; *NW* (November 21, 1966): 50–51; *Time* (November 18, 1966): 95.

21. Harrison E. Salisbury, *A Time of Change: A Reporter's Tale of Our Time* (New York: Harper & Row, 1988), 116–183; Talese, *The Kingdom and the Power*, 446–451; Hammond, *Public Affairs*, 247–279; Goulding, *Confirm or Deny*, 52–92; Joseph C. Goulden, *Fit to Print*, 142–145; James Boylan, "Survey: A Salisbury Chronicle," *Columbia Journalism Review* 5 (winter 1966–67): 10–14; Wyatt, *Paper Soldiers*, 153–155.

22. Goulding, *Confirm or Deny*, 92. Goulding also wrote that no story during his four years in office "so disturbed me, and none so disturbed my associates in government," 79.

23. *WP* (December 28, 1966): 1.

24. Harrison E. Salisbury, oral history, 31, LBJL.

25. *NYT* (December 28, 1966): 1–4.

26. *Time* (January 6, 1967): 14. *Newsweek* was more favorable to Salisbury in its January 9, 1967 issue, 17–18.

27. *GRD* (November 7, 1967): 1–2.

28. Tom Johnson to Lyndon Johnson, January 10, 1967, box 348, PR 16 and Dixon Donnelly to Bill Moyers, January 12, 1967, box 223, ND19CO312, LBJL. William Hammond, in *Public Affairs*, 276–277, saw the press as more evenly split while James Aronson agreed with the State Department in *The Press and the Cold War* (Indianapolis: Bobbs-Merrill, 1970), 255–258.

29. Rostow to Johnson, box 7, Rostow Memos, NS File Name file, LBJL; Boylan, "Survey," 13; Goulding, *Confirm or Deny*, 13.

30. For information on this campaign and how it contributed to disillusionment after the Tet Offensive in 1968, see Small, *Johnson, Nixon, and the Doves*, 122–124.

31. DeBenedetti, *An American Ordeal*, 172–174; Zaroulis and Sullivan, *Who Spoke Up?* 108–111; Powers, *The War at Home*, 160–163; Herbert Shapiro, "The Vietnam War and the American Civil Rights Movement," *Journal of Ethnic Studies* 16 (winter 1989): 117–141.

32. *NYT* (April 5, 1967): 1; *WP* (April 5, 1967): 1,13. See also *DT*, (April 5, 1967): 36.

33. *NW* (April 14, 1967): 32; *Time* (April 10, 1967): 32.

34. On the importance of "inflammatory" rhetoric to maintain group morale, see Margolis and Burtt, "Revolutionaries of the Status Quo," 199.

35. DeBenedetti, *An American Ordeal*, 174–177; Zaroulis and Sullivan, *Who Spoke Up?* 110–116; Powers, *The War at Home*, 181–184; Sale, *SDS*, 322–333;

Dotson Rader, *I Ain't Marchin' Anymore* (New York: David McKay, 1969), 17–34; Halstead, *Out Now*, 271–286.

36. Dotson Rader describes violent actions in which he took part with revolutionary contingents that chose not to follow the parade route or marshals' orders. Rader, *I Ain't Marchin'*, 29–34.

37. *GRD* (April 22, 1967): 1–2.

38. Ibid., 3. See also *VV* (April 20, 1967): 1, 31. Perhaps because the *Voice* was becoming more and more a mass circulation publication (and thus more commercial?), it tended to be a bit more colorful than the *Guardian*. For example, on this occasion, unlike the more sectarian *Guardian*, it devoted more attention to Stokely Carmichael's flamboyant speech than to King's gentler oration.

39. *NYT* (April 16, 1967): 1; *WP* (April 16, 1967): 1.

40. *DT* (April 17, 1967): 14.

41. *NW* (April 24, 1967): 27–28; *Time* (April 21, 1967): 20. For comments on *Time*'s conservatism in this period, see Hans Koning, *Nineteen Sixty-Eight: A Personal Report* (New York: Norton, 1987), 22.

42. Marvin Watson to Johnson, April 16, 1967, box 54, HU-4 Freedoms, confidential, LBJL. For a contrary view, see the report of Margaret Mead through Walt Rostow to the president. Rostow to Johnson, April 26, 1967, reel 6, PDS.

43. Mail Summaries, box 2, LBJL. See also WDT, box 234, LBJL.

44. Mailer, *The Armies of the Night*; Anti-Vietnam Demonstrations of October 21–22, 1967, Personal Papers of Warren Christopher, LBJL; David Caute, *Sixty-Eight: The Year of the Barricades* (London, U.K.: Hamish Hamilton, 1988), xi–xv; DeBenedetti, *An American Ordeal*, 196–199; Powers, *The War at Home*, 232–243; Zaroulis and Sullivan, *Who Spoke Up?* 135–142; Sale, *SDS*, 383–387; Calvert, *Democracy from the Heart*, 244–254; Halstead, *Out Now*, 333–340; Russ Braley, *Bad News*, 289–290; Rader, *I Ain't Marchin' Anymore*, 61–74; Goulding, *Confirm or Deny*, ix–x.

45. Small, *Johnson, Nixon, and the Doves*, 122–124.

46. Dellinger, *From Yale to Jail*, 311–312.

47. Mailer thought the crowd was half as large as that which attended the 1963 civil rights march in Washington. Mailer, *Armies of the Night*, 115.

48. Ibid., 281.

49. Dellinger, *More Power Than We Know*, 126.

50. Press release, November 13, 1967, box 29, Ramsey Clark papers, LBJL.

51. Press release, October 25, 1967, Anti-Vietnam Demonstrations, Christopher papers, LBJL.

52. Mailer, *The Armies of the Night*, 243. See also Mailer's report of Dellinger worrying about what the media would say about the predemonstration negotiations, ibid., 266.

53. Gitlin, *The Whole World Is Watching*, 228 n.53.

54. *NYT* (October 21, 1967): 8.

55. Gans, *Deciding What's News*, 175.

56. *VV* (October 26, 1967): 1, 40; *GRD* (October 28, 1967): 1, 6–7.

57. *NYT* (October 21, 1967): 1, 8.

58. *NYT* (October 22, 1967): 58.

59. Ibid., 59.

60. *NYT* (October 23, 1967): 1.
61. Ibid., 32.
62. Ibid., 1
63. Notes of meeting, November 2, 1967, box 2, Meeting Notes file, LBJL.
64. *WP* (October 22, 1967): 1, 11.
65. *WP* (October 23, 1967): 1.
66. Ibid., 16.
67. *DT* (October 21, 1967): 1.
68. *DT* (October 23, 1967): 1, 19.
69. *MD* (October 23, 1967): 1.
70. *MD* (October 25, 1967): 1.
71. *Time* (October 27, 1967): 26–27.
72. Ibid., 28.
73. *NW* (October 30, 1967): 84–90.
74. Ibid., 20–21.
75. Ibid., 26–27.
76. See Vietnam public-relations activity files, NSCVN, LBJL; and material for September and October 1967 on reel 1, PDS.
77. Notes of meeting on September 20, 1967, box 2, Meeting Notes file, LBJL.
78. Notes of October 4 cabinet meeting, box 10, Cabinet Meeting papers, LBJL.
79. Small, *Johnson, Nixon, and the Doves*, 112–113.
80. See Clark to Johnson, October 4, 1967, Anti-Vietnam Demonstrations, Christopher papers, LBJL.
81. Wilkins to Clark, October 5, 1967, ibid.
82. October 18, 1967 memo, ibid.
83. David E. McGiffert to Army Chief of Staff, October 10, 1967, ibid.
84. Califano to Johnson, October 16, 1967, box 229, ND19CO312, LBJL.
85. Notes of cabinet meeting of October 18, 1967, box 11, Cabinet papers, LBJL.
86. Clark to Johnson, October 21, 1967, box 29, Clark papers, LBJL.
87. Notes of meeting on October 31, 1967, box 2, Meeting Notes file, LBJL.
88. See box 14, Office Files of Matthew Nimetz, in general, and Califano to Johnson, October 21, 1967, in that file, LBJL.
89. Watson to Johnson, October 21, 1967, box 13, ND19CO312, LBJL.
90. Califano to Johnson, October 21, 1967, box 80, President's Appointment File, Diary Backup, LBJL.
91. Mjdr(?) to Johnson, October 21, 1967, ibid.
92. Stephen Pollak to Clark, October 22, 1967, box 29, Clark papers, LBJL.
93. Van Cleve to Clark, October 30, 1967, ibid.
94. Califano to Johnson, October 26, 1967, box 57, Hu-4 Freedoms, confidential, LBJL.
95. Califano to Johnson, October 23, 1967, box 360, PR 18, LBJL.
96. Panzer to Johnson, October 26, 1967, ibid.
97. Notes of meeting of November 2, 1967, box 2, Meeting Notes file, LBJL.
98. Harold Kaplan memo to Rostow and others, October 31, 1967, box 12, Office Files of George Christian, LBJL.

99. Notes of meeting of November 25, 1967, box 1, Tom Johnson's Notes of Meetings, LBJL.

100. J. Walter Yeagley to Ramsey Clark, October 26. 1967, box 29, Clark papers, LBJL.

101. Howard to Marvin Watson, October 23, 1967, box 232, ND19CO312, LBJL.

102. WDT, box 232, LBJL.

103. Walt to Wallace Greene in Greene to Watson, November 6, 1967, box 360, PR 18, LBJL.

104. Box 2, Mail Summaries, LBJL.

105. Box 180, Panzer files, LBJL.

6. Exit Johnson, Enter Nixon

1. David Hawk, in Joan Morrison and Robert K. Morrison, eds., *From Camelot to Kent State: The Sixties Experience in the Words of Those Who Lived It* (New York: Times Books, 1987), 135.

2. *NYT* (October 16, 1969): 1.

3. Quoted in Small, *Johnson, Nixon, and the Doves*, 110.

4. Halstead, *Out Now*, 386–392; Zaroulis and Sullivan, *Who Spoke Up?* 168–170; Lyttle, *The Chicago Anti-Vietnam War Movement*, 100–105.

5. *NYT* (April 26, 1968): 1; *WP* (April 27, 1968): 3; *Time* (May 3, 1968): 23; *NW* (May 6, 1968). *Newsweek* did run pictures of Coretta Scott King and the crowd of eighty thousand in Central Park, "evidence the war is still a prime concern of the nation."

6. *GRD* (April 27, 1968): 2–4.

7. *VV* (April 27, 1968): 1, 10–12. Becoming a mass circulation weekly, the *Voice* had already exhibited a tendency to ape its sensation-seeking competitors by presenting more photographs and copy on counterdemonstrators and violence than the *Guardian*.

8. *NYT* (April 27, 1968): 1; *WP* (April 27, 1968): 3.

9. DeBenedetti, *An American Ordeal*, 223–229; David Farber, *Chicago '68* (Chicago: University of Chicago Press, 1988); Halstead, *Out Now*, 410–418; Gitlin, *The Sixties*, 322–332; Zaroulis and Sullivan, *Who Spoke Up?* 183–198; Sale, *SDS*, 474–476; Dellinger, *More Power*, 186; Dellinger, *From Yale to Jail*, 321–337. Tom Hayden, *Reunion: A Memoir* (New York: Random House, 1988), 291–326; Lyttle, *The Chicago Anti-Vietnam War Movement*, 105–128; Daniel Walker, *Rights in Conflict* (New York: New American Library, 1968); Reuven Frank, *Out of Thin Air*, 267–285; Marty Jezer, *Abbie Hoffman: An American Rebel* (New Brunswick, N.J.: Rutgers University Press, 1992), 147–171.

10. Michael J. Arlen, *The Living Room War*, 239–240; Thomas Whiteside, "Corridors of Mirrors: The Television Editorial Process, Chicago," *Columbia Journalism Review* 7 (winter 1968–69): 35–54.

11. For an earlier example of how official brutality turned public opinion against the authorities, see Thomas Weber, "'The Marchers Simply Walked Forward Until Struck Down'": Nonviolent Suffering and Conversion," *Peace and Change* 18 (July 1993): 267–289.

12. *GRD* (April 31, 1968): 7.

13. Castleman and Podrazik, *Watching TV*, 205.

14. Small, *To Kill A Messenger*, 208; John P. Robinson, "Public Reaction to Political Protest: Chicago, 1968," *Public Opinion Quarterly* 34 (spring 1970): 1–9.

15. *NW* (September 9, 1968): 70.

16. Chet Huntley, oral history, 24–25, LBJL.

17. *VV* (August 29, 1968): 41, (September 5, 1968): 23–24; *NW* (September 9, 1968): 38; *Time* (September 6, 1968): 21. See also the *Guardian* (August 31, 1968): 1–2, 7; and the headline of a wire-service story in *The Daily Tribune* (August 29, 1968): 1, "HHH Denounces Police Tactics." Using the same wire-service material, however, the *Macomb Daily* generally supported the police in its front-page story.

18. Salisbury, *A Time of Change*, 180–181.

19. See, for example, box 7, LG Chicago, LBJL.

20. Panzer to Johnson, September 17, 1968, ibid.

21. Panzer to Johnson, September 4, 1968, box 233, ND19CO312, LBJL.

22. Box 2, Mail Summaries, LBJL; Epstein, *News from Nowhere*, 59; Farber, *Chicago '68*, 205; Small, *To Kill a Messenger*, 210.

23. Lesher, *Media Unbound*, 98.

24. Christian, *The President Steps Down*, 196.

25. Zaroulis and Sullivan, *Who Spoke Up?* 200.

26. DeBenedetti, *An American Ordeal*, 245–246.

27. *GRD* (April 12, 1969): 3, 6; *VV* (April 10, 1969): 1, 10, 12.

28. *NYT* (April 6, 1969): 1; *WP* (April 6, 1969): 1; *Time* (April 11, 1969): 18. *The Daily Tribune* offered only a photograph on page 14 in its April 9 issue and the *Macomb Daily* did not cover the demonstration.

29. Summary of Sunday Newspaper Coverage, April 6, 1969, box 30, Annotated News Summaries (hereafter ANS), President's Office Files (hereafter POF), NP.

30. Weekly Survey of Television Coverage, April 6–13, 1969, ibid.

31. Zaroulis and Sullivan, *Who Spoke Up?* 65.

32. Gitlin, *The Whole World Is Watching*, 217–220.

33. The official Nixon administration roundup recorded demonstrations in over two hundred cities. Memo, October 17, 1969, Demonstration 10/15/69 folder, box 81, John Dean files, NP.

34. The *Boston Globe* devoted ten pages to the event on October 16. Zaroulis and Sullivan, *Who Spoke Up?* 271.

35. The far less popular Saddam Hussein of Iraq also made that error when he publicly saluted Western peace marchers in his interview with CNN's Peter Arnett on January 28, 1991.

36. *GRD* (October 25, 1969): 4.

37. Gitlin, *The Whole World Is Watching*, 221.

38. Because of that favorable coverage, there is no need here for a counterpoint from the two left-wing sources. See *GRD* (October 25, 1969): 4–5; and *VV* (October 23, 1969): 1.

39. *NYT* (October 16, 1969): 1.

40. Ibid., 19–20.

41. *NYT* (October 17, 1969): 1, 20–21.

42. *WP* (October 16, 1969): 1, 18.

43. *DT* (October 15, 1969): 1; *MD* (October 15, 1969): 1.

44. *MD* (October 16, 1969): 1; *DT* (October 16, 1969): 1.

45. *DT* (October 16, 1969): 20.

46. *Time* (October 17, 1969): 17–22.

47. Ibid., 19.

48. Ibid.

49. *Time* (October 24, 1969): 16–20.

50. Ibid., 16.

51. *NW* (October 13, 1969): 35–36.

52. The issue of October 20 had the Moratorium in lead position but it was another advance story.

53. *NW* (October 27, 1969): 30. In the story, the magazine's reporters referred to a "great silent majority" of people concerned about the war.

54. Ibid., 34.

55. Magruder to Haldeman, October 17, 1969, box 141, Haldeman files, NP.

56. There is some conflicting evidence on the speech's origin in ANS, October 16, 1969, box 31, NP.

57. Haldeman note, October 15, 1969, box 40, Haldeman personal notes, Haldeman files, NP.

58. News Summaries, October 15, 1969, October, 1969 folder, NP.

59. Ibid.

60. October 16, 1969, ibid.

61. Several network specials were also judged to be balanced. ibid.

62. Bill Gavin to Haldeman, October 16, 1969, Moratorium Response folder, box 130, Haldeman files, NP.

63. News Summaries, October 16, 1969, October, 1969 folder, NP.

64. ANS, October 16, 1969, box 31, NP.

65. News Summaries, October 16, 1969, October, 1969 folder, NP.

66. ANS, October 16, 1969, box 31, NP.

67. Magazine Report, October 26, 1969, News Summaries, October, 1969 folder, NP.

68. Moynihan to Nixon, October 16, 1969, Moratorium Response folder, box 130, Haldeman files, NP.

69. Paul McCracken to Nixon, November 10, 1969, box 3, POF, NP.

70. Press and Media folder, box 141, Haldeman files, NP.

71. ANS, October(?), 1969, box 31, NP.

7. Nixon versus the Media

1. "A Socialist Analysis of the November 15, 1969, Mass Anti-War Demonstration," in G. Louis Heath, ed., *Mutiny Does Not Happen Lightly: The Literature of the American Resistance to the Vietnam War* (Metuchen, N.J.: Scarecrow Press, 1976), 498.

2. *Time* (November 21, 1969): 23.

3. Spiro T. Agnew, *Go Quietly or Else* (New York: William Morrow, 1980), 27.

4. Klein, *Making It Perfectly Clear*, 2, 27.

5. Magruder, *An American Life*, 58–59; Small, "Containing Domestic Enemies," 132–136.

6. Kissinger, *White House Years*, 289, 292.

7. Ibid., 291.

8. Klein, *Making It Perfectly Clear*, 127.

9. Spear, *Presidents and the Press*, 42. See also Lashner, *The Chilling Effect in TV News*, Appendix A, for a list of 256 incidents of media intimidation that occurred during the Nixon administration, with October through December, 1969, being among the most active periods.

10. Efron, *The News Twisters*; Pat Buchanan to Bruce Kehrli, October 15, 1971, in Oudes, ed., *From: The President*, 328.

11. Spear, *Presidents and the Press*, 40.

12. Magruder, *An American Life*, 87–90; Porter, *Assault on the Media*, 40–51; Powledge, *The Engineering of Restraint*, 9; Spear, *Presidents and the Press*, 113–118.

13. Small, *Johnson, Nixon, and the Doves*, 187–190; Safire, *Before the Fall*, 172–174.

14. *DT* (November 4, 1969): 1–2.

15. *WP* (November 4, 1969): 1, and (November 5, 1969): 1, 6.

16. *NYT* (November 4, 1969): 1, 17.

17. *Time* (November 14, 1969): 15–16. *Newsweek* generally agreed with *Time*. *NW* (November 17, 1969): 35–36.

18. Nixon, *In the Arena*, 216; Nixon, *RN*, 410–411.

19. Of course, Nixon had not helped his case by withholding advance copies of his speech from the media.

20. Keogh, *President Nixon and the Press*, 138. For transcripts of the networks' analyses, see 171–190. Magruder also claims that the television coverage was not unfavorable. Magruder, *An American Life*, 57.

21. Klein, *Making It Perfectly Clear*, 69–70. See also Kissinger, *White House Years*, 307.

22. Robert J. Donovan and Ray Scherer, *Unsilent Revolution: Television News and American Public Life, 1948–1991* (New York: Cambridge University Press, 1992), 118.

23. Nixon to Haldeman, October 26, 1969, box 229, Presidential Memos, Haldeman files, NP.

24. Klein to Haldeman, November 3, 1969, box 54, Memos from Herb Klein, October, 1969 folder, Haldeman files, NP.

25. New Summaries, November 4, 1969 folder, NP. See also memo, November 3, 1969, box 40, personal notes, Haldeman files, NP, for Pat Buchanan's comments on unfair criticism of CBS's Sevareid and Marvin Kalb and for the follow-up note of November 5 in which aide Peter Flanigan was deputized to call William Paley to complain.

26. News Summaries, November 5, 1969 folder, NP.

27. Keogh memo, November 5, 1969, box 79, Memoranda for the President, POF, NP.

28. Butterfield to Nixon, November 7, 1969, News Summaries, November 7, 1969 folder, NP.

29. William Hopkins to Larry Higby and Haldeman, December 4, 1969, box 129, mail operation folder, Haldeman files, NP. The administration also directed the United

States Information Agency to send out "The Silent Majority," a fifteen–minute film, to 104 countries.

30. News Summaries, November 10, 1969 folder, Editorial and Column Reaction to the President's Vietnam Speech (reported on November 7), NP.

31. Klein, *Making It Perfectly Clear*, 168.

32. Thomas Whiteside, "Corridor of Mirrors," 41; Safire, *Before the Fall*, 352.

33. Safire, *Before the Fall*, 177.

34. Powledge, *The Engineering of Restraint*, 11.

35. William S. Paley, *As It Happened*, 335. See, for confirmation, Burch's advice to Nixon on the networks quoted in Oudes, ed., *From: The President*, xviii–xix.

36. Powledge, *The Engineering of Restraint*, 10.

37. For a transcript of the speech see John R. Coyne, Jr., *The Impudent Snobs: Agnew vs. the Intellectual Establishment* (New Rochelle, N.Y.: Arlington House, 1972), 265–270. Coyne's study is a defense of Agnew's charges.

38. Klein, *Making It Perfectly Clear*, 170.

39. For the reasons behind this see Smith, *Paley*, 493. See also Frank, *Out of Thin Air*, 293–299.

40. Agnew, *Go Quietly or Else*, 28.

41. Schorr, *Clearing the Air*, 40; Gans, *Deciding What's News*, 283. See also Efron, *The News Twisters*, 133–142; and Coyne, *The Impudent Snobs*, 50.

42. William Hopkins to Higby, December 1, 1969, Haldeman, mail operation folder, box 129, Haldeman files, NP.

43. Keogh, *President Nixon and the Press*, 138.

44. Coyne, *The Impudent Snobs*, 1.

45. Safire, *Before the Fall*, 353; Klein, *Making It Perfectly Clear*, 174; Price, *With Nixon*, 189.

46. Powledge, *The Engineering of Restraint*, 31–32.

47. Gitlin, *The Whole World Is Watching*, 278–279.

48. Safire, *Before the Fall*, 353; Schorr, *Clearing the Air*, 40. See Klein, *Making It Perfectly Clear*, 211–115, for comments on CBS as enemy number one among the networks.

49. Donovan and Scherer, *Unsilent Revolution*, 118.

50. Castleman and Podrazik, *Watching TV*, 220.

51. Colson, *Born Again*, 41–42. See also Schorr, *Clearing the Air*, 43; and Gary Paul Gates, *Air Time: The Inside Story of CBS News* (New York: Harper & Row, 1978), 297–298, for the failed attempt to intimidate Dan Rather.

52. Gans, *Deciding What's News*, 264; Frank D. Russo, "A Study of Bias in TV Coverage of the Vietnam War: 1969 and 1970," *Public Opinion Quarterly* 35 (winter 1971–72): 539–543.

53. Two years later, Nixon was on the warpath against the media again, threatening to bring antitrust suits against the networks. Ehrlichman to Nixon, September 19, 1971, in Oudes, ed., *From: The President*, 315–316.

54. DeBenedetti, *An American Ordeal*, 260–264; Gitlin, *The Whole World Is Watching*, 222–228; Gitlin, *The Sixties*, 394–395; Halstead, *Out Now*, 506–521; Zaroulis and Sullivan, *Who Spoke Up?* 277–299; Richard G. Kleindienst, *Justice: The Memoirs of Attorney General Richard Kleindienst* (Ottowa, Ill.: Jameson Books, 1985), 73.

55. Gitlin, *The Whole World Is Watching*, 224–226; Zaroulis and Sullivan, *Who Spoke Up?* 278.

56. This group played into Nixon's hands. He wanted the media to focus on their activities and they used their affiliation with the demonstration to obtain media coverage. Gitlin, *The Whole World Is Watching*, 224.

57. That record has been challenged by kazoo-playing members of the Eugene V. Debs Society, who fill the Tiger Stadium bleachers in Detroit once a year to serenade the rest of the crowd.

58. Gitlin, *The Whole World Is Watching*, 227–228.

59. *WP* (November 16, 1969): 19.

60. *NYT* (November 15, 1969): 1.

61. Ibid., 26.

62. *NYT* (November 16, 1969): 1.

63. Ibid., 60.

64. Ibid., 61.

65. *WP* (November 16, 1969): 1.

66. Ibid., 14.

67. Ibid., 17.

68. Ibid., 18.

69. *DT* (November 13, 1969): 1.

70. *DT* (November 15, 1969): 1.

71. *MD* (November 15, 1969): 1.

72. Ibid., 4.

73. *DT* (November 17, 1969): 1, 19.

74. *DT* (November 14, 1969): 19.

75. *GRD* (November 22, 1969): 2–5; *VV* (November 20, 1969): 1, 48, 50, 66, 67.

76. *VV* (November 20, 1969): 48.

77. Ibid., 50.

78. Ibid., 66–67.

79. *Time* (November 21, 1969): 16–17, 18–22.

80. Ibid., 23–26.

81. Ibid., 25.

82. Ibid., 26.

83. *NW* (November 17, 1969): 35–36.

84. Ibid., 37.

85. *NW* (November 24, 1969): 31–32, 34–35. This demonstration had drawn the most glittering array of music makers of any antiwar activity.

86. Ibid., 31.

87. Ibid., 32.

88. Ibid., 34.

89. Ibid., 34–35.

90. News Summaries, November 17, 1969, folder, NP.

91. Buchanan memo, ca. November 15, 1969, November 15, 1969 folder, box 54, general memoranda, Haldeman files, NP.

92. News Summaries, Special Report, Analysis of Television, submitted by Mort Allin, NP.

93. News Summaries, November 20, 1969, folder, NP.

8. The Movement Rebounds

1. Ken Wachsberger, "A Tradition Continues: The History of East Lansing's Underground Press, 1965–Present," in his *Voices from the Underground*, 247–248.

2. *NYT* (May 4, 1971): 1, 32.

3. He spoke so frequently on television during the period that antiwar critics successfully petitioned the FCC for equal time. Samuel Kernell, *Going Public: New Strategies of Presidential Leadership*, 2nd ed. (Washington: Congressional Quarterly Press, 1993), 111.

4. Moratorium organizer David Hawk commented: "We had achieved the first time around what we had hoped to do in another six, seven, or eight months. We had made our contribution and had shot our wad." Quoted in Morrison and Morrison, eds., *From Camelot to Kent State*, 135.

5. Zaroulis and Sullivan, *Who Spoke Up?*, 311; Halstead, *Out Now*, 531–534; DeBenedetti, *An American Ordeal*, 270–271.

6. *NYT* (April 16, 1970): 1.

7. *WP* (April 16, 1970): 16; *DT* (April 16, 1970): 39. Similar themes dominated the newsweeklies' stories with *Time* (April 27, 1970): 27, headlined "Using the Moratorium for Their Own Ends," and *Newsweek* (April 27, 1970): 33–34, headed by "Moratorium: The Radicals Move in." See also the *Guardian* (April 25, 1970): 3, for a characteristically more accurate account.

8. News Summaries, April 16, 1970 folder; Magazine Summaries for the week of April 20, 1970, NP.

9. He was also determined to demonstrate to the Senate, which had just rejected the second of his two Supreme Court nominations, that it could not continue to push him around.

10. Zaroulis and Sullivan, *Who Spoke Up?* 324–329; Halstead, *Out Now*, 544–556; Gitlin, *The Sixties*, 410; Dan Rather and Gary Paul Gates, *The Palace Guard* (New York: Warner, 1975), 216–217; Price, *With Nixon*, 169–174.

11. For Nixon's account, see Nixon memo, May 13, 1970, Memoranda from the President, PPF, NP.

12. *VV* (May 14, 1970): 1, 10. The *Guardian* (May 23, 1970): 6–7), was more upbeat, perhaps because it concentrated on protests in other parts of the country and not on the Washington centerpiece.

13. *NYT* (May 9, 1970): 1–8, 9.

14. *NYT* (May 10, 1970): 1, 24.

15. Ibid., 25.

16. Braley, *Bad News*, 349–350.

17. *WP* (May 10, 1970): 1, 11–14.

18. *DT* (May 9, 1970): 1, 9.

19. *DT* (May 11, 1970): 17.

20. *MD* (May 9, 1970): 1.

21. *Time* (May 18, 1970): 6–15.

22. *NW* (May 18, 1970): 26–28.

23. Castleman and Podrazik, *Watching TV*, 220.

24. Magruder, *An American Life*, 131.

25. Klein, *Making It Perfectly Clear*, 125.

26. Notes of May 10 meeting, box 41, Haldeman notes, Haldeman files, NP.

27. Nixon to Haldeman, May 11, 1970, Memos from the President folder, box 138, Haldeman files, NP; Nixon to Haldeman, May 11, 1970, in Oudes, ed., *From: The President*, 125–126; ibid., 135–136. See also, Nixon to Haldeman, May 25, 1970, ibid., 139–140, complaining about a New York proadministration demonstration that CBS covered in one minute while devoting on the same program two to three minutes to a story on one thousand left-wing lawyers.

28. Notes of a May 9 meeting, box 41, Haldeman notes, Haldeman files, NP.

29. Krogh to Ehrlichman, May 9, 1970, box 70, Memoranda for the President, POF, NP; Nixon to Haldeman, May 13, 1970, in Oudes, ed., *From: The President*, 127–134; John Brown III to Haldeman, June 11, 1970, ibid., 141–142.

30. News Summaries, May 11, 1970, folder, NP.

31. Allin to Magruder, Lynn Nofziger, and Colson, May 11, 1970, box 129, Haldeman files, NP.

32. "The Public Appraises the Nixon Administration," box 262, Haldeman files, NP.

33. Allin to Colson and others, ca. July 70, found tucked away in News Summaries material, NP.

34. Hopkins, "'May Day' 1971"; DeBenedetti, *An American Ordeal*, 295–310; Halstead, *Out Now*, 605–607; Zaroulis and Sullivan, *Who Spoke Up?* 355–364; Wachsberger, "A Tradition Continues," 244–254; Micheal Clodfelter, *Mad Minutes and Vietnam Months: A Soldier's Memoirs* (Jefferson, N.C.: McFarland, 1988), 226–228; Vincent Nobile, Jr., "Political Opposition in the Age of Mass Media: GI's and Veterans against the War in Vietnam," (Ph.D. dissertation, University of California-Irvine, 1987), 252–274; Kleindienst, *Justice*, 74–80.

35. Clodfelter, *Mad Minutes*, 226.

36. Even former Attorney General Richard Kleindeinst estimated that at least four hundred thousand showed up that day. Kleindeinst, *Justice*, 74. San Francisco doves also boasted a record turnout that day. From 150,000 to 350,000 marched from the Embarcadero to Golden Gate Park for a rally.

37. Price, *With Nixon*, 150–151.

38. *NYT* (April 23, 1971): 1, 4.

39. *NYT* (April 24, 1971): 12.

40. *NYT* (April 25, 1971): 1, 58.

41. *NYT* (April 26, 1971): 31.

42. *WP* (April 23, 1971): 1, 8.

43. *WP* (April 24, 1971): 1.

44. Ibid., 8. Other stories appeared on page 9.

45. *WP* (April 25, 1971): 1.

46. Ibid., 23.

47. *VV* (April 29, 1971): 1, 9, 44–45.

48. *GRD* (May 5, 1971): 1, 3, 15.

49. *DT* (April 23, 1971): 20.

50. *DT* (April 24, 1971): 14. Two pictures of Friday's medal return appeared on page 22.

51. *DT* (April 26, 1971): 1.

52. Ibid., 14.

53. *MD* (April 24, 1971): 7.
54. *MD* (April 25, 1971): 1.
55. *Time* (April 26, 1971): 16.
56. *Time* (May 3, 1971): 10–13.
57. Ibid., 12–13.
58. *NW* (April 26, 1971): 29–20.
59. *NW* (May 3, 1971): 24–25.
60. Allin to Colson, April 12, 1971, Mort Allin April 1971 file, box 76, Haldeman files, NP. Allin had surveyed network treatment of stories on Laos and Vietnam from February 1 through April 8.
61. Colson to Haldeman, April 14, 1971, box 2, Colson, Haldeman memos, Haldeman files, NP.
62. Colson to Haldeman, April 22, 1971, April 1971 folder, box 76, Haldeman files, NP.
63. News Summaries, April 21, 1971, folder, NP.
64. Ibid., April 22, 1971, folder, NP.
65. Buchanan to Haldeman, April 21, 1971 in Oudes, ed., *From: The President*, 240.
66. New Summaries, April 23, 1971 folder, NP.
67. Haldeman to Colson, April 23, 1971, April 1971 folder, box 76, Haldeman files, NP.
68. Notes from meetings on April 23, 1971, box 43, Haldeman notes, Haldeman files, NP.
69. News Summaries, April 24, 1971 folder, NP.
70. Meeting of April 25, 1971, box 43, Haldeman notes, Haldeman files, NP.
71. News Summaries, April 25, 1971, April 1971 folder, NP.
72. News Summaries, April 29, 1971, folder, NP.
73. Allin to Colson, April 26, 1971, box 1, Buchanan files, NP.
74. Colson to Haldeman, April 29, 1971, box 2, Colson papers, NP.
75. Colson to Haldeman, April 26, 1971, Colson, April 1971 folder, box 76, Haldeman files, NP.
76. *VV* (May 13, 1971): 9, 12; *GRD* (May 12, 1971): 1–3.
77. *NYT* (May 4, 1971): 41.
78. *NYT* (May 5, 1971): 32.
79. *NYT* (May 6, 1971): 26.
80. *WP* (May 4, 1971): 12.
81. Ibid., 13.
82. *WP* (May 5, 1971): 14.
83. *DT* (May 3, 1971): 18.
84. *DT* (May 4, 1971): 1.
85. *DT* (May 4, 1971): 1; (May 5, 1971): 32.
86. *MD* (May 4, 1971): 1; (May 5, 1971): 1
87. *Time* (May 10, 1971): 11.
88. Ibid., 12–13.
89. *Time* (May 17, 1971): 13–15.
90. Ibid., 13.
91. Ibid., 15.
92. *NW* (May 10, 1971): 25–27.

93. *NW* (May 17. 1971): 24.

94. Ibid., 26.

95. Ibid., 28.

96. Ken Wachsberger, "A Tradition Continues: East Lansing's Underground Press, 1965–Present," in his *Voices from the Underground*, 246.

97. ANS, May 3, 1971, box 33, POF, NP.

98. Colson to Haldeman, May 5, 1971, January–June 1971 folder, box 2, Haldeman memos, Haldeman files, NP.

99. Nixon to Haldeman, May 9, 1971, President's Memo folder, box 228, Haldeman files, NP.

9. Conclusion

1. For a discussion of this subject, see David Farber, "The Counterculture and the Antiwar Movement," in Small and Hoover, eds., *Give Peace a Chance*, 7–21.

2. In a comparable vein, I once complained over a dinner table to the former publisher of the *Detroit Free Press*, David Lawrence, about errors of fact and irresponsible statements in several Joseph Sobran columns that appeared on his op-ed page. He agreed with my critiques but did not accept the notion that Sobran should be dropped; after all, "he sure got your dander up, didn't he?" Lawrence was not overly concerned about journalistic standards in this case. Sobran sold papers because of his slashing, bully-boy style.

3. According to one Vietnamese diplomat, Hanoi *was* encouraged, though the communists expected the antiwar forces to grow in the United States as the war dragged on, just as they had in France in the early 1950s. See Small, *Johnson, Nixon, and the Doves*, 88–89. In addition, there is no doubt that newsreels and press reports of American mass protests viewed in North Vietnam helped buoy the spirits of citizens there who made so many sacrifices in their interminable war.

4. See Appendix B.

Appendix A

1. *NYT* (April 10, 1989): 1.

2. Trisha Penly, letter to the editor, *Detroit Free Press* (April 17, 1989): 8A.

3. On the evening of April 9, ABC and NBC devoted four and two minutes respectively to generally favorable accounts of the rally in their evening newscasts and made it their lead stories. Both followed it up with material on where the abortion question stood at the Supreme Court.

4. *Detroit Free Press* (April 13, 1989): 11a.

Appendix B

1. *NYT* (January 27, 1971): 17.

2. *WP* (January 27, 1992): 1, 21, 24–25.

3. Looking at a broader span of Gulf War coverage, Bethami A. Dobkin found that television journalists were not very interested in the political arguments offered by doves to explain their opposition to the war. Bethami A. Dobkin, "Constructing News

Narratives: ABC and CNN Cover the Gulf War," in Robert E. Denton, Jr., ed., *The Media and the Persian Gulf War* (Westport, Conn.: Praeger, 1993), 118–119. For an interesting sampling of media issues relating to the Gulf War see the special issue of *Film and History* 22 (February–May 1993).

4. *DT* (January 27, 1991): 7a.

5. *Time* (January 28, 1991): 34–37; (February 4, 1991): 42–45, 58–59, 74.

6. *NW* (January 28, 1991): 36–39; (February 4, 1991): 58.

7. *VV* (February 5, 1991): 25.

8. *VV* (February 5, 1991): 27–28.

Selected Bibliography

Unpublished Sources

Interviews Conducted by the Author

Lewis Bateman, Washington, D.C., June 21, 1991
Bui Xuan Ninh, New York, New York, June 15, 1983
George Christian, Austin, Texas, February 20, 1989
Rudolph DiFazio, February 2, 1989, telephone

Archival Sources

CBS News Archives, New York City
Lyndon B. Johnson Presidential Library, Austin, Texas
Nixon Presidential Materials Project, National Archives, Alexandria, Virginia
Vanderbilt University Television News Archive, Nashville, Tennessee

Oral Histories from the Lyndon B. Johnson Presidential Library

Stewart J. Alsop
Peter Benchley
George Christian
Katherine Graham
Dan Rather
George Reedy
Harrison E. Salisbury
Tom Wicker

Oral History from the Nixon Presidential Materials Project

Charles Colson

Ph.D. Dissertations

Bailey, George Arthur. "The Vietnam War According to Chet, David, Walter, Harry, Bob, Howard and Frank: A Content Analysis of Journalistic Performance by the Network Television Evening News Anchormen 1965–1970." University of Wisconsin, 1973.

Nobile, Vincent, Jr. "Political Opposition in the Age of Mass Media: GI's and Veterans against the War in Vietnam." University of California-Irvine, 1987.

Published Primary Materials

Documents

CBS News. *CBS News Daily News Broadcasts*. Ann Arbor, MI.: University Microfilms, 1963–.

Heath, G. Louis, ed. *Mutiny Does Not Happen Lightly: The Literature of the American Resistance to the Vietnam War*. Metuchen, N.J.: Scarecrow Press, 1976.

Menashe, Louis, and Ronald Radosh, eds. *Teach-Ins U.S.A.: Reports, Opinions, Documents*. New York: Praeger, 1967.

Oudes, Bruce, ed. *From: The President: Richard Nixon's Secret Files*. New York: Harper & Row, 1989.

Presidential Documents Series. *Vietnam, the Media, and Public Support for the War*. Selections from the Holdings of the Lyndon Baines Johnson Library. Frederick, Md.: University Publications of America, 1986.

Memoirs and Autobiographies

Agnew, Spiro T. *Go Quietly . . . Or Else*. New York: William Morrow, 1980.

Berrigan, Daniel. *To Dwell in Peace: An Autobiography*. New York: Harper & Row, 1987.

Calvert, Gregory Nevala. *Democracy from the Heart: Spiritual Values, Decentralism, and Democratic Idealism in the Movement of the 1960s*. Eugene, Ore.: Communitas Press, 1991.

Christian, George. *The President Steps Down: A Personal Memoir of the Transfer of Power*. New York: Macmillan, 1970.

Clodfelter, Micheal. *Mad Minutes and Vietnam Months: A Soldier's Memoirs*. Jefferson, N.C.: McFarland, 1988.

Colby, William. *Lost Victory: A Firsthand Account of America's Sixteen-Year Involvement in Vietnam*. Chicago: Contemporary Books, 1989.

Colson, Charles W. *Born Again*. New York: Bantam, 1976.

Dellinger, David. *From Yale to Jail: The Life Story of a Moral Dissenter*. New York: Pantheon, 1993.

———. *More Power Than We Know: The People's Movement Toward Democracy*. Garden City, N.Y.: Doubleday, 1975.

Ehrlichman, John. *Witness to Power*. New York: Simon & Schuster, 1972.

Friendly, Fred W. *Due to Circumstances beyond Our Control*. New York: Random House, 1967.

Halstead, Fred. *Out Now: A Participant's Account of the American Movement against the Vietnam War*. New York: Monad Press, 1978.

Hayden, Tom. *Reunion: A Memoir*. New York: Random House, 1988.

Healey, Dorothy, and Maurice Isserman: *Dorothy Healey Remembers: A Life in the American Communist Party*. New York: Oxford University Press, 1990.

Kelman, Steve. *Push Comes to Shove*. Boston: Houghton Mifflin, 1970.

Kissinger, Henry A. *White House Years*. Boston: Little, Brown, 1979.

Klein, Herbert. *Making It Perfectly Clear*. Garden City, N.Y.: Doubleday, 1980.

Kleindienst, Richard G. *Justice: The Memoirs of Attorney General Kleindienst*. Ottowa, Ill.: Jameson Books, 1985.

Lens, Sidney. *Unrepentant Radical: An American Activist's Account of Five Turbulent Decades*. Boston: Beacon Press, 1980.

McPherson, Harry. *A Political Education*. Boston: Little, Brown, 1972.

Magruder, Jeb Stuart. *An American Life: One Man's Road to Watergate*. New York: Atheneum, 1974.

Mailer, Norman. *The Armies of the Night: History as Novel, The Novel as History.* New York: New American Library, 1968.

Morrison, Joan, and Robert K. Morrison, eds. *From Camelot to Kent State: The Sixties Experience in the Words of Those Who Lived It.* New York: Times Books, 1987.

Nixon, Richard M. *In the Arena.* New York: Simon & Schuster, 1990.

————. *RN: The Memoirs of Richard Nixon.* New York: Warner, 1978.

Paley, William S. *As It Happened: A Memoir.* Garden City, N.Y.: Doubleday, 1979.

Price, Raymond. *With Nixon.* New York: Viking, 1977.

Rader, Dotson. *I Ain't Marchin' Anymore.* New York: David McKay, 1969.

Reedy, George. *Lyndon B. Johnson: A Memoir.* New York: Andrews and McMeel, 1982.

Rubin, Jerry. *Do It! Scenarios of the Revolution.* New York: Ballantine, 1970.

Safire, William. *Before the Fall: An Inside View of the Pre-Watergate White House.* Garden City, N.Y.: Doubleday, 1975.

Salisbury, Harrison E. *A Time of Change: A Reporter's Tale of Our Time.* New York: Harper & Row, 1988.

Schorr, Daniel. *Clearing the Air.* Boston: Houghton Mifflin, 1977.

Willenson, Kim. *The Bad War: An Oral History of the Vietnam War.* New York: New American Library, 1987.

Secondary Sources

Books

Altheide, David L. *Creating Reality: How TV News Distorts Events.* Beverly Hills: Sage, 1976.

————. *Media Power.* Beverly Hills: Sage, 1985.

Ambrose, Stephen A. *Nixon: The Triumph of a Politician, 1962–1972.* New York: Simon & Schuster, 1989.

Arlen, Michael J. *The Living-Room War.* New York: Viking, 1969.

Aronson, James. *Deadline for the Media: Today's Challenges to Press, TV and Radio.* Indianapolis: Bobbs-Merrill, 1972.

————. *The Press and the Cold War.* Bobbs-Merrill: Indianapolis, 1970.

Berry, Nicholas O. *Foreign Policy and the Press: An Analysis of the New York Times's Coverage of U.S. Foreign Policy.* Westport, Conn.: Greenwood, 1990.

Borg, Dorothy. *The United States and the Far Eastern Crisis of 1933–1938.* Cambridge: Harvard University Press, 1964.

Braestrup, Peter. *Big Story: How the American Press and Television Reported and Interpreted the Crises of Tet in Vietnam and Washington.* Boulder, Colo.: Westview, 1977.

Braley, Russ. *Bad News: The Foreign Policy of the "New York Times."* Chicago: Regnery Gateway, 1984.

Branch, Taylor. *Parting the Waters: America in the King Years 1954–1963.* New York: Simon & Schuster, 1988.

Breines, Wini. *Community and Organization in the New Left, 1962–1968: The Great Refusal.* New York: Praeger, 1982.

Broder, David. *Behind the Front Page: A Candid Look at How the News Is Made.* New York: Simon & Schuster, 1987.

Califano, Joseph A., Jr. *The Triumph and Tragedy of Lyndon Johnson: The White House Years.* New York: Simon & Schuster, 1991.

Castleman, Harry, and Walter J. Podrazik. *Watching TV: Four Decades of American Television.* New York: McGraw Hill, 1982.

Caute, David. *Sixty-Eight: The Year of the Barricades.* London, U.K.: Hamish Hamilton, 1988.

Chatfield, Charles, with Robert Kleidman. *The American Peace Movement: Ideals and Activism.* New York: Twayne, 1992.

Cohen, Bernard C. *The Press and Foreign Policy.* Princeton, N.J.: Princeton University Press, 1963.

———. *The Public's Impact on Foreign Policy.* Boston: Little, Brown, 1973.

Cooper, Sandi E. *Patriotic Pacifism: Waging War on War in Europe,* 1815–1914. New York: Oxford University Press, 1991.

Coyne, John R., Jr. *The Impudent Snobs: Agnew vs. the Intellectual Establishment.* New Rochelle, N.Y.: Arlington House, 1972.

Davis, Douglas. *The Five Myths of Television Power Or Why the Medium Is not the Message.* New York: Simon & Schuster, 1993.

DeBenedetti, Charles, with Charles Chatfield. *An American Ordeal: The Antiwar Movement of the Vietnam Era.* Syracuse, N.Y.: Syracuse University Press, 1990.

Diamond, Edwin. *The Tin Kazoo: Television, Politics, and the News.* Cambridge: MIT Press, 1975.

Donovan, Robert J., and Ray Scherer. *Unsilent Revolution: Television News and American Public Life, 1948–1991.* New York: Cambridge University Press, 1992.

Efron, Edith. *The News Twisters.* Los Angeles: Nash, 1971.

Epstein, Edward Jay. *Between Fact and Fiction: The Problem of Journalism.* New York: Vintage, 1975.

———. *News from Nowhere: Television and the News.* New York: Random House, 1973.

Farber, David. *Chicago '68.* Chicago: University of Chicago Press, 1988.

Felsenthal, Carol. *Power, Privilege and the* Post: *The Katherine Graham Story.* New York: G.P. Putnam's Sons, 1993.

Frank, Reuven. *Out of Thin Air: The Brief Wonderful World of Network News.* New York: Simon & Schuster, 1991.

Gans, Herbert. *Deciding What's News: A Study of "CBS Evening News," "NBC Nightly News," "Newsweek" and "Time."* New York: Random House, 1980.

Garrow, David J. *Bearing the Cross: Martin Luther King, Jr., and the Southern Christian Leadership Conference.* New York: Morrow, 1986.

Gates, Gary Paul. *Air Time: The Inside Story of CBS News.* New York: Harper & Row, 1978.

Gitlin, Todd. *The Sixties: Years of Hope, Days of Rage.* New York: Bantam, 1987.

———. *The Whole World Is Watching: Mass Media in the Making and Unmaking of the New Left.* Berkeley: University of California Press, 1980.

Goulden, Joseph C. *Fit to Print: A. M. Rosenthal and His Times.* New York: Lyle Stuart, 1988.

Goulding, Phil G. *Confirm or Deny: Informing the People on National Security.* New York: Harper & Row, 1969.

Graber, Doris A. *Mass Media and American Politics*. Washington: Congressional Quarterly Press, 1980.

Grossman, Michael Baruch, and Martha Joynt Kumar. *Portraying the Presidents: The White House and the News Media*. Baltimore: Johns Hopkins University Press, 1981.

Halberstam, David. *The Powers that Be*. New York: Knopf, 1979.

Hallin, Daniel C. *The "Uncensored War": The Media and Vietnam*. New York: Oxford University Press, 1986.

Halloran, James D., Philip Eliott, and Graham Murdock. *Demonstrations and Communication: A Case Study*. Harmondsworth, U.K.: Penguin, 1970.

Hammond, William M. *Public Affairs: The Military and the Media, 1962–1968*. Washington, D.C.: Center for Military History, 1988.

Herman, Edward S., and Noam Chomsky: *Manufacturing Consent: The Political Economy of the Mass Media*. New York: Pantheon, 1988.

Iynegar, Shanto, and Donald R. Kinder. *News That Matters: Television and American Opinion*. Chicago: University of Chicago Press, 1987.

Jezer, Marty. *Abbie Hoffman: An American Rebel*. New Brunswick, N.J.: Rutgers University Press, 1992.

Johnson, Richard Tanner. *Managing the White House: An Intimate Study of the Presidency*. New York, Harper & Row, 1974.

Katz, Andrew. *Public Opinion, Congress, President Nixon, and the Termination of the Vietnam War*. Baltimore: Johns Hopkins University Press, 1986.

Katz, Elihu, and Paul F. Lazarsfeld. *Personal Influence: The Part Played by People in the Flow of Communications*. Glencoe, Ill.: Free Press, 1955.

Kearns, Doris. *Lyndon Johnson and the American Dream*. New York: Signet, 1977.

Keogh, James. *President Nixon and the Press*. New York: Funk and Wagnalls, 1972.

Kernell, Samuel. *Going Public: New Strategies of Presidential Leadership*. 2nd ed. Washington: Congressional Quarterly Press, 1993.

Koning, Hans. *Nineteen Sixty-Eight: A Personal Report*. New York: Norton, 1987.

Lapham, Lewis H. *The Wish for Kings: Democracy at Bay*. New York: Grove Press, 1993.

Lashner, Marilyn A. *The Chilling Effect in TV News: Intimidation by the Nixon White House*. New York: Praeger, 1984.

Lesher, Stephen. *Media Unbound: The Impact of Television on the Public*. Boston: Houghton Mifflin, 1982.

Levy, David W. *The Debate Over Vietnam*. Baltimore: Johns Hopkins University Press, 1991.

Lyttle, Bradford. *The Chicago Anti-Vietnam War Movement*. Chicago: Midwest Pacifist Center, 1988.

MacNeil, Robert. *The People Machine: The Influence of Television on American Politics*. New York: Harper & Row, 1968.

McQuaid, Kim. *The Anxious Years: America in the Vietnam-Watergate Era*. New York: Basic Books, 1989.

Merrill, John C., and Harold A. Fisher. *The World's Great Dailies: Profiles of Fifty Newspapers*. New York: Hastings House, 1980.

Miller, James. *"Democracy Is in the Streets:" From Port Huron to the Siege of Chicago*. New York: Simon & Schuster, 1987.

Mueller, John F. *War, Presidents, and Public Opinion*. New York: John Wiley, 1973.

Nacos, Birgitte Lebens. *The Press, Presidents, and Crises*. New York: Columbia University Press, 1990.

O'Heffernan, Patrick. *Mass Media and American Foreign Policy: Insider Perspectives on Global Journalism and the Foreign Policy Process*. Norwood, N.J.: Ablex, 1991.

Paletz, David L., and Robert M. Entman. *Media Power Politics*. New York: Free Press, 1981.

Parenti, Michael. *Inventing Reality: The Politics of the Mass Media*. New York: St. Martin's Press, 1986.

Podhoretz, John. *Hell of a Ride: Backstage at the White House Follies, 1989–1993*. New York: Simon & Schuster, 1993.

Porter, William E. *Assault on the Media: The Nixon Years*. Ann Arbor: University of Michigan Press, 1976.

Powers, Thomas. *The War at Home: Vietnam and the American People, 1964–1968*. New York: Grossman, 1973.

Powledge, Fred. *The Engineering of Restraint: The Nixon Administration and the Press*. Washington, D.C.: Public Affairs Press, 1971.

Rachlin, Allan. *News as Hegemonic Reality: American Political Culture and the Framing of News Accounts*. Westport, Conn.: Praeger, 1988.

Rather, Dan, and Gary Paul Gates. *The Palace Guard*. New York: Warner, 1975.

Reedy, George C. *The Twilight of the Presidency*. rev. ed. New York: New American Library, 1987.

Reeves, Richard. *President Kennedy: Profile of Power*. New York: Simon & Schuster, 1993.

Rorabaugh, W. J. *Berkeley at War: The 1960's*. New York: Oxford University Press, 1989.

Rozell, Mark. *The Press and the Carter Presidency*. Boulder, Colo.: Westview, 1989.

Sale, Kirkpatrick. *SDS: Ten Years toward a Revolution*. New York: Random House, 1973.

Schneiders, James C. *Should America Go to War? The Debate Over Foreign Policy in Chicago, 1939–1941*. Chapel Hill: University of North Carolina Press, 1989.

Searle, John R. *The Campus War: A Sympathetic Look at the University in Agony*. New York: World, 1971.

Skolnick, Jerome. *The Politics of Protest*. New York: Simon & Schuster, 1969.

Skornia, Harry J. *Television and the News: A Critical Appraisal*. Palo Alto, Cal.: Pacific Books, 1968.

Small, Melvin. *Johnson, Nixon, and the Doves*. New Brunswick, N.J.: Rutgers University Press, 1988.

Small, Melvin, and William D. Hoover, eds. *Give Peace a Chance: Exploring the Vietnam Antiwar Movement*. Syracuse, N.Y.: Syracuse University Press, 1992.

Small, William. *To Kill a Messenger: Television News and the Real World*. New York: Hastings House, 1970.

Smith, Sally Bedell. *In All His Glory: The Life of William S. Paley*. New York: Simon & Schuster, 1990.

Spear, Joseph. *Presidents and the Press: The Nixon Legacy*. Cambridge: MIT Press, 1984.

Steel, Ronald. *Walter Lippmann and the American Century.* New York: Vintage, 1981.

Talese, Gay. *The Kingdom and the Power.* New York: World Publishing, 1969.

Turner, Kathleen J. *Lyndon Johnson's Dual War: Vietnam and the Press.* Chicago: University of Chicago Press, 1985.

Viorst, Milton. *Fire in the Streets: America in the 1960's.* New York: Simon & Schuster, 1980.

Walker, Daniel. *Rights in Conflict.* New York: New American Library, 1968.

Westin, Av. *Newswatch: How TV Decides the News.* New York: Simon & Schuster, 1982.

Wober, J. Mallory, and Barrie Gunter. *Television and Social Control.* Aldershot, U.K.: Brookfield, 1988.

Wyatt, Clarence R. *Paper Soldiers: The American Press and the Vietnam War.* New York: Norton, 1993.

Zaroulis, Nancy, and Gerald Sullivan. *Who Spoke Up? American Protest against the War in Vietnam, 1963–1975.* Garden City, N.Y.: Doubleday, 1984.

Articles

Berkowitz, William. "The Impact of Anti-Vietnam Demonstrations upon National Public Opinion and Miltary Indicators." *Social Science Research* 2 (March 1973): 1–14.

Blumberg, Nathan. "Misreporting the Peace Movement." *Columbia Journalism Review* 9 (winter 1970–71): 28–32.

Bosso, Christopher J. "Setting the Agenda: Mass Media and the Discovery of Famine in Ethiopia." In Michael Margolis and Gary A. Mauser, eds., *Manipulating Public Opinion: Essays on Public Opinion as a Dependent Variable* (Pacific Grove, Cal.: Brooks-Cole, 1989), 153–174.

Boylan, James. "Survey: A Salisbury Chronicle." *Columbia Journalism Review* 5 (winter 1966–67): 10–14.

Cohen, Stanley. "Mods and Rockers: The Inventory as Manufactured News." In Stanley Cohen and Jock Young, eds., *The Manufacture of News: Social Problems, Deviance, and the Mass Media* (Beverly Hills: Sage, 1981), 263–279.

Converse, Philip E., Warren E. Miller, Jerold G. Rusk, and Arthur C. Wolfe. "Continuity and Change in American Politics: Parties and Issues in the 1968 Election." *American Political Science Review* 63 (December 1969): 1083–1105.

DeBenedetti, Charles. "Lyndon Johnson and the Antiwar Opposition." In Robert A. Divine, ed., *The Johnson Years* Vol. 2 (Lawrence: University of Kansas Press, 1987), 23–53.

Dobkin, Bethami A. "Constructing News Narratives: ABC and CNN Cover the Gulf War," In Robert E. Denton, Jr., ed., *The Media and the Gulf War* (Westport, Conn.: Praeger, 1993), 107–123.

Duscha, Julius. "The White House Watch Over TV and the Press." *New York Times Magazine* (August 20, 1972): 9, 92–93, 95–97, 100.

Elegant, Robert. "How to Lose a War: Reflections of a Foreign Correspondent." *Encounter* 57 (August 1981): 73–90.

Entman, Robert M., and David L. Paletz. "The War in Southeast Asia: Tunnel Vision on Television." In William C. Adams, ed. *Television Coverage of International Affairs* (Norwood, N.J.: Ablex, 1982), 181–201.

Erbring, Lutz, Edie N. Goldenberg, and Arthur H. Miller. "Front Page News and Real World Cues: A New Look at Agenda Setting by the Media." *American Journal of Political Science* 24 (February 1980): 16–49.

Film and History 22 (February-May 1993).

Fishman, Mark. "Crime Waves as Ideology." In Cohen and Young, eds., *The Manufacture of News*, 98–117.

Fowler, Joseph F. and Stuart W. Showalter. "Evening News Selection: A Confirmation of Judgement." *Journalism Quarterly* 51 (winter 1974): 712–715.

Frank, Reuven. "On Tiananmen Square: Echoes of Chicago." *New York Times* (June 4, 1989): sec. 2, 27.

Galtung, Johann, and Mari Ruge. "Structuring and Selecting News." In Cohen and Young, eds., *The Manufacture of News*, 52–63.

Goodman, Walter. "When Gay Images and Reality Conflict." *New York Times* (July 20, 1993): B3.

Gottlieb, Sanford. "Discussion." In Leon Friedman and William F. Levantrosser, eds., *Watergate and Afterward: The Legacy of Richard M. Nixon* (Westport, Conn.: Greenwood, 1992), 144–147.

Hall, Stuart. "A World at One with Itself." In Cohen and Young, eds., *The Manufacture of News*, 147–156.

Hersh, Seymour. "Nixon's Last Cover-up: The Tapes He Wants the Archives to Suppress." *New Yorker* (December 14, 1992): 76–95.

Hopkins, George W. "'May Day' 1971: Civil Disobedience and the Vietnam Antiwar Movement." In Small and Hoover, eds., *Give Peace a Chance*, 71–90.

Jacobs, Travis Beal. "Roosevelt's Quarantine Speech." *Historian* 24 (August 1962): 483–502.

Kettl, Donald F. "The Economic Education of Lyndon Johnson: Guns, Butter and Taxes." In Divine, ed., *The Johnson Years*, 54–78.

Lee, Martin, and Tiffany Devitt. "Gulf War Coverage: Censorship Begins at Home." *Newspaper Research Journal* 12 (winter 1991): 14–22.

Lemert, James B. "Content Duplication by the Networks in Competing Evening Newscasts." *Journalism Quarterly* 51 (summer 1974): 238–244.

Lichty, Lawrence W. "Video Versus Print." *Wilson Quarterly* 6 (1982): 49–57.

Lipsky, Michael. "Protest as a Political Resource." *American Political Science Review* 62 (December 1968): 1144–1159.

McClure, Robert D., and Thomas E. Patterson. "Print vs Network News." *Journal of Communication* 26 (spring 1976): 23–28.

McCombs, Maxwell, and Sheldon Gilbert. "News Influence on Our Pictures of the World." In Jennings Bryant and Dolf Zillman, eds., *Perspectives on Media Effects* (Hillsdale, N.J.: Lawrence Erlbaum, 1986), 1–14.

McNulty, Thomas. "Vietnam Specials: Policy and Content." *Journal of Communication* 25 (August 1975): 173–180.

Mandelbaum, Michael. "Vietnam: The Television War." *Daedalus* 3 (fall 1982): 157–169.

Margolis, Michael, and Robert E. Burtt. "Revolutionaries of the Status Quo: The Denominational Ministry Strategy, the Unemployed, and the Powers That Be." In Margolis and Mauser, eds. *Manipulating Public Opinion*, 175–202.

Mohr, Charles. "Once Again—Did the Press Lose Vietnam?" *Columbia Journalism Review* 22 (November 1983): 51–56.

Molotoch, Harvey, and Marilyn Lester. "Accidental News: The Great Spill." *American Journal of Sociology* 81 (September 1975): 235–260.

———. "News as Purposive Behavior: On the Strategic Use of Routine Events, Accidents and Scandals." In Cohen and Young, eds., *The Manufacture of News*, 118–137.

Moss, George Donelson. "News or Nemesis: Did Television Lose the Vietnam War?" In his *A Vietnam Reader* (Englewood Cliffs, N.J.: Prentice Hall, 1991): 245–300.

Murdock, Graham. "Political Deviance: The Press Presentation of a Militant Mass Demonstration." In Cohen and Young, eds., *The Manufacture of News*, 206–225.

Neuman, Johanna. "The Media: Partners in the Revolution of 1989." Washington, D.C.: Atlantic Council, 1991.

Page, Benjamin I., and Robert Y. Shapiro. "Effects of Public Opinion on Policy." *American Political Science Review* 77 (March 1983): 175–195.

———. "What Moves Public Opinion." *American Political Science Review* 81 (March 1987): 23–43.

Patterson, Oscar III. "An Analysis of Television Coverage of the Vietnam War." *Journal of Broadcasting* 28 (fall 1984): 397–404.

———. "Television's Living-Room War in Print: Vietnam in the News Magazines." *Journalism Quarterly* 61 (spring 1984): 35–40.

Pride, Richard A., and Barbara Richards. "Denigration of Authority? Television News Coverage of the Student Movement." *Journal of Politics* 36 (August 1974): 637–660.

Robinson, John P. "Public Reaction to Political Protest: Chicago 1968." *Public Opinion Quarterly* 34 (spring 1970): 1–9.

Russo, Frank D. "A Study of Bias in TV Coverage of the Vietnam War: 1969 and 1970." *Public Opinion Quarterly* 35 (winter 1971–72): 539–543.

Schreiber, E. M. "Anti-War Demonstrations and American Public Opinion on the War in Vietnam." *British Journal of Sociology* 27 (June 1976): 225–236.

Shapiro, Herbert. "The Vietnam War and the American Civil Rights Movement." *Journal of Ethnic Studies* 16 (Winter 1989): 117–141.

Sheppard, Robert. "Lots of Ballyhoo, Not Much Audience." *The Globe and Mail* (Toronto), (August 18, 1993): A21.

Sidle, Winant. "The Role of Journalists in Vietnam: An Army General's Perspective." In Harrison E. Salisbury, ed., *Vietnam Reconsidered* (New York: Harper, 1984), 110–112.

Singer, Benjamin D. "Violence, Protest, and War in Television News: The U.S. and Canada Compared." *Public Opinion Quarterly* 34 (winter 1970–71): 612–616.

Small, Melvin. "Containing Domestic Enemies: Richard M. Nixon and the War at Home." In David L. Anderson, ed., *Shadow on the White House: Presidents and the Vietnam War, 1945–1975* (Lawrence: University of Kansas Press, 1993), 131–151.

———. "Impact of the Antiwar Movement on Lyndon Johnson: A Preliminary Report." *Peace and Change* 10 (spring 1984): 1–22.

———. "The *New York Times* and the *Toronto Globe and Mail* View the Anti-Vietnam War Demonstrations." *Peace and Change* 14 (July 1989): 324–349.

————. "Public Opinion on Foreign Policy: The View from the Johnson and Nixon White Houses." *Politica* 16 (1984): 184–200.

Smith, Jack A. "The *Guardian* Goes to War." In Ken Wachsberger, ed., *Voices from the Underground: Insider Histories of the Vietnam Era Underground Press* (Tempe, Ariz.: Mica Press, 1993), 99–106.

Spiegelman, Robert. "Media Manipulation of the Movement." *Social Policy* 13 (summer 1982): 9–16.

Trinkl, John. "Something to Guard," *Crossroads* 29 (March 1993): 27–31.

Wachsberger, Ken. "A Tradition Continues: The History of East Lansing's Underground Press, 1965–Present." In his *Voices from the Underground*, 233–258.

Weaver, Paul H. "Newspaper News and Television News." In Douglass Cater and Richard Adler, eds., *Television as a Social Force: New Approaches to TV Criticism* (New York: Praeger, 1975), 81–94.

Weber, Thomas. "'The Marchers Simply Walked Forward Until Struck Down'": Nonviolent Suffering and Conversion." *Peace and Change* 18 (July 1993): 267–289.

Whiteside, Thomas. "Annals of Television: Shaking the Tree." *New Yorker* (March 17, 1975): 41–91.

————. "Corridors of Mirrors: The Television Editorial Process, Chicago." *Columbia Journalism Review* 7 (winter 1968–69): 35–54.

Witcover, Jules. "The Press and Chicago: The Truth Hurt." *Columbia Journalism Review* 7 (fall 1968): 5–8.

INDEX

ABC, 17, 27, 29, 31, 91, 139, 151, 189n50; on Agnew speech, 113, archives of, 6; on Bosnia, 183n38; on Cambodia–Kent State protests, 135; on Gulf War protest, 173; on Mayday, 157, 158–159; on Moratorium, 95–96, 103, 104; on Moratorium and Mobilization, 1969, 117, 119, 125; on NPAC demonstration, 153; on Pro-Choice demonstration, 170; ratings of, 6; on Silent Majority speech, 110, 111; on VVAW protests, 143–144, 152

Abernathy, Ralph David, 97, 118, 142

ABM (anti-ballistic missile), 186n1

Abzug, Bella, 142

AFL-CIO, 48

African Americans, 58, 97, 98, 99, 142

Agnew, Spiro T., 32, 100, 102, 103, 107, 108, 119, 123, 142, 150; Des Moines speech of, 109, 112–114, 122, 123, 124, 125, 126

air force, 65

Alaskan oil spill, 170

Algeria, 36

Allen, James, 138

Allen, Woody, 93

Allin, Mort, 30, 31, 125, 138, 139, 154

Alsop, Joseph, 26, 66

American Friends of Vietnam, 45

American Opinion Survey, 27, 30, 56–57, 66, 67, 69

"America the Beautiful," 95, 136

Anderson, Jack, 30, 104

Annenberg, Walter, 32

anti-nuclear demonstrations, 190n6

anti-Vietnam War movement, 1, 2, 9, 15, 18, 35; agenda of, 1, 164; and bombing of North Vietnam, 35; decline of, 8; development of, 61; influence of media on, ix, 1; origins of, 8, 34–35; and radicals, 49, 52, 53, 57, 62–63, 70, 81, 83, 105, 114, 144, 163, 166; tactics and strategies, 2, 9–10, 11, 19, 23, 67–68, 84, 92, 130, 140, 161, 168; women leaders in, 191n33

anti-Vietnam War movement activities: Cambodia–Kent State protests, 130–140, 145, 165; Chicago Democratic Party Convention, 21, 88–90, 160; counter-inaugural, 90; First International Days of Protest, 9, 46–57, 62, 63, 64, 167; Fulbright hearings, 21, 61–62, 63, 64, 167; Harvard riot, 21, 64–65, 129; London demonstration, 1968, 24; Martin Luther King, Jr., speaks out, 66–68, 167; Mayday, 127–128, 143, 149, 154–160, 161; Mobe demonstrations, 1968, 86–88; Moratorium, 9, 85–86, 92–106, 108, 122, 125, 126, 139, 165; Moratorium and Mobilization, 1969, 9, 31, 107–108, 113, 114–126, 135, 138, 141, 147, 149; Moratorium and Mobilization, 1970, 128–130; NPAC demonstration, 142–143, 148–149, 159, 165; Resistance and Renewal demonstrations, 90–92, 164; Salisbury reports, 65, 66, 167; SANE demonstration, 34, 57–59, 167; SDS demonstration, 8, 35–41, 43, 47, 161; Second International Days of Protest, 62–64, 163–164, 167; siege of Pentagon, 9, 60–61, 70–84; Spring Mobilization, 67, 68–70, 79; VVAW protests, 141–149, 156, 159, 165; Washington teach-in, 41–46, 49, 167; WSP-WILPF picket, 8, 35

About the Author

Melvin Small, a professor of history at Wayne State University and a former president of the Council on Peace Research in History, is the author of many books and articles on public opinion, foreign policy, and international conflict, including *Was War Necessary* (1980) and *Johnson, Nixon, and the Doves* (1988).